W9-CDM-501

Keep Talking that Book!

Booktalks to Promote Reading
Grades 2-12

VOLUME III

Carol Littlejohn
with Cathlyn Thomas

PROFESSIONAL GROWTH SERIES®

A Publication of THE BOOK REPORT & LIBRARY TALK
Professional Growth Series

Linworth Publishing, Inc.
Worthington, Ohio

Library of Congress Cataloging-in-Publication Data

Littlejohn, Carol.
    Keep talking that book! / Carol Littlejohn
        p. cm.--(Professional growth series)
    "Booktalks to promote reading, volume three."
    "This book is a companion to: Talk that book : booktalks to promote reading"--Introd.
    Includes indexes.
    ISBN 1-58683-020-1
    1. Book talks. 2. Best books. I. Title. II. Series.

Z716.3 .L58 2000
028'.9--dc21

                                                                00-023064

Published by Linworth Publishing, Inc.
480 East Wilson Bridge Road, Suite L
Worthington, Ohio 43085

Series Information:
        From The Professional Growth Series

ISBN 1-58683-020-1

5 4 3 2 1

Table of Contents

Table of Contents continued

Table of Contents continued

Table of Contents continued

Table of Contents continued

Table of Contents continued

Introduction

As librarians and teachers, we always will need to help individuals find the "perfect" book—the book that will enchant the reader, or at least encourage future reading. *Keep Talking That Book! Booktalks to Promote Reading, Grades 2-12, Volume III,* by author and library media specialist Carol Littlejohn, aims to help media specialists and others use booktalks or brief book chats to stimulate interest among individuals of all ages and ultimately match the right readers with the right books. This is the third booktalk-related title Littlejohn has written for Linworth Publishing's *Progressive Growth Series.* This time, the author collaborated with school librarian and writer Cathlyn Thomas to make Volume 3 a valuable booktalk resource.

Previously, Littlejohn wrote *Talk That Book! Booktalks to Promote Reading* and *Keep Talking That Book: Booktalks to Promote Reading, Volume 2.* While some of the content in this third volume is similar to that in prior versions, new content has been added and an easy-to-use organization format has been applied. This guide is designed to help you give successful booktalks to readers of all ages.

The text is divided into five Parts.

Part I presents a list of book awards. Since most of the booktalks are based on books from recommended reading lists, background information on the various awards may be helpful.

Part II offers an alphabetical list of tips and strategies educators and others can use to effectively plan and conduct booktalks.

Part III provides genre and subject headings for the booktalks in this volume. The headings *Bullies, Holidays, Mental Illness, Moving, Nature, Seasons,* and *Transportation* were not listed in the two prior booktalk series volumes.

Part IV presents myriad booktalks for all readers. The booktalks included in Part IV are presented alphabetically by the author's last name, and followed by bibliographic information, age/grade suitability, any known book awards, genre, subjects, and related books. After the booktalk, a "Note" provides additional information about the author, book, genre, or maturity content (even regarding the inclusion of profanity). At times a "Note" may reveal the ending of the book, however, do not reveal the ending to students. The ending of a book should never be shared with students since the purpose of booktalks is to *encourage* reading.

Part V comprises a set of useful author, title, reading level, genre, and subject indexes. You can use the Genre and Subject indexes provided in Part V to help locate books or booktalks that will help you further stimulate students' interest in reading in a particular genre or subject. The indexes are designed to match related books for booktalking themes and book recommendations.

The reading level index separates the booktalks by grade level. For instance, elementary reading levels are separated into Lower Elementary (Grades 2–3, short chapter books or picture books) and Upper Elementary (Grades 4–6, developing readers) groups. Middle School titles have more developed plots and some may include mild profanity. High School titles are for the "mature reader," that is, the reader who can understand a story's context.

The American Library Association, the International Reading Association, and other organizations that sponsor book awards, provide immense help in selecting quality books. Booktalks are useful ways to help promote reading and help individual readers find the right books. Booktalking allows readers the free choice to select books that interest them. It's important that a person giving a booktalk provide a variety of reading levels and genres so each reader can find at least one book of high interest.

Many librarians and teachers complain that computers have replaced good, old-fashioned reading. In spite of advanced technology, however, students continue to read books. Who would have believed that three children's books in J.K. Rowling's *Harry Potter* series would remain the top three sellers in the year 2000? The repercussions can only be good for young adult and children's literature. Our job as educators is to recommend quality books so we can keep students reading.

So, as we continue into the new millennium, let's keep talking those books!

Carol Littlejohn
and Cathyln Thomas

About the Authors

Carol Littlejohn is on a mission to promote reading. During the early hours she is a library media specialist at the Deer Lakes Middle School in Russellton, Pennsylvania. Then, as darkness descends, she becomes a writer. Sometimes the two identities merge, and have thus far produced two other books about booktalking: *Talk That Book! Booktalks to Promote Reading* and *Keep Talking That Book: Booktalks to Promote Reading, Volume 2.* She also has contributed articles to Library Talk, The Book Report, *JOYS, VOYA, the ALAN Review,* and other journals.

Cathlyn Thomas, who previously has worked as a medical, public, and school librarian, has seen the effectiveness of booktalks with readers of all ages. Currently, she is a library media specialist at Isenberg Elementary School in Salisbury, North Carolina.

Acknowledgments

CAROL:

Once again, I thank the Linworth staff, including Betty J. Morris (our new editor), Marlene Woo-Lun, Wendy Medvetz, Amy Robison, and all the others who supported this book.

Special thanks to Principal Bill McClarnon and the students, teachers, and staff at the Deer Lakes Middle School in Russellton, Pennsylvania. You have all encouraged me to keep reading and writing booktalks. It's been a pleasure working with all of you.

I would also like to express a special thank-you to the friends and colleagues with whom I exchange ideas: Nikki Fieser, Sarah Conaster, Jeanette Gerlach, Connie Maxwell, Professor Magdaleen Bester, Margie Bragg, and Kate Fleming.

As always, my family has encouraged me to do and be the best I can. Thanks again, Mike, Karl, and Drew!

CATHLYN:

Thanks to my family and Bob Moffet. Thanks also to Pamela Murphy and the teachers and students at Isenberg Elementary School in Salisbury, North Carolina.

Book Awards

ABBY AWARD

The American Booksellers Association's annual selection of recommended adult and juvenile books.

ALA/ALSC NOTABLE CHILDREN'S BOOKS

Annual list of recommended children's books provided by the American Library Association (ALA) and the Association for Library Service to Children.

ALEX AWARD

Annual list of recommended young adult books selected by the ALA division of the Young Adult Library Service Association (YALSA).

BLUE RIBBON AWARD

Presented annually by *The Bulletin of the Center for Children's Books* for the best children's book.

BOOK LINKS' LASTING CONNECTIONS

Annual list of books for young people as selected by the editors of *Book Links* magazine.

BOOKLIST EDITORS' CHOICE

Annual list of recommended books provided by the editorial staff of *Booklist*, published by the American Library Association.

BOSTON GLOBE/HORN BOOK AWARDS

Awarded annually since 1967 to an author of fiction, an author of nonfiction, and an illustrator.

CALDECOTT AWARD

Awarded annually by the ALA for the best illustrations in a children's book by an American author.

CARNEGIE AWARD
Awarded annually by the British Library Association for the best children's book by a British author.

CHILDREN'S BOOKS OF THE YEAR
Annual recommended book list presented by the Child Study Children's Book Committee at Bank Street College in New York. The committee includes educators, librarians, authors, illustrators, psychologists, and specialists in related fields.

COOPERATIVE CHILDREN'S BOOK CENTER SELECTION
Annual recommended list provided by the Cooperative Children's Book Center, a library of the School of Education at the University of Wisconsin, to bring children's literature to the attention of adults.

CORETTA SCOTT KING AWARD
Awarded annually by the ALA to honor the best African-American author and illustrator for excellence in children's literature.

EDGAR ALLAN POE AWARD
Awarded annually by the Mystery Writer's Association for the best children's and young adult mystery.

HORN BOOK FANFARE AWARD
Sponsored by the editors of *Horn Book* and awarded annually for the best children's book.

HUGO AWARD
Presented annually by the members of the current World Science Fiction Convention for the best science fiction book.

IRA/CBC CHILDREN'S CHOICES
Project sponsored jointly by the International Reading Association and the Children's Book Council; annually polls 10,000 youngsters on their favorite books of the year to provide a list of titles proven to be appealing to children.

IRA CHILDREN'S BOOK AWARD
Awarded annually by the International Reading Association for excellence in children's literature.

JANE ADDAMS BOOK AWARD
Awarded annually by the Jane Addams Peace Association to promote peace and social justice.

LOS ANGELES TIMES AWARD
Annual list of young adult titles recommended by the *Los Angeles Times*.

MICHAEL L. PRINTZ AWARD FOR EXCELLENCE IN YOUNG ADULT LITERATURE
New award named for the Topeka, Kansas, school librarian known for discovering and promoting quality books for young adults; presented annually by the ALA.

NATIONAL COUNCIL FOR THE SOCIAL STUDIES SELECTION
Annual list of notable books concerned with multicultural experiences and sensitivity to human relations; selected by the NCSS.

NEBULA AWARD
Awarded annually by the Science Fiction and Fantasy Writers of America for the best science fiction book.

NEW YORK TIMES BOOK SELECTION
Annual list of notable books selected by the editors of *The New York Times*.

NEWBERY AWARD
Awarded annually by the ALA for the best children's or young adult book by an American author.

PARENTS' CHOICE AWARDS
Awarded annually by The Parents' Choice Foundation for toys and children's media for youngsters from birth to 12 years old. Selections are made by children, parents, teachers, and librarians.

PUBLISHER WEEKLY'S BEST BOOKS
Annual list of recommended books selected by the editors of *Publishers Weekly*.

SLJ'S BEST BOOKS
Annual list of recommended books provided by the Book Review editors of *School Library Journal*.

SOCIETY OF SCHOOL LIBRARIANS INTERNATIONAL LIST
Annual list of recommended books that meet schools' instructional curriculum in language arts, science and social studies; presented by the SSLI.

SYDNEY TAYLOR JEWISH AWARD
Children's book awarded annually by the National Association of Jewish Libraries.

VOYA AWARD
Annual award of the best young adult books; provided by the editors of the *Voice of Youth Advocates (VOYA)*.

WHITBREAD AWARDS
Since 1971, these annual awards have celebrated and promoted the best of contemporary British writing.

YALSA'S RECOMMENDED LISTS
Annual lists of recommended young adult books selected by members of the ALA's Young Adult Library Service Association (*as follows*):
BEST BOOKS FOR YOUNG ADULTS
TEENS TOP TEN BEST BOOKS
POPULAR PAPERBACKS FOR YOUNG ADULTS
QUICK PICKS FOR RELUCTANT YOUNG ADULT READERS
10 QUICK PICKS FOR YOUNG ADULTS

The ABCs of Booktalking:
Tips and Strategies
From A to Z

A   **AUTHOR**. Tell something about the author that would interest students. Any personal details will add spice to a booktalk (e.g., Edgar Allan Poe married his 13-year-old cousin, Louisa May Alcott wrote mystery thrillers under a pen name).

B   **BANNED BOOKS**. Discuss books that have been banned for one reason or another (***To Kill a Mockingbird, Huckleberry Finn, The Giver***, and ***Harry Potter and the Sorcerer's Stone*** qualify). What is it about these books that stirs such controversy? Should any book be banned in a democracy? This could be discussed in September during Banned Books Week.

C   **COMMERCIALS.** Think of booktalks as brief advertisements or commercials that stress the book's appeal. When writing a booktalk, begin with a teaser that will capture interest, try to mention the book's title somewhere in the talk, and end with a slam-bam finish!

D   **DIALOGUE.** During booktalking, keep the audience involved through dialogue. Ask questions; expect answers, even from groups who don't usually talk. The students will provide valuable information about book trends, favorite authors, and reading levels.

E   **EASY CHAPTER BOOKS.** Booktalk easy chapter books for beginning readers. These books offer minimal characters, a limited vocabulary, and simple plots. They can transform a reader of words into a reader of text. Perhaps the best known easy reader is Else Homelund Minarik's **Little Bear** series. Recently, award-winning authors Cynthia Rylant, Katherine Paterson, Jane Yolen and others have also contributed to this thriving field.

F **FOLKLORE.** Many scholars believe that literacy derives from hearing the patterns, rhythms, and themes of traditional favorites. Folklore can be read or told at every age level and during each presentation. Introduce complicated stories, such as **The Fisherman and His Wife, Wicked John and the Devil,** and **Faust,** then observe students' reactions. Discuss the morals and themes with your audience. Don't forget the fractured fairy tales; older elementary and middle school students appreciate those twisted tales.

G **GENRES.** Define genres during booktalks. If helpful, use a video store's subject headings (e.g., *Action* for adventure, *Comedy* for humor). Differentiate between historical fiction and nonfiction, collective biographies and individual biographies, mysteries and horror, and so on.

H **HOLIDAYS AND SEASONS.** Booktalk during seasons and holidays. During autumn, booktalks can include scary stories, urban legends, stories by Washington Irving and Edgar Allan Poe, any Native American folktale and football stories. Winter booktalks can include ice hockey, chilling adventures, Jack London's books, Alaska stories, or books on any cold climate, mountain climbing, ice skating, or skiing. Spring booktalks can include books on baseball, swimming, fishing, nature, Easter, and rabbits, and also include fantasies like *Alice's Adventures in Wonderland*. Summer books can include topics such as boats, water sports, beaches, baseball, and tennis. Stay creative and each season should bring up new books as well as recyclable favorites.

I **ILLUSTRATORS AND ILLUSTRATIONS.** Some books are enhanced by the illustrations. Give the illustrators their deserved glory. Mention their names, techniques, and style.

J **JOKES.** Open a booktalk with some humor. Tell or read some riddles or jokes, preferably related to the genre, topic, or books to be used.

K **KNOWLEDGE.** Import some information about the book's subject matter that will increase students' knowledge. Include anecdotes about the book's time period or subject matter. (In Part Four of this book, refer to the *Note* section after each booktalk to answer any questions you or the reader might have).

L **LAMINATE.** Laminate book jackets and place your booktalk behind the cover. You can read the booktalk while the students look at the jacket.

M **MATURE READERS.** When selecting books for booktalking, always assume that there are some mature readers. Mature readers can read the text and can grasp most of its subtle nuances. Select some classics that never become dated or, if they are anachronistic, retain the power to enchant. Some booktalks could include *Alice's Adventures in Wonderland* by Lewis Carroll, *The Adventures of Tom Sawyer* by Mark Twain, *Little Women* by Louisa May Alcott and *Pride and Prejudice* by Jane Austen.

N **NEWBERY AWARDS AND OTHER HONORS.** Booktalk Newbery and Caldecott books, even the Honor books. The Newbery and Caldecott, awarded by the American Library Association, honor the best American author and illustrator. Use these award-winning books as a launching pad to introduce other countries and their book awards (e.g., Great Britain: the Carnegie; South Africa: SALIS).

O **ONLINE.** Go online to get book reviews and booktalks. Amazon <*Amazon.com*> and Barnes and Noble <**Barnesandnoble.com**> supply book reviews from prestigious journals including *Booklist, Kirkus Reviews,* and *The Horn Book Magazine.* To buy out-of-print books (without reviews), try <**www.bookfinder.com/**> and for booktalks, use Nancy Keane's Booktalks—Quick and Simple site at <**http://rms.concord.k12.nh.us/booktalks/**>.

P **PEER BOOKTALKING.** Students make excellent booktalkers. Have them booktalk their favorites to their peers. You'll be surprised at some of their picks and how "professional" they sound (with instruction, that is).

Q **QUEST.** Many of the classics involve a quest. For example, Odysseus' search for his home and King Arthur's quest for the Holy Grail. Many modern novels, such as Stephen King's **The Girl Who Loved Tom Gordon** and Christopher Paul Curtis' **Bud, Not Buddy**, also involve a journey. Why not use the theme of adventurous quests for your next program of booktalks?

R **RELUCTANT READER.** A reluctant reader does not read voluntarily, either because of poor reading skills or the lack of motivation. Booktalks may motivate reluctant readers. For these individuals, always booktalk the high interest, entertaining books. Note when a reluctant reader enjoys a book, and then recommend books that are similar either in style, characterization, or plot. (The *Related books* section in the booktalks provided in Part Four will be helpful for making book recommendations as well as answering that question: "Can I have a book like the last one?")

S **SHAKESPEARE.** Occasionally, slide in some Shakespeare. Let the students know that Shakespeare was an actor and entertainer, and not some boring writer no one understands. Some great adaptations might lead a reader to the real thing (e.g., **Othello** by Julius Lester; **Shakespeare Stories** by Geraldine McCraughton; **Top Ten Shakespeare Stories** by Terry Deary).

T **TWO-WAY BOOKTALKS.** To liven up booktalks, use a partner, such as a teacher or student. The partner could read a poem or chapter from a book, or do a booktalk.

U **URBAN LEGENDS.** These folktales will always appeal to young adults, maybe because they are told by teens to other teens. The **Scary Stories** series, collected by Alvin Schwartz, should be in every library. Throw in some horror books by Stephen King and Dean Koontz, with some romantic thrillers by Lois Duncan and Joan Lowery Nixon. Then, watch the students practically grab the books out of your hands!

V **VARIETY.** Choose a wide variety of books for successful booktalking. Choose all reading levels, genres, and cultures, so everyone is included.

W **WEB PAGE.** With your students, develop a library Web page that contains booktalks and book recommendations by you as well as by your students. If you decide to scan book jackets for your site, remember you must contact the publisher for permission.

X **X-FILES.** Booktalk any topic related to the *X-Files* television series: aliens; telepathy; Bermuda Triangle; any conspiracy topics; the FBI; anything supernatural, fiction or nonfiction. Like magic, books will disappear!

Y **YOUNG ADULTS.** This is the term adolescents prefer—not *teens, teenagers, kids,* or *children.*

Z   **ZERO ILLITERACY.** Illiteracy is still a problem. Our goal as educators should be to achieve *zero illiteracy.* Voluntary reading leads to higher overall scores, not just reading scores. Do your part to eliminate illiteracy! Talk that book!

PART 3

Genres and Subjects for Booktalking

GENRES

Adventure	Historical Fiction	Realistic Fiction
Biography	Horror	Romance
Classics	Humor	Science Fiction
Fantasy	Mysteries/Thrillers	Short Stories
Folklore	Nonfiction	Sports
	Poetry	

SUBJECTS

Abuse	Caribbean and Latin America	Ecology
Aging	China	End-of-the-World
Adoption	Civil War, 1860-1865	Ethics
Africa	Class Conflicts	Europe
African Americans	Computers	Family
American Revolutionary War	Crime	France
Animals	Death	Friendship
Asia	Diaries	Great Britain
Asian Americans	Disability	Hispanic Americans
Australia	Divorce	Hobbies
Bullies	Eating Disorders	Holidays

Holocaust

Homeless

Homosexuality

Illness

Immigrants

Interracial Relations

Ireland

Jews

Love

Magic

Men's Issues

Mental Illness

Middle Ages

Middle East

Movies

Moving

Music

Native Americans

Nature

Orphans

Peer Pressure

Pioneer Life

Politics

Pregnancy

Problem Parents

Racism

Religion

Religious Prejudice

Responsibility

Revenge

Rites of Passage

Rivalry

Runaways

Russia

School

Science

Secrets

Self-Identity

Sex and Sexuality

Sexual Abuse

Show Business

Single Parents

Sports

Stepparents

Substance Abuse

Suicide

Supernatural

Survival

Time Travel

Transportation

Trust

Vietnam War

War

Women's Issues

Work

World War I

World War II

PART 4

Booktalks for
All Readers

Alderson, Bruce. *Touchdown Trivia: Secrets, Statistics, and Little Known Facts About Football.*

Illustrated by Harry Pulver Jr. Lerner, 1998, 61pp. Lower Elementary & Up. Fourth book in **Trivia** *series;* **Hat Trick Trivia; Slam Dunk Trivia; Grand Slam Trivia** *precede.*

- ■ **NONFICTION AND SPORTS.** *African Americans; sports (football); women's issues.*
- ■ **RELATED BOOKS: Hat Trick Trivia, Slam Dunk Trivia,** and **Grand Slam Trivia** by Bruce Alderson.

Note: *Pulver's illustrations perfectly complement the humorous and informative text. Includes brief biographies of sports heroes as well as a chapter about women in football. Recommended for beginning or reluctant readers who enjoy sports.*

Here's some "Touchdown Trivia" about football. Did you know that football was first played in 11th-century England with rocks and human skulls? (Ugh.) Later, they got sensible and used inflated pig bladders. Then, presto, the term "pigskin." (Double ugh.) Everybody was so into kicking the ball that they didn't *pass* the ball until 1906. (Obviously no one wanted to pass human skulls while running down the field!)

See how well you know **Touchdown Trivia** about the history and players of football—it's the best game in town.

Almond, David. *Skellig.*

Delacorte, 1999, 182pp. First published in Great Britain by Hodder Children's Books, 1998. Upper Elementary & Up. Michael R. Printz Award for Excellence in Young Adult Fiction (Honor Book); ALA Notable Children's Book; Publishers Weekly's Best Books; SLJ's Best Books; Cooperative Book Center choice; Book Links' Lasting Connections selection; Horn Book Fanfare; Booklist Editors' Choice.

- ■ **FANTASY.** *Friendship; illness (physical); moving; secrets; supernatural.*
- ■ **RELATED BOOKS: Owl in Love** by Patrice Kindl; **Maura's Angel** by Lynne Reid Banks; **The van Gogh Café** by Cynthia Rylant; **A Wrinkle in Time** series by Madeleine L'Engle; **Harry Potter** series by J. K. Rowling.

Note: *Main character, Michael narrates gothic fantasy of Skellig, the man-owl-angel, whose history and reason for being are open to interpretation. His friend, Mina is a home schooled girl who constantly quotes the poet William Blake, adding to mysticism. Recommended as a read aloud, group reading (great for discussions) or for fantasy lovers, especially* **Harry Potter** *fans.*

I'll never forget the day I found Skellig. I thought he was dead. He was small, covered in dust and webs, lying in a dark corner in my family's deserted garage. I shined the flashlight on his pale face and black suit.

His voice squeaked, like he hadn't spoken in years: "What do you want?"

"What are you?" I whispered. Somehow I sensed this mystical creature was more than he seemed.

He turned his face away. I left quickly, wondering what I should do. Should I tell my parents that a withered old man was in our garage? It was a bad time for them. My baby sister was deathly ill. I did tell my new friend, Mina. She helped me move Skellig to safety.

One magical day Mina removed Skellig's black jacket. Beneath the jacket were wings. The wings began to unfurl from his shoulder blades. "Ooh, you're beautiful," Mina whispered.

She repeated my question: "**Skellig**, what are you?"

Anderson, Christopher. *The Day John Died.*

William Morrow, 2000, 303pp. Middle School & Up.

■ **BIOGRAPHY.** *Death; family; love; politics; show business; single parents.*

■ **RELATED BOOKS: Jack and Jackie** and **Jackie After Jack** by Christopher Anderson; **Prince Charming: The John F. Kennedy Jr. Story** by Wendy Leigh and Stephen Karten; **The J.F.K. Jr. Scrapbook** by Stephen J. Spignesi.

 Note: *Written by a Time and People former editor who provides both gossip and substance, this book is perfect for reluctant readers who are required to read a biography. Also, John Kennedy Jr. is an excellent role model as one who lived his life in the spotlight.*

Where were you the day John died?

Like his father's assassination, the tragic death of John F. Kennedy Jr. will remain an unforgettable moment in history.

We remember John as a toddler who saluted his father's coffin. Then he grew into "The Sexiest Man Alive," according to *People* magazine. He became a devoted husband and respected magazine publisher of *George.* Then, on July 16, 1999, he vanished with his wife, Carolyn Bessette, and her sister in a plane crash that he piloted. The Federal Aviation Administration proclaimed the accident was due to "spatial disorientation." Ironically, all he had to do was punch two buttons and the plane would have landed safely on autopilot.

From history's most famous salute to the tragic plane crash, John's story is both distressing and inspiring. That's why none of us will ever forget **The Day John Died.**

Anderson, Janet S. *Going Through the Gate.*

Dutton, 1977, 134pp. Upper Elementary & Up.

■ **FANTASY.** *Animals; nature; responsibility; school; self-identity; supernatural.*

■ **RELATED BOOKS: The Giver** by Lois Lowry; **Animal Farm** by George Orwell; **A Door in the Wall** by Heather Quales.

Note: *The characters' lives are told vividly, with issues of alienation and empathy poignantly highlighted. Recommended by Newbery winner Lloyd Alexander, especially for animal and nature lovers as well as fantasy lovers.*

"Going through the gate."

That's what people in town said when someone disappeared, never to be seen again. Becky wondered what they meant. All she knew was that she and other sixth graders had to pass some kind of test. Everyone who went through the test never talked about it again and never mentioned the students who failed.

What happened beyond the town's gate that changed people forever? If you dare, join Becky's class as they, one by one, experience **Going through the Gate.**

Anderson, Laurie Halse. *Speak.*

Farrar, Straus, and Giroux, 1999, 198pp. High School & Up. National Book Award nominee; Michael R. Printz Award for Excellence in Young Adult Fiction (Honor Book); YASLA Quick Picks for Reluctant Young Adult Readers; Top 10 Best Books for Young Adults; SLJ's Best Books; YALSA Best Books for Young Adults; Book Links' Lasting Connection selection.; Booklist Editor's Choice

■ **REALISTIC FICTION.** *Ethics; responsibility; school; sexual abuse; sex and sexuality.*

■ **RELATED BOOKS: What Jamie Saw** by Carolyn Coman; **The Facts Speak for Themselves** by Brock Cole; **Yolanda's Genius** by Carol Fenner.

 Melinda Sordino becomes an outcast when she calls 911 from a teen drinking party. No one knows she was raped at that party and, eventually, Melinda loses her voice. The ending is triumphant when Melinda recovers her voice and confronts the rapist. Because of its serious content, recommended for the mature reader.

I am an Outcast.

As I enter high school, I am clanless. I'm not a Martha, Jock, Country Clubber, Cheerleader, Thespian, or Goth. I'm an Outcast.

No one speaks to me. Last summer I called the police during a rowdy party and everybody was busted. Even my best friend doesn't speak to me.

Now I can't speak. My throat is always sore and my lips are raw. Every time I try to talk, I freeze. It's like I have spastic laryngitis.

I wish I could talk. I would tell my secret. I would tell *why* I called the police and why I can never trust anyone again.

I believe that when I tell my secret, I'll be able, once again, to **Speak.**

Anderson, M. T. *Burger Wuss.*

Illustrated by David Butler. Candlewick Press, 1999, 208pp. Middle School & Up.

■ **REALISTIC FICTION.** Bullies; love; men's issues; rivalry; revenge; sex and sexuality; sports (baseball); work.

■ **RELATED BOOKS: Thirsty** by M. K. Anderson; **the perks of being a wallflower** by Stephen Chbosky; **How I Spent My Last Night on Earth** by Todd Strasser; **Tex** by S. E. Hinton.

> *Note:* High school student Anthony devises a plan of revenge for his rival after Turner dates his girlfriend. Anthony's first-person narrative in staccato prose adds to the story. The author's experience of working in a fast-food restaurant is also hilariously incorporated. Reluctant young adult readers, especially males, will identify with Anthony's teenage angst in this realistic novel.

You have to be ferocious to be a teenager in America. Being Mr. Nice Guy has got me exactly jack, so it's time to drop-kick "nice." Now it's high time for revenge.

Turner was the reason I was applying for a job at O'Dermott's. He had stolen my girlfriend Diana, and I intended to make his life miserable.

Meanwhile, I had a few things occupying my mind. I had never experienced anything like the lunch rush at a fast-food place. People kept ordering things and wouldn't stop. "I'd like a Happy Meal . . . no, make that two Happy Meals, one without cheese, a chocolate shake, no, make that strawberry . . . ."

To make it worse, Turner kept muttering mean things to me under his breath. "Anthony, you are a complete wuss. Make that a 'Burger Wuss.'"

"Turner, shut your face," I warned. "Oh, yes, Ma'am?"

"Hi, I'll have an O'Chicken meal. Wait. Is that a meal? Maybe the Chicken Special. What's the difference? I'll try that, I guess. A large coke. No, make that small."

Turner, in passing, says: "Hey, wuss, do you like ballet? I bet you and Diana played shuffleboard for fun."

"Turner, I mean it . . . Oh, yes, sir?"

During orders for burgers and Chicken Specials, I thought of a wonderful plan for revenge. It would be huge and ornate, like a torture machine. It would hurt Turner in many spots at once. Then I could reclaim my name. Hello, Anthony—goodbye, **Burger Wuss**!

Atwater-Rhodes, Amelia. *In the Forests of the Night.*

Delacorte, 1999, 147pp. Middle School & Up. ALA Popular Paperbacks for Young Adults.

■ **HORROR.** *Death; revenge; supernatural (vampires).*

■ **RELATED BOOKS: Companions of the Night** by Vivian Vande Velde; **Blood and Chocolate** by Annette Curtis Klause; **Interview With the Vampire** by Anne Rice (for mature readers).

The vampire myths are so confused. There is little truth and many lies.

I do dislike the smell of garlic, but doesn't everyone? I sleep in a bed, not a coffin. Brightness hurts my eyes, but I don't burn in sunlight. Silver does not burn me. Holy water and crosses do not bother me.

Since I am speaking from personal experience. I should introduce myself. I was born to the name Rachel Weatere in 1684, more than 300 years ago. After I was changed, I became Risika. Like most vampires, I was transformed against my will.

How did this happen? Here is my story, from Rachel to Risika, from human to vampire, roaming **In the Forests of the Night.**

 Note: *Either before or after the booktalk, explain that author wrote this vampire book when she was 13. The brief, well-written book alternates between the year 1701, when Risika was changed, and the present. The time switch may be confusing at times, but the plot is captivating. Risika, a 300-year-old vampire, finds a black rose on her pillow—the same flower she was given the day before her mortal death. Risika believes fellow vampire Aubrey was responsible for her brother's murder and Risika seeks revenge. Recommended for mature horror lovers, especially reluctant readers.*

Auch, Mary Jane. *Frozen Summer.*

*Henry Holt, 1998, 202pp. Upper Elementary & Up . First in a series; **Journey to Nowhere** follows. Children's Books of the Year selection.*

■ **HISTORICAL FICTION.** *End-of-the-world; mental illness; pioneer life; problem parents; responsibility; school; women's issues.*

■ **RELATED BOOKS: Journey to Nowhere** by Mary Jane Auch; **Prairie Songs** by Pam Conrad; **Preacher's Boy** by Katherine Paterson; **Sarah, Plain and Tall** and **Skylark** by Patricia MacLachlan; **A Day No Pigs Would Die** by Robert Newton Peck.

 Note: *Author's notes inform us that New England's cold winter was due to a faraway volcano in Indonesian Islands, and that she based the story and characters on diaries of several pioneer women. Reading the first volume is not required, but it can lend understanding of the heroine's moral character development. Recommended for readers looking for a resourceful heroine coping with a parent's mental illness.*

People still talk about that bitterly cold New York winter in 1815. It was so cold that some people like Mrs. Foster were convinced that it was God's vengeance on the sinners. *Take heed!* proclaimed the local preachers. *The end of the world is coming!*

As for me, I have more important things to think about. Like my Mama who's been acting strangely since she had my baby sister. Or my Papa's insistence that nothing is wrong with her. Or my realization that boys have more rights than girls.

We survived that winter. Could we make it through a **Frozen Summer?**

Auch, Mary Jane. *I Was a Third Grade Science Project.*

Illustrated by Herm Auch. Holiday House, 1998, 80pp. Upper Elementary & Up. Children's Books of the Year selection.

■ **HUMOR.** *Animals (dogs, cats); school; science (projects).*

■ **RELATED BOOKS: Serious Science: An Adam Joshua Story** by Janice Lee Smith; **Puppy's Sister** by S. E. Hinton; **A Year with Butch & Spike** by Gail Gauthier; **Regarding the Fountain** by Kate Klise; **The Llama** series by Johanna Hurwitz.

Note: *Recommended for readers who like humorous stories that have a scientific slant. Illustrations add to hilarity. Good as a read-aloud, especially before a science project.*

Some kids call me "Birdbrain." Not that I'm dumb, but because I hang around the class genius nicknamed "Brain." Next to him, I don't look so smart. Who would? Anyway, "Birdbrain" I am.

Maybe I deserve my nickname. I must have been out of my mind to let Brain talk me into joining him on his science project. He got the bright idea of hypnotizing his dog into thinking it was a cat. It worked all right, but not on his dog! All of a sudden I craved catnip, climbed trees and coughed up hairballs!

Come to think of it, maybe they should call me "Catbrain" instead of "Birdbrain."

Especially after **I Was a Third Grade Science Project**!

Austen, Jane. *Pride and Prejudice.*

First published in 1813. Tom Doherty Associates, 1988, 295pp. Middle School & Up. YALSA Popular Paperbacks.

■ **CLASSICS AND ROMANCE.** *Ethics; Great Britain; love.*

■ **RELATED BOOKS: Sense and Sensibility** by Jane Austen; **Jane Austen's World** by Maggie Lane; **Portrait of a Lady** by Henry James; **Age of Innocence** by Edith Wharton; **Madame Bovary** by Gustave Flaubert.

Note: *First published in 1813, this has been imitated endlessly, but none have the elegant style or dry wit of this classic. The style and language might be difficult for some readers, so recommend to mature readers. As a supplement, the BBC TV production, starring Colin Firth and Jennifer Ehle, is true to the book and very entertaining.*

From the beginning, Miss Elizabeth Bennet disliked the handsome, wealthy Thomas Darcy. She considered him arrogant and conceited because he made no attempt to hide his selfish disdain for others. Indeed, her instincts were confirmed when the insensitive Mr. Darcy interfered with her beloved sister's romance as well as a dear friend's fortune.

However, Mr. Darcy was rather intrigued with the pretty Miss Bennet, although he certainly knew that her station and family were not up to his standards. Miss Bennet possessed neither property nor proper breeding. Yes, to be certain, her family was an embarrassment to a person of his manner born. Yet, there was something about Miss Bennet's eyes . . .

Pride and Prejudice. With such handicaps, what are the chances of romance?

Avi. *Abigail Takes the Wheel.*

Illustrated by Don Bolognese. HarperCollins, 1999, 64pp. Lower Elementary & Up.

■ **HISTORICAL FICTION AND ADVENTURE.** *Nature; responsibility; transportation; women's issues.*

■ **RELATED BOOKS: Mirette on the High Wire** by Emily Arnold McCully; **First Farm in the Valley: Anna's Story** by Anne Pellowski; **Little House Chapter Books** series by Laura Ingalls Wilder.

Note: *Avi bases the story on an account given in an 1881 St. Nicholas magazine. Illustrations capture the nautical atmosphere and include a simple map of the Hudson Bay area. Recommended for beginning readers who love adventure stories.*

Every day her father takes Abigail and her brother to school, from New Jersey to New York City, more than 20 miles away. You're probably wondering: What's so special about that? That happens every day.

Abigail's daily trip is special because the year is 1880, more than a hundred years ago. In those days, there were no trucks or trains. Instead, Abigail's family traveled by freight boat.

One day the first mate becomes very ill. Someone who is very responsible and reliable is needed to guide the boat. Take a guess who saves the day when **Abigail Takes the Wheel**.

Avi. *Beyond the Western Sea: Book One, The Escape From Home.*

*Orchard, 1996, 295pp. Middle School & Up. First book of the **Beyond the Western Sea** series; **Lord Kirkle's Money** follows.*

■ **HISTORICAL FICTION AND ADVENTURE.** *Class conflict; family; Great Britain (Ireland); immigrants; Ireland; runaways.*

■ **RELATED BOOKS: The True Confessions of Charlotte Doyle** and **Lord Kirkle's Money** by Avi; **Journey of the Shadow Bairns** by Margaret Anderson; **The House on Hound Hill** by Maggie Prince; **Oliver Twist** by Charles Dickens.

*Note: Author provides authentic flavor to 1850s Liverpool. Like Charlotte Doyle in Avi's **The True Confessions of Charlotte Doyle**, Maure is a spunky heroine. The sequel is required for the completion of the story. Excellent for a group read or read-aloud because each chapter ends with a cliffhanger. Recommended for historical fiction readers as well as fans of Victorian novels.*

"Look! The stars look like a pilgrimage," said Patrick to his older sister.

"All the stars are leading us to the Promised Land," agreed Maure. It would be a long journey to America, and she wanted to keep up Patrick's spirits.

Sometimes she didn't feel as brave as she sounded. In Ireland, her life was predetermined. Now she couldn't predict anything from one moment to the next. There was danger lurking around every corner of the Liverpool docksides, from thieves to corrupt officials. Although she was often frightened, she also felt a strange excitement.

Maure knew she was beginning a new life **Beyond the Western Sea**, leading to her **Escape From Home**.

Banks, Kate. *Howie Bowles, Secret Agent.*

Illustrated by Issac Millman. Frances Foster Books, 1999, 96pp. Lower Elementary & Up. Cooperative Children's Book Center selection.

■ **REALISTIC FICTION AND HUMOR.** *Moving; peer pressure; school; self-identity; sports (baseball).*

■ **RELATED BOOKS: Harriet the Spy** by Louise Fitzhugh; **Coffin on a Case** by Eve Bunting; **The Pink Hotel** by Carol Ryrie Brink; **The Dark Stairs** by Betsy Byars.

 Note: New student Howie becomes a secret agent to gain attention and respect from his third grade class. His self-identity crisis is both humorous and poignant. Recommended for fans of humorous realistic fiction and as a read-aloud.

It's not easy being a secret agent. Howie Bowles should know.

Howie has to remain on the job all day. He has to write down all that's going on in school. Things like guys picking their noses, girls chewing gum, and people writing on desks. Howie's latest case was to find who put chewing gum in the water fountain at school. Howie is a very busy secret agent.

Howie doesn't mind. Being a secret agent is a lot easier than being just plain Howie. For the first time, his classmates pay attention to him. Maybe for the rest of his life he would stay **Howie Bowles, Secret Agent**.

Banks, Lynne Reid. *Maura's Angel.*

Avon, 1998, 128pp. Upper Elementary & Up.

■ **HISTORICAL FICTION.** *Family; Ireland, mental illness; politics; religion; supernatural; war.*

■ **RELATED BOOKS: Angela and Diabola** and **Melusine** by Lynne Reid Banks; **Torn Away** by James Heneghan.

 *Note: Banks, author of The **Indian in the Cupboard** series, weaves unusual plot with supernatural elements. The author presents thought-provoking issues, such as violence in modern-day Belfast, Ireland, and the limitations of spiritual guides. Recommended for fantasy lovers as well as for group reads or as a read-aloud.*

"Ma, this is my friend from school," said Maura. "She got scared when the bomb went off at school. I invited her home. What's wrong?"

Maura's mother gasped, "It's my baby!" Then she calmed down. "What am I saying? My baby has been dead for years. She looks just like my baby. What's your name, darling?"

"Angela," the girl replied.

Maura's mother looked as if she were going to faint. "Angela! That was her name!"

Who was Angela? A ghost? A spiritual guide?

To find out, meet **Maura's Angel**.

Bauer, Joan. *Backwater.*

G. P. Putnam's Sons, 1999, 185pp. Middle School & Up. Society of School Librarians International Honor book; Children's Books of the Year selection.

■ **REALISTIC FICTION.** *Animals (birds); family; love; nature; survival.*

■ **RELATED BOOKS: The Rules of the Road** by Joan Bauer; **My Side of the Mountain** by Jean Craighead George; **Into the Wild** by Jon Krakauer; **Between a Rock and a Hard Place** by Alden R. Carter.

> *Note:* This warm, humorous novel offers a plucky heroine (Ivy Breedlove), a survival adventure, and a brief romance that guarantees enjoyable reading. The story also touches on complex issues, such as personal and historical honesty, connections between generations, and tolerance for eccentric individuals. Recommended for all types of readers and as a group read, especially for mothers and daughters.

History takes time to discover. I respect history. You can't rush connecting to the past, you've got to respect it.

When I made a gravestone rubbing of my great-great-great-great grandfather's tombstone, I took my time. When I researched my family's family tree, my aunt Tib and I carefully plotted our trail back to our early roots in England. I never worked harder at anything in my life.

Then I heard about the missing link in the Breedlove family—my aunt Josephine. I applied my best detective skills to find this amazing woman whose determination and individuality reminded me of myself. I would have to hire a mountain guide to take me to the wild and wintry Adirondack Mountains—into the **Backwater**.

This project will take time and effort, but I'm ready to try.

When I find Josephine Breedlove, will I also find myself?

Baum, L. Frank. *The Wizard of Oz.*

*Pictures by W. W. Denslow. First published in 1900. Ballantine Books, 1979, 240pp. For all libraries. First book in the series; **The Marvelous Land of Oz**; **Ozma of Oz** follow, as well as 14 by Baum and 18 more titles by Ruth Plumly Thompson.*

■ **CLASSICS AND FANTASY.** *Ethics; family; friendship; movies; self-identity.*

■ **RELATED BOOKS: The Lion, The Witch, and the Wardrobe** series by C. S. Lewis; **Harry Potter** series by J. K. Rowling; **A Wrinkle in Time** series by Madeleine L'Engle.

> *Note:* According to Marjorie N. Allen's book, **100 Years of Children's Books in America** (Facts on File, 1996), Baum's fantasy series was never appreciated by many children's librarians, including Anne Carroll Moore. However, perhaps because of the classic movie, this series has endured, becoming as legendary as Lewis Carroll's **Alice's Adventures in Wonderland**. Recommended also as a read-aloud for younger elementary students.

"Come along, Toto," said Dorothy, "we must go to the Emerald City and ask the great Oz how to get back to Kansas."

She took off her leather shoes and tried on the silver ones that had belonged to the Witch of the East. Within a short time she was walking down the paved road with yellow brick.

Now, let's stop right here. Many of you know the rest of the story because you've seen the movie *The Wizard of Oz*. Still, the book came first and you might have noticed that I said Dorothy's slippers were silver, not ruby. Don't be so sure you know this story. Yes, the Scarecrow, Tin Man and Cowardly Lion are here. But so are the yellow Winkies, the Queen of the Field Mice, and other fascinating characters that the movie didn't have.

Come on down, let's follow the yellow brick road to **The Wizard of Oz!**

Beatty, Theresa M. *Foods and Recipes of China.*

*Rosen, 1999, 23pp. Kids in the Kitchen series: **Foods and Recipes of Africa; Foods and Recipes of Greece; Foods and Recipes of Japan; Foods and Recipes of Mexico; Foods and Recipes of the Caribbean**. Lower Elementary & Up.*

■ **NONFICTION.** *Asia (China); China; hobbies (cooking).*

■ **RELATED BOOKS: Kids in the Kitchen** series, all by Theresa M. Beatty; **Betty Crocker's New Chinese Cookbook** with recipes by LeeAnn Chin; **It's Disgusting and We Ate It: True Food Facts From Around the World** by James Solheim.

Note: *Colorful layout includes maps, pronunciation of words, and history of China, as well as cooking safety tips. The booktalk could include either bringing in food or cooking utensils.*

China is one of the oldest civilizations in the world, containing more people than any other country. The food is just as fascinating as its history.

For instance, the Chinese discovered that cooking vegetables in water or sauce was healthy. They also created noodles for their dishes and served them with rice, water chestnuts, ginger root, and pork.

You, too, can create meals fit for an emperor as you read **Foods and Recipes of China**.

Billingsley, Franny. *The Folk Keeper.*

Atheneum, 1997, 176pp. Middle School & Up. ALA Notable Children's Book; SLJ's Best Books; Bulletin of the Center for Children's Books Blue Ribbon Award; Book Links' Lasting Connections selection; Children's Books of the Year selection; Publishers Weekly's Best Books; Booklist's Editors' Choice.

■ **FANTASY.** *Diaries; Great Britain (Ireland); Ireland; orphans; revenge; secrets; supernatural (gremlins).*

■ **RELATED BOOKS: Well Wished** by Franny Billingsley; **Hob and the Goblins** by William Mayne; **Harry Potter** series by J. K. Rowling; **The Borrowers** series by Mary Norton; **The Boggart** series by Susan Cooper.

Note: *The text is written in the poetic style of a journal. The main character, 15-year-old Corrina Stonewall, discovers her heritage as a seal maiden as well as her validity as the Folk Keeper. The acclaimed author bases the unusual plot on Selkie folklore and songs that her father sang to her as a child. Recommended for fantasy lovers and readers looking for a strong, self-reliant heroine.*

I have great secret powers. I am never cold, I always know what time it is, and my hair grows two inches while I sleep. That's why I have the most important job in Rhysbridge—in fact, all of the Mainland.

I am the Folk Keeper. I watch over The Folk. The Folk are fierce, wet-mouthed, cave-dwelling gremlins. These gremlins sour milk, rot cabbage, and make farm animals sick. I sit with the Folk and draw off their anger as a lightning rod draws off lightning. The Folk are no match for my power.

I am also Corinna Stonewall. My secrets run as deep as my powers. No one knows that I am a girl disguised as a boy and that I have no official training as a Folk Keeper. Yet I am strong enough to defeat them all: the sassy yet attractive Lord Finian Hawthorne, the snobbish Sir Edward and all the vicious Folk.

Whatever happens, I am and will remain **The Folk Keeper**.

Billingsley, Franny. *Well Wished.*

Atheneum, 1997, 170pp. Upper Elementary & Up. ALA Notable Children's Book; YASLA Best Books for Young Adults.

■ **FANTASY.** *Disability (crippled); orphans; rivalry; secrets; supernatural.*

■ **RELATED BOOKS: The Wish Giver: Three Tales of Coven Tree** and others in **The Coven Tree** series by Bill Brittain; **Switching Well** by Penni R. Griffin; **Tuck Everlasting** by Natalie Babbitt.

> *Note:* First-time author addresses self-identity questions without losing story's suspense. Nuria uses the Wishing Well to wish for her friend Catty Winter to walk again, but her wish lands Nuria in Catty's body, confined to a wheelchair. Recommended for readers who enjoy fantasy with supernatural elements.

Be careful what you wish because it just might come true.

Nuria had always heard that saying, and in the village of Bishop Mayne, it is particularly true. The Wishing Well grants your wish, no matter how silly. That's why there were no children in the village. Some fool had made a wish, and as usual, the wish came true.

Despite her grandfather's warnings, however, Nuria made a wish. She was lonely and needed a friend. After Nuria's wish, like magic, her new friend appeared—Catty Winter.

Of course, one wish always leads to another. Catty wanted to be released from her wheelchair so she could skate like Nuria. Nuria decided to help her friend, but the wish went wrong. Very, very wrong.

Bockris, Victor, and Roberta Bayley. *Patti Smith: An Unauthorized Biography.*

Simon and Schuster, 1999, 336pp. Middle School & Up.

■ **BIOGRAPHY.** *Music; show business; women's issues.*

■ **RELATED BOOKS: Woolgathering** by Patti Smith; **Two Times Intro: On the Road With Patti Smith** by Michael Stipe; **Patti Smith Complete: Lyrics, Reflections & Notes for the Future** by Patti Smith; **Edie** edited by Jean Stein and George Plimpton.

> *Note:* Book also provides fascinating tidbits on rock royalty (Bob Dylan, the Rolling Stones, Debbie Harry, Marianne Faithfull) and popular artists (Andy Warhol, photographer Robert Mapplethorpe, playwright Sam Shepherd, Beat writer William Burroughs). Recommended for music lovers and as a biography about a creative, inspiring woman.

On February 10, 1971, a poet delivered her first public reading. Only Patti Smith wasn't exactly reading. Her language had a cadence, much like rap music. She repeated words, over and over, fusing poetry and rock. On that February night, Patti began her climb to rock stardom, becoming the godmother of punk.

Inevitably, she fell from stardom—literally, as she tumbled offstage during a 1977 performance. With that fall, she disappeared from the public. When she reappeared, she had reinvented herself. She was a subservient suburban Detroit housewife. Then she disappeared again. Later, a widow with two children, she returned to the stage as a middle-aged survivor.

Who is this rock priestess who reincarnates herself each decade? How many more lives are left for **Patti Smith**?

Bouzereau, Laurent and Jody Duncan. *Star Wars: The Making of Episode 1, The Phantom Menace.*

Ballentine, 1999, 160pp. For all libraries.

■ **NONFICTION AND SCIENCE FICTION.** *End-of-the-world; movies.*

■ **RELATED BOOKS: Star Wars: Episode 1, The Phantom Menace** by Terry Brooks; **Star Wars: Episode 1, The Phantom Menace** by Patricia Wrede; **The Suicide of Star Wars** by Jeanne Cavelos.

> *Note:* *Lavishly illustrated with hundreds of drawings and colored photographs, this will also appeal to movie and science fiction fans.*

At first, it was a secret known only to a few. After 16 years, following the 1983 release of *The Return of the Jedi,* the new *Star Wars* movie was now in production. George Lucas had finally written the prequel to *Star Wars,* and, in the summer of 1997, began directing *Star Wars: Episode One, The Phantom Menace.*

Once the media leaked the secret, interest accelerated. During those 16 years, *Star Wars* had gained a new generation of admirers who were even more enthusiastic than their predecessors. They wanted all the details—the more, the better.

Here's the behind-the-scenes story of a movie phenomenon: **Star Wars: The Making of Episode 1, The Phantom Menace**. May the Force be with you.

Bridges, Ruby, and Margo Lundell (editor). *Through My Eyes.*

Scholastic Trade, 64pp. For all libraries. ALA Notable Children's Books selection; Parents' Choice Gold Award winner; SLJ's Best Books; Bulletin of Center of Children's Books Blue Ribbon award; Cooperative Children's Books Center choice; New York Times Notable Book; Children's Books of the Year selection; Publishers Weekly's Best Books.

■ **BIOGRAPHY.** *African Americans; ethics; interracial relations; racism; school; self-identity.*

■ **RELATED BOOKS: The Story of Ruby Bridges** by Robert Coles; **Ruby Bridges** by Scott Correntino, et al; **If a Bus Could Talk: The Story of Rosa Parks** by Faith Ringgold.

> *Note:* *This memoir, told in the voice of bewildered compassion, combines sepia-tone photographs, newspaper articles, and commentaries from her teacher and psychologist. The story is significant because the hero is a courageous six-year-old child who had no idea she was making history. Highly recommended as group read or read-aloud.*

When I was six, I made history.

I made history by beginning the first grade at a New Orleans school. Of course, many students did that; however, I was the first African American to attend a white school. On November 14, 1960, as I walked toward the school door, surrounded by four federal marshals, white people yelled and threw things at me. I ignored them. Unknown to me, my picture (without my name, Ruby Bridges) appeared in newspapers all over the world.

When I was 18, I saw the painting of me by Norman Rockwell (*see page 25, Through My Eyes*) that was inspired by the words of John Steinbeck. I learned people were touched by the story of a black child who was so alone that day. Interest in my story keeps growing, and it's not because I'm promoting it. Now it's time for me to share my story and my place in history. I will try to give you the bigger picture **Through My Eyes.**

B

Bronte, Charlotte. *Jane Eyre.*

First published in 1847. Mass Market Paperback, 1994, 466pp. Middle School & Up.

■ **CLASSICS AND ROMANCE.** *Abuse; class conflict; death; disability (blindness); Great Britain; love; mental illness; orphans; secrets.*

■ **RELATED BOOKS: Wuthering Heights** by Emily Bronte; **Rebecca** by Daphne du Maurier; **Romeo and Juliet** by William Shakespeare.

 *This story was first published in 1847 and written in the archaic yet forthright voice of an intense, plucky, self-aware young heroine named Jane Eyre. Recommended as a logical progression from Louisa May Alcott's **Little Women** and Jane Austen's novels. A definite must-read for romance lovers.*

My name, Jane Eyre, is all I own.

Orphaned at only 10 years of age, I was a dependent of my aunt and her family. I had no money; my father left me none. For that reason, I was called naughty and tiresome, sullen and sneaking, from morning to noon, and from noon to night.

Sent to a charity school, I stayed for eight years. My life was uniform, but I had the means of an excellent education.

At 18, I had my name, my education, and my pride. Armed with these small possessions, I became a governess to the ward of Edward Rochester of Thornfield. This man possessed strange moods and seemed to be living under some dark shadow. Nevertheless, I cannot help but love this man.

Eventually Mr. Rochester asked my hand in marriage. The day of the wedding I learned Mr. Rochester's secret, a secret so terrible I felt forced to leave Thornfield for what I assume is forever.

Now, dear reader, I will leave you to ponder the outcome of this proud orphan, this young woman called **Jane Eyre.**

Bronte, Emily. *Wuthering Heights.*

First published in 1847. Bantam Classic, 1983, 315pp. Middle School & Up.

■ **CLASSICS AND ROMANCE.** *Class conflict; death; Great Britain; love; supernatural.*

■ **RELATED BOOKS: Jane Eyre** by Charlotte Bronte; **Pride and Prejudice** by Jane Austen; **Tess of the D'Urbervilles** by Thomas Hardy; **Rebecca** by Daphne du Maurier; **Turn of the Screw** by Henry James.

Set in untamed Yorkshire moors, Bronte's tragic love story is forerunner of today's romance novels and soap operas. Emily, like her sister Charlotte and Anne, used a pen name, Ellis Bell. Unfortunately, Emily Bronte died in 1848, a year after its publication, at the age of 30, believing her work to be a failure. After Emily's death, Charlotte edited her sister's book. A must-read for all romance lovers.

I was determined to stop the gutsy wind from allowing the fir branch to tap against my snow-covered window. To my horror, instead of grasping the impertinent limb, I clasped a child's ice-cold hands!

As I tried to withdraw, a melancholy voice whispered, "Oh, please let me in! Let me in! Let me in! I am Catherine Linton."

"Who the devil is that?" I bellowed, still trembling from fear.

"It's me, Catherine! I've come home. At last. After losing my way among the moors for 20 years. Let me in!"

"The devil I will!" I retorted. "To the devil with you and those ghosts like you!" I slammed the shutters. After retiring to an uneventful sleep, I decided that I must have conjured up this ghost in my dreams.

That is, until I saw Mr. Heathcliff the next morning and told him about my adventurous night. His face became ghostly white. "Catherine? Catherine's come back home, you say?"

Consumed with curiosity, I received the complete tale from his housekeeper. This love story is filled with passion, betrayal, and revenge that would illuminate Catherine and Heathcliff's love beyond life itself.

I beg you to listen to my story of the two lovers from **Wuthering Heights.**

Brooks, Bruce. *The Moves Make the Man.*

First published in 1984. Mass Market Paperback, 1995, 256 pp. Middle School & Up. Newbery Honor, ALA Notable Children's Book, YASLA Best Books for Young Adults, Boston Globe/Horn Book Award, Best '80s YA novel (English Journal), 100 Favorite Paperbacks (IRA/CBC); Children's Books of the Year selection.

■ **REALISTIC FICTION AND SPORTS.** *African Americans; interracial relations; mental illness; problem parents (mental illness); racism; rivalry; school; runaways.*

■ **RELATED BOOKS: Midnight Hour Encores** by Bruce Brooks; **On the Devil's Court** and **Painting the Black** by Carl Deuker; **Danger Zone** by David Klass; **Bull Catcher** by Alden R. Carter; **Blue Star Rapture** by James W. Bennett.

Note: First published in 1984 and recommended for sports fans and readers looking for realistic fiction about interracial friendships. Author brings up many issues such as stepparents, rivalry, racism and family mental illness. Warning: Narrator Jerome Foxworthy uses street lingo and racially offensive terms such as "nigger" and "Sambo."

I gotta tell Bix River's story. If I don't, who will? Not his crazy mamma or his mean stepfather. It's me who gets to tell the truth. Truth can sometimes cut deep and leave wounds.

Bix and me shoot basketball just like we move through life. I use a lotta fake moves 'cause I like to think of myself as mysterious and unpredictable. Bix refuses to teach his body to trick people. He likes to play the game straight, clean. Truth is a big thing with Bix. Maybe too big, 'cause his truth may be too real for others. Either way, both of us learned that if someone is faking it, another one is taking it.

Watch us fake it and take it. We got game. That game will move us straight through life because **The Moves Make the Man**.

Bruchac, Joseph. *The Arrow Over the Door.*

Illustrated by James Watling. Dial, 1998, 96 pp. Lower Elementary & Up. Children's Books of the Year selection; National Council for Social Studies Notable Trade Books; Children's Crown Award.

■ **HISTORICAL FICTION.** *American Revolutionary War; Native Americans (Abenaki); racism; religion (Quakers); religion prejudices; war.*

■ **RELATED BOOKS: Saturnalia** by Paul Fleischman; **The Sign of the Beaver** and **Calico Captive** by Elizabeth George Speare; **The Courage of Sarah Noble** by Alice Dalgliesh.

Note: In alternating chapters, author describes two 14-year-old boys, one a Quaker, one an Abenaki Indian. Based on actual events in 1777 before the Battle of Saratoga, the "Saratoga meeting," or the "Easton meeting" brought the Quakers and Indians together for a pledge of peace. Author's notes include background on the Quakers and Abenakis, including the incident. Recommended for intermediate readers who enjoy historical fiction, especially about Native Americans.

Indians! Samuel thought. Two of them right in the middle of our Quaker prayer meeting! How safe are we?

Samuel had heard all about Indians. How cruel and bloodthirsty Indians were. How they hated white people and found pleasure in torturing them. How they fought with King George against his family and all the other Loyalists. Samuel also remembered what the Quakers taught him: the light of God was in Indians, too.

One of the Indians, Stands Straight, knew nothing about Quakers. He knew only that he hated the people who killed his mother and brother. He would make the white people pay for this. He felt angry and defiant when he and his father's tribe silently surrounded the Quaker meeting house.

Meanwhile, Samuel and the Quakers waited inside, deep in prayer. Within minutes, the Indians will attack.

When enemies meet, what will be the outcome?

Brunvand, Jan Harold. *Too Good to Be True: The Colossal Book of Urban Legends.*

W. W. Norton, 1999, 480pp. Middle School & Up.

■ **FOLKLORE.** *Crime; death; love.*

■ **RELATED BOOKS: Scary Stories to Tell in the Dark** series by Alvin Schwartz; **Spiders in the Hairdo: Modern Urban Legends** collected and retold by David Holt and Bill Mooney; other books by Jan Harold Brunvand, such as **The Big Book of Urban Legends, The Baby-Sitter's Nightmare**, and **Curses! Broiled Again!**

> *Note:* Brunvand tells all the latest urban legends, and also analyses them, noting that urban legends express a society's subconscious fears and desires. Recommended for all types of readers, especially reluctant readers.

Have you heard "The Elevator Story"?

Eddie Murphy was in an elevator with 10 of his bodyguards. An elderly lady was there too. One of the bodyguards said, "Hit the floor." The lady dropped to the floor, shaking and trembling. The men, including Eddie, started laughing. The guy had only wanted the woman to push the elevator button. ("Hit the floor," get it?) The next day, the lady received a dozen roses from Eddie Murphy who told her that she provided his laugh for the day.

Guess what? That never happened. That story is an urban legend. A friend of a friend tells a friend a story that's "absolutely true," and an urban legend is born.

Try reading the latest urban legends. These stories are just **Too Good to be True!**

Burgess, Melvin. *Smack.*

*With glossary. Originally published in Great Britain in 1996 under the title **Junk.** Henry Holt, 1998, 327pp. Middle School & Up. Carnegie Award; Guardian Prize for Fiction; VOYA award; YALSA Best Books for Young Adults; SLJ's Best Books; Publishers Weekly's list; Children's Books of the Year selection.*

■ **REALISTIC FICTION.** *Great Britain; runaways; substance abuse (heroin).*

■ **RELATED BOOKS: Go Ask Alice** by Anonymous; **Beauty Queen** by Linda Glovach; **the perks of being a wallflower** by Stephen Chbosky.

>
> *Note:* The text is based on actual people and events. The author uses multiple narrators who tell of their slow descent into drug addiction. Only the hard facts are presented without resorting to didacticism. Unforgettable; highly recommended for mature readers.

Here it is—what you've all been waiting for—*Gemma Brogan's Handbook to Running Away from Home*:

1. Bring these essential items—clothes, plenty of keep-warm stuff. A sleeping bag. money, your father's bank card and PIN number.

2. Your wits. You'll need 'em.

3. Leave a note telling them you're gone for good. Otherwise, your parents will think you've been kidnapped. They'll call the police and that means trouble.

4. Once you hit the streets, stay away from smack. Speaking from experience, I can say that heroin, known as smack or junk, will destroy what's left of your wits.

That's it. My advice. I'm speaking from experience. Don't end up like me. Don't end up on **Smack.**

Cadnum, Michael. *Rundown.*

Viking, 1999, 168pp. High School & Up. Quick Picks for Reluctant Young Adult Readers; Children's Books of the Year selection.

■ **REALISTIC FICTION.** *Rivalry; secrets; sexual abuse.*

■ **RELATED BOOKS: Are You in the House Alone?** by Richard Peck; **After the Fall** by Robert Cormier; **Jacob Have I Loved** by Katherine Paterson; **The Tribe of Palo Alto** by Joy Nicholson.

 Note: *Main character, Jennifer Thayer, is jealous of her sister, Cassandra, and has a desperate need to communicate with her controlling parents. Jennifer constructs a lie that, while jogging at dusk, she was the victim of an attempted rape. Because of the content, recommend this page-turner to mature readers.*

One month before my sister's wedding I did a terrible thing. I started a lie. I reported a crime that never happened. I made myself the victim.

Now I know I did it for my parents' attention. I got their attention, all right. I also became a local celebrity with way too much attention. This is totally out of control.

Help!

Card, Orson Scott. *Ender's Game.*

*First published in 1977. Tom Doherty, 1991, 324pp. Middle School & Up. First in a series: **Speaker for the Dead; Xenocide; Children of the Mind;** and **Ender's Shadow** follow. Hugo Award; Nebula Award.*

■ **SCIENCE FICTION.** *Bullies; computers; rites of passage; rivalry; science; war.*

■ **RELATED BOOKS: Foundation Trilogy** series: **Foundation; Foundation and Empire** and **Second Foundation** by Isaac Asimov; **Stranger in a Strange Land** by Robert Heinlein.

Note: *A gifted boy, Andrew "Ender" Wiggin is selected by government agencies to become a military leader and to fight "buggers" or aliens. He leaves behind his sadistic older brother, Peter and his devoted sister, Valentine, both of whom will forge an alliance to change the Earth's future. The fast-moving plot involves aliens and computer games, and may appeal to those who think they don't like science fiction. This novel is also a must-read series for the serious science fiction fan.* **Warning:** *Profanity.*

"Ender, I'm director of the Battle School in the Belt. I'm inviting you to enter the school."

"What's it like there?" Ender asked.

"Hard work. Strategy and tactics. And, above all, the Battle Room."

"What's the Battle Room?"

"War games. In zero gravity, there are mock battles. It's like playing aliens and astronauts—except you have weapons that work and the whole future of the human race depends on how well you fight. The aliens may seem like a game to you, Ender, but they almost wiped us out last time. We need to prepare for our next war. We think you may be our future leader."

Ender had trouble listening because the thought of fighting the aliens was frightening. "I don't want to go, but I will. Let me tell Mother and Father goodbye."

Ender started his new life at the Battle School, beginning **Ender's Game.** He was only six-years-old!

Carroll, Lewis (Charles Dodgson). *Alice's Adventures in Wonderland: The Ultimate Illustrated Edition.*

Compiled and arranged by Cooper Edens. Illustrated by John Tenniel, et al. Chronicle Books, 2000, 152pp. For all libraries. Part of a series: Alice Through the Looking Glass follows. 2000 ALA Notable; Horn Book Fanfare; Cooperative Children's Book Center choice.

■ **CLASSICS AND FANTASY.** *Great Britain; magic; movies; time travel.*

■ **RELATED BOOKS: Alice Through the Looking Glass** by Lewis Carroll; **The Phantom Tollbooth** by Norton Juster; **Alice** by Whoopi Goldberg; **Charlie and the Chocolate Factory** series by Roald Dahl; **In His Own Write** by John Lennon (for mature readers).

Note: This edition is highly recommended since vintage illustrations are gathered from the late 19th and early 20th century. Work from many artists, from the classic Tenniel to Dali, is dramatically presented, resembling an art gallery. The large-print text is reader-friendly, and the book also makes a good read-aloud for younger readers.

Later, Alice blamed the White Rabbit.

If that rabbit hadn't been running around, checking his watch, mumbling, "Oh dear! Oh dear! I shall be late!" she wouldn't have followed him. When the White Rabbit jumped down the rabbit hole, Alice jumped, too, and her adventures began in Wonderland.

Have you seen a cat without a grin or a grin without a cat? What about a deck of cards that changes into people? While we're on the topic, who stole the tarts from the Queen of Hearts? Why is the Queen always yelling, "Off with her head!"

Escape to **Alice's Adventures in Wonderland.** Your world will never look the same again!

Cart, Michael (compiler). *Tomorrowland: 10 Stories About the Future.*

Scholastic Trade, 1999, 244pp. Middle School & Up. VOYA award; Book Links' Lasting Connections selection; YASLA Quick Picks for Reluctant Young Adult Readers; YALSA Best Books for Young Adults.

■ **SCIENCE FICTION AND SHORT STORIES.** *Computers; ecology; end-of-the-world.*

■ **RELATED BOOKS: Trapped!** edited by Lois Duncan; **War of the Worlds** and **The Time Machine** by H. G. Wells; **Ender's Game** by Orson Scott Card.

Note: Ten award-winning authors (Lois Lowry, Katherine Paterson, Jon Scieszka, Ron Koertge, Rodman Philbrick, Gloria Skurzynski, Jacqueline Woodson, et al) view the future. Only three stories are traditional science fiction: Gloria Skurzynski's Martian Cain and Abel adventure; Katherine Paterson's story about a "pod man's" discovery of what may be Earth's last dog; and Rodman Philbrick's futuristic tale reminiscent of **Fahrenheit 451.** Recommended for all types of readers because of the versatility of the stories.

Suppose you could see the future. I call that "Tomorrowland." What would you see? Do you foresee a heavenly, peaceful planet (*utopia*) or a distressed, dire world (*distopia*)?

Some of your favorite authors have created their vision of Tomorrowland. Jon Scieszka takes us back to 33,001 B.C., when Neanderthal-bashing brutes begin the tradition of a rowdy bash. Many thousands of years from now, author Ron Koertge believes that in a robot world: "There are two things that are never gonna change. There's always going to be a spring dance, and guys are always gonna play ball." Rodman Philbrick describes a future like the one depicted in Ray Bradbury's *Fahrenheit 451*, where books and word processors are a thing of the past.

Your future is waiting. Welcome to **Tomorrowland: 10 Stories About the Future.**

Cavelos, Jeanne. *The Science of Star Wars.*

St. Martins, 1999. 224pp. High School & Up.

■ **NONFICTION.** *Animals; movies; science (astronomy, geology, physics).*

■ **RELATED BOOKS: Empire Building: Remarkable Real-Life Story of Star Wars** by Garry Jenkins; **Star Wars Episode 1: What's What** by Daniel Wallace; **George Lucas** by Christopher Rau.

> **Note:** NASA scientist, **Star Wars** fan, and author Jeanne Cavelos includes information on four **Star Wars** films (**Star Wars, Empire Strikes Back, Return to Jedi,** and **Phantom Menace**) as well as **Star Wars** comic books. Recommended for science fiction fans, science lovers and movie buffs.

How accurate is *Star Wars*? Could there be intelligent life in outer space? Would aliens look like the aliens from *Star Wars*? Is The Force real?

When George Lucas created his vision of *Star Wars*, he was more accurate about interplanetary life than scientists realized at the time. Yesterday's science fiction often becomes tomorrow's reality. At last, science is finally catching up with *Star Wars*.

Hop aboard to discover the **Science of Star Wars.**

Chbosky, Stephen. *the perks of being a wallflower.*

Pocket Books, 1999, 213pp. High School & Up. YASLA Quick Picks for Reluctant Young Adult Readers; YALSA Best Books for Young Adults.

■ **REALISTIC FICTION.** *Diaries; homosexuality; sex and sexuality; sexual abuse; suicide; substance abuse (LSD, marijuana, and others).*

■ **RELATED BOOKS: The Catcher in the Rye** by J. D. Salinger; **Tribute to Another Dead Rock Star** by Randy Powell; **Rats Saw God** by Rob Thomas; **The Falcon** by Jackie French Koller.

> **Note:** In this debut novel, reviewers compared this to Salinger's **The Catcher in the Rye**, Chbosky uses Charlie's letters to describe his first year of high school, including his first love, family tensions, homosexuality between two classmates, drug experiments, and most of all, a friend's suicide. Highly recommended for mature readers.

Dear friend,

I am a wallflower. I admit it.

There are certain perks to being a wallflower at my high school. No one notices me, but I notice everyone else. That's why these letters are filled with details. Because I do notice things.

For instance, I walk around the school hallways and look at the teachers. What were they like when they were 15? I look at the students, too, and wonder about them. Who had their heart broken today? Who is gay and who is straight? (I thought our football hero was straight until I learned differently.)

I wonder about my family and friends, too. Why did my best friend, Michael commit suicide? What secret was my Aunt Helen hiding from me? How can I be in love with a friend named Sam (who's a girl)?

I'll tell you all I know and see. That's one of **the perks of being a wallflower.**

Christopher, Matt. *Stranger in Right Field.*

Illustrated by Bert Dodson. Little, Brown, 1997, 61pp. Lower Elementary & Up. Last book in the **Peach Street Mudders** *series:* **All-Star Fever; Centerfield Ballhawk; Hit-Away Kid; Man Out at First; Shadow Over Second; Spy on Third Base; Zero's Slider.**

■ **SPORTS.** *Friendship; responsibility; rivalry; sports (baseball).*

■ **RELATED BOOKS: Peach Street Mudders** series and **Dirt Bike Racer** by Matt Christopher; **Thank You, Jackie Robinson** by Barbara Cohen; **The Trading Game** by Alfred Slote; **Orp Goes to The Hoop** by Suzy Kline.

 Note: *Christopher's stories always discuss ethical issues. Recommended for beginning readers who enjoy sports.*

OK, Alfie wasn't the best baseball player in the world. He missed some fly balls in the right field and struck out a few times, but he was getting better.

So why does a new kid, who has never played baseball, get picked to be on the team? Why did Alfie have to teach this greenhorn how to play when he had his own troubles? Worse still, was this new kid going to end up replacing him?

Find out what else Alfie had to endure from the **Stranger in Right Field**.

Ciencin, Scott. *Dinoverse.*

Illustrated by Mike Fredericks. Random House, 1999, 282pp. Upper Elementary School & Up.

■ **FANTASY.** *Animals (dinosaurs); science; survival.*

■ **RELATED BOOKS: Dinotopia** series (**Windchaser; Lost City; Thunder Falls**) by Scott Ciencin; horror books by Paul Zindel: **Reef of Death; Loch; Raptor.**

 Note: *This humorous, fast-paced fantasy is also useful for its informative "Dinoverse" glossary and bibliography on dinosaurs. A sure-fire winner for reluctant readers.*

This book should be titled *I Was a Teenage Dinosaur.*

Four teens travel back in time—and body. They all become prehistoric dinosaurs. Betrum is no longer a nerd; he's a spiky Ankylosaurus (ANG-kih-luh-saw-rus). Beauty queen Candayce becomes a huge Leptoceratops (lep-tuh-SER-uh-tops). Football hero Mike becomes a T. Rex. Janine finds her bliss soaring on the wings of a handsome Pterodactyl (ter-o-DAK-til).

How do these four escape certain extinction and get back to Wetherford Junior High? Find out in **Dinoverse**.

My rating? Two claws up!

Cleary, Beverly. *Ramona's World.*

Illustrated by Alan Tiegreen. Morrow Junior Books, 1999, 192pp. Upper Elementary & Up. Last book in the series; **Beezus and Ramona; Ramona the Pest; Ramona the Brave; Ramona and Her Father; Ramona and Her Mother; Ramona Quimby, Age 8;** *and* **Ramona Forever** *precede. Children's Books of the Year selection.*

■ **HUMOR.** *Family; friendship; school.*

■ **RELATED BOOKS: Ellen Tibbets** series by Beverly Cleary; **Tales of a Fourth Grade Nothing** series by Judy Blume; the **Aldo** series by Johanna Hurwitz.

 Note: In Cleary's first **Ramona** book in 15 years, the beloved spitfire Ramona is now nine and ready to face the best year of her life. Of course, everything goes wrong, as it only can with Ramona. This is a great read-aloud for younger readers.

Ramona's baaaack!

Many of you know Ramona and her older sister, Beezus. Now Ramona has a new baby sister and a new fourth grade teacher. Life should be perfect, but for Ramona, life is never that simple.

First of all, Ramona can't spell. One of her misspelled words was "couch." She spelled it C-O-A-C-H. That's "coach." Her secret crush, Danny, known as Yard Ape, teased her, "What kind of coach did you sit on? Baseball or football?"

Ramona's school pictures didn't turn out well either. Maybe because she said "peas" instead of "cheese." Still, Yard Ape's valentine read, "If you are eating peas/Think of me before you sneeze."

Be warned: Funny things are always happening in **Ramona's World.**

Clements, Andrew. *The Landry News.*

Illustrated by Sal Murdocca. Simon & Schuster, 1999, 128pp. Upper Elementary & Up. Parents' Choice Silver Award; ALA Notable Children's Book; Society of School Librarians International Honor Book; SLJ's Best Books; Children's Books of the Year selection.

■ **REALISTIC FICTION.** *Divorce; ethics; hobbies (writing); moving; school; responsibility; work.*

■ **RELATED BOOKS: Frindle** by Andrew Clement; **Nothing But the Truth** by Avi; **Harriet the Spy** by Louise Fitzhugh; **The Turnabout Shop** by Colby F. Rodowsky.

Note: New girl Cara Landry writes a scathing editorial about her fifth grade teacher that leads to a classroom newspaper and the school board's evaluation of Mr. Larson's teaching techniques. The Christopher Award-winning author presents all sides through three narratives—the students, the teachers, and principal. The ending may be predictable, but it raises issues about the First Amendment, the Constitution, and fairness vs. honesty. Recommended for all types of readers and especially as a group read since it should provide stimulating discussions.

Mr. Larson is the kind of teacher about whom parents write letters to the principal. Letters like:

Dear Mr. Barnes:
We know our child is only in the second grade this year, but, in the future, please be sure that he (or she) is **not** *placed in Mr. Larson's fifth grade class.*

Sincerely,
Mr.-and-Mrs.-Everybody-Who-Lives-in-Carlton

However, no one had taken a public stand against Mr. Larson until the arrival of the new fifth grade student. Cara Landry was a budding journalist who liked to report The Truth as she saw it. When she decided to post her editorial comment in the *The Landry News* about Mr. Larson, she was surprised at the response. Not only did she hear from students, the parents, and th Principal, she received an answer from Mr.-Bad-Teacher himself!

Pick up a copy of **The Landry News** to see what all the fuss is about.

Clinton, Catherine (editor). *I, Too, Sing America: Three Centuries of African American Poetry.*

Illustrated by Stephen Alcorn. Clarion Books, 1998, 128pp. For all libraries. VOYA award; YALSA Best Books for Young Adults; Children's Books of the Year selection.

■ **POETRY.** *African Americans; Civil War; holidays (Martin Luther King Jr. Day); politics; racism.*

■ **RELATED BOOKS: The Middle Passage** by Tom Feelings; **To Be a Slave** by Julius Lester; **Celebrate America: In Poetry and Art** edited by Nora Panzer.

 Note: Read Langston Hughes' "Harlem" which inspired Lorraine Hansberry's **Raisin in the Sun**. *The book also includes biographical sketches of 25 African-American poets with stunning illustrations. Highly recommended for social studies and language arts classes.*

The African-American poet Langston Hughes called himself a "literary sharecropper" because he had to work so hard for his success. Nevertheless, he never underestimated his worth: "I, too, sing America/I am the darker brother/They'll see how beautiful I am/And be ashamed/I, too, am America."

Join Langston Hughes and other poets who expressed their rage, defiance and pride in their African-American heritage in **I, Too, Sing America**.

Conford, Ellen. *Annabel the Actress Starring in Gorilla My Dreams.*

*Illustrated by Renee W. Andriani. Simon & Schuster, 1999, 64pp. Lower Elementary & Up. First of **Annabel the Actress** series; **Annabel the Actress Starring in Just a Little Extra** follows.*

■ **HUMOR AND REALISTIC FICTION.** *Animals (gorillas); friends; show business; work.*

■ **RELATED BOOKS: Dynamite Dinah** series by Claudia Mills; **Ramona Quimby, Age 8,** and other **Ramona** books by Beverly Cleary; **Class Clown** series by Johanna Hurwitz.

 Note: Adriani's illustrations add to the hilarity. Recommended for beginning readers looking for a spunky heroine in a humorous setting.

Annabel knew that someday she was going to be a famous actress. She was always willing to suffer for her art. For instance, she always watched TV to study how actors acted and practiced making faces in the mirror every day. She even put an ad in the town newspaper every week that read:

ANNABEL THE ACTRESS
NO PART TOO BIG OR SMALL

Of course, dressing up in a gorilla suit at a birthday party was not exactly what she had in mind. It was hard enough wearing a gorilla costume that kept falling apart, but acting like an ape in front of rowdy five-year-old boys was a real challenge.

Hey, not to worry. Annabel is a professional. The show must go on for **Annabel the Actress**!

Conford, Ellen. *Diary of a Monster's Son.*

Illustrated by Tom Newsom. Little, Brown, 1999, 76pp. Upper Elementary & Up. Society of School Librarians International Best Book.

■ **HUMOR.** *Family; holidays (Halloween); supernatural.*

■ **RELATED BOOKS: Ma and Pa Dracula** by Ann M. Martin; **Bunnicula** series by Deborah and James Howe; **The Vampire in My Bathtub** by Brenda Seabrooke.

Note: *While booktalking, show some illustrations that humorously display the father's monstrous hairy paw, but never reveal his face. Underlying the humor is irony that the main character, Bradley Fentriss, responds to his father's caring character, unaware that his father is a physical beast. Highly recommended as a read-aloud during Halloween or autumn, even to the younger readers.*

My father is special.

He gives great advice. "Bradley, always take care of your fangs and your fangs will take care of you."

"I don't have fangs," I tell him. "I just have plain little teeth."

"And you never will have fangs," he warns, "if you don't eat all of your fungus. I went to a lot of trouble to dig it up. That lizard is cooked just the way you like it. Follow my advice and you'll grow up to be like me, big and hairy."

That's my father, always concerned and caring. I don't understand why people don't stick around long enough to get to know him. When they see him, they always seem to running or gasping for breath.

My advice to people? Don't judge a father by the size of his claws. My father is special. Read my **Diary of a Monster's Son**.

Cooper, Susan. *King of Shadows.*

Simon & Schuster, 1999, 186pp. Middle School & Up. VOYA award; Horn Book Fanfare; YASLA Best Books for Young Adults; Children's Books of the Year selection; Booklist Editors' Choice; Best Books; ABBY Pick of the Lists; Publishers Weekly's Best Book.

■ **FANTASY AND HISTORICAL FICTION.** *Great Britain; illness (bubonic plague); orphans; time travel.*

■ **RELATED BOOKS: The Shakespeare Stealer** by Gary Blackwood; **William Shakespeare & the Globe** by Aliki; **A Midsummer Night's Dream** by William Shakespeare; **The House of Hound Hill** by Maggie Prince.

Note: *This award-winning author realistically conveys sights, sounds and smells of Elizabethan England as, like many of Shakespeare's plays, two characters switch identities. Nathan Fields is a young actor playing Puck when he suddenly travels back in time several centuries to become another Nathan Fields who will play Puck to Shakespeare's Oberon. Cooper's depiction of staging the play A Midsummer's Night Dream might send readers to Shakespeare's play. (The title comes from the line in the play: "Believe me, King of Shadows, I mistook.") Queen Elizabeth also makes a brief appearance. Recommended for all types of readers, especially those studying English history or Shakespeare. Warning: Some profanity.*

"Where am I?" Nat asked weakly.

"Th'art Nathan Field, come to our new Globe Theatre in London. Th'art a wonderful actor who joined us yesterday. You took sick suddenly. I was sore afraid th'art had the plague."

The plague? Nat thought. Nobody has had the plague for centuries. And what did he mean by calling the Globe Theatre new? Shakespeare's theatre must be hundreds of years old. How can that be? The only explanation is that I've time traveled back to the year 1599!

Meanwhile, another Nathan Field was in a modern London hospital. The doctor ordered immediate isolation. "I know this will be hard to believe in this modern age. I think we have a case of bubonic plague."

Is this some Midsummer's Night Dream from which both Nathans will never awake? Methinks this book **King of Shadows** will clarify.

Cormier, Robert. *Frenchtown Summer.*

Delacorte, 1999, 113pp. Middle School & Up. Los Angeles Times Book Prize; SLJ's Best Books; Cooperative Children's Book Center Choice; Book Links' Lasting Connection selection; Children's Books of the Year selection; Publishers Weekly's Best Books.

■ **POETRY.** *Family; death; suicide; secrets; men's issues.*

■ **RELATED BOOKS: Out of the Dust** by Karen Hesse; **Stop Pretending** by Sonya Sones; **Foreign Exchange** and other books by Mel Glenn.

 Note: *Memoir in blank verse about the French-Canadian district of Monument called Frenchtown, familiar to Cormier fans from Fade, Heroes, and Tunes for Bears to Dance To. Main character, Eugene, observes the 1920s world around him—a near suicide; the death of a classmate; and his silent, enigmatic father. Recommended especially for reluctant readers who think they don't like poetry.*

It was the summer of my 12th birthday,
That summer in Frenchtown
In the days
When I knew my Name
But did not know who I was.
That was the summer of my first paper route,
Of Sister Angela
And my brother Raymond,
But especially my Uncle Mel
And my father.
And, finally,
It was the summer
Of the airplane.
It was my **Frenchtown Summer**.

Couloumbis, Audrey. *Getting Near to Baby.*

G. P. Putnam, 1999, 211pp. Upper Elementary & Up. Newbery Honor Award; ALA Notable Children's Book; SLJ's Best Books.

■ **REALISTIC FICTION.** *Death; disability (speech); single parent.*

■ **RELATED BOOKS: Snowdrops for Cousin Ruth** by Susan Katz; **The Barn** by Avi; **Toning the Sweep** by Angela Johnson; **Beat the Turtle Drum** by Constance Greene.

Note: *The story is loosely based on the author's childhood experience. Twelve-year-old Willa Jo's grief and her sister's temporary speech loss is poignantly handled. Recommended for realistic fiction fans and readers coping with a family death.*

Right now I got it pretty bad. My little sister hasn't said a word since my Mom lost her baby. Worse still, we were sent to Aunt Patty's home to live until Mom recovers.

That's why I'm sitting on Aunt Patty's roof and refuse to come down. I don't like her. She's so bossy and has crazy rules. Like us not buying peanut butter and not letting us enter through her front door.

I just overheard Aunt Patty saying to a neighbor, "I am going out of my mind with those two children, and I have only had them here for three weeks!"

I thought I was the only one counting the days until Mom returns.

Cummins, Julie, and Roxie Munro (co-author and illustrator).
The Inside-Outside Book of Libraries.

Dutton, 1996, 45pp. **Inside-Outside** *series:* **Inside-Outside Book of Paris** *and* **Inside-Outside Book of New York City** *by Roxie Munro. Lower Elementary & Up.*

■ **NONFICTION.** *Hobbies (reading); school; work.*

■ **RELATED BOOKS: Books and Libraries** by Jack Knowlton; **My Hometown Library** by William Jaspersohn; **How a Book Is Made** by Aliki.

Note: *Munro's ink and watercolor illustrations add to the fascinating text by New York Public Librarian Cummins. Specific libraries in New York City are described, such as the Chatham Square Library in Chinatown, the Explorers Club Library, and the Andrew Heiskell Library for the Blind and Physically Handicapped. The book also describes the Library of Congress in Washington, D.C., the Folsom State Prison Library, the Berkeley Public Library Tool Lending Library, and others. Excellent for classroom use or as a read-aloud during National Library Week. Also recommended for library and book lovers.*

Where would we be without libraries? Libraries show us where we have been and what we might be in the future. They collect all kinds of information and come in all shapes and sizes.

For instance, the United States has libraries with a Braille collection for the blind, a historical map collection for explorers, and even a tool collection for workers! Libraries are in hospitals, prisons, and on ships. Even the Internet is called a "library without walls" because it contains information you can use.

So check out what libraries have to offer inside and out!

Cunningham, Michael. *The Hours.*

Farrar, Straus, & Giroux, 1998, 230pp. High School & Up. Pulitzer Prize Winner; ALA Notable Adult Book.

■ **HISTORICAL FICTION.** *Eating disorders (anorexia); Great Britain; homosexuality; illness (mental, AIDS); suicide; women's issues; work (writing).*

■ **RELATED BOOKS: Mrs. Dalloway** and **To the Lighthouse** by Virginia Woolf; **Virginia Woolf** by Hermione Lee; **Home at the End of the World** and **Flesh and Blood** by Michael Cunningham.

Note: *The original story intertwines Woolf's life with two other female writers contemplating life and death—1950s Laura Brown and contemporary Clarissa Vaughn. The author brilliantly uses a stream-of-consciousness technique to capture Woolf's literary style. The text also includes passages from* **Mrs. Dalloway** *as well references to the Bloomsbury Group. You may wish to also share Virginia's actual suicide note (see page 6,* **The Hours***). Recommended for Virginia Woolf fans, mature readers, and readers who enjoy classic literature. Also, good for discussion groups on women's studies.* **Warning:** *Profanity.*

1941
My lovely husband Leonard,

You only remember me as a pale and tall young girl called Virginia Stephens who caught your fancy 20 years ago. The world knows me as Virginia Woolf, author of *To the Lighthouse* and *Mrs. Dalloway.* However, my voices tell me that I live a lie. I am not a gifted writer, just a gifted eccentric. I cannot finish my latest novel, so my characters must come alive through someone else's pen.

It will only be a few more hours until I, like my character Mrs. Dalloway, will be no more. I will succumb to the darkness of the ocean to escape life's endless hours that go on and on, hours riddled with failure and guilt.

When I am gone to the deep jaws of death, will anyone remember me as anything but a failure?

Love,
Virginia

C

Curtis, Christopher Paul. *Bud, Not Buddy.*

Delacorte, 1999, 245pp. Upper Elementary & Up. Newbery Award; Coretta Scott King Award; ALA Children's Notable Book; YALSA Best Books for Young Adults; SLJ's Best Books; Book Links' Lasting Connections selection; Cooperative Children's Book Center Choice; New York Times Notable Children's Book; Children's Books of the Year selection; Publishers Weekly's Best Books.

■ **HISTORICAL FICTION.** *Abuse; African Americans; music; orphans; runaways.*

■ **RELATED BOOKS:** ***The Watsons Go to Birmingham—1963*** *by Christopher Paul Curtis;* ***Holes*** *by Louis Sachar;* ***The Great Gilly Hopkins*** *by Katherine Paterson;* ***Maniac Magee*** *by Jerry Spinelli.*

 Note: Set in 1936 in Flint, Michigan, during the Great Depression, this Newbery winner has laugh-out-loud humor and wonderful characters. Great read-aloud.

Here I go again.

I'm on the move again. Since I've been six, I've been going from one foster home to another. It's always the same. Some family needs the government money for my upkeep. Some kid beats up on me because he doesn't want to share his room with a 10-year-old orphan. I get called Buddy, a name I despise. I'm Bud, not Buddy.

All I've got is my suitcase, my father's picture, and my memories. In the picture, my father's standing next to a giant fiddle that's taller than him. There are two men beside him, one playing drums, the other one blowing a horn. After I found this flyer on my mama's dresser, I lost my mamma.

Now I'm on a quest. I will find my father and nothing will stop me—not hunger, fear, or vampires. When I find my father, I will find my past, present and future. Join me on my journey. Call me **Bud, not Buddy**.

D

Danziger, Paula. *Amber Brown Is Feeling Blue.*

G. P. Putnam, 1998, 133 pp. Upper Elementary & Up. Eighth book in the **Amber Brown** *series; others include:* **Amber Brown Is Not a Crayon; Amber Brown Goes Forth;** *and* **Forever Amber Brown.** *Children's Books of the Year selection.*

■ **REALISTIC FICTION AND HUMOR.** *Animals (dogs); divorce; holidays (Halloween, Thanksgiving); rivalry; school; single parents.*

■ **RELATED BOOKS:** ***Amber Brown*** *series and* ***My Cat Ate My Gymsuit*** *by Paula Danziger;* ***Aldo Applesauce*** *by Johanna Hurwitz;* ***Anastasia*** *series by Lois Lowry;* ***The Watsons Go to Birmingham – 1963*** *by Christopher Paul Curtis (mentioned in text).*

Note: The story covers multiple problems, such as divorce, rivalry, and even racism when character writes a book report on **The Watsons Go to Birmingham – 1963.** *Recommended for readers who enjoy realistic fiction with a humorous slant.*

Amber Brown used to hate her name. Nobody else had a two-color name like Amber Brown. However, as time passed, Amber began to think of her name as a colorful name for a colorful person.

That's why Amber didn't like the idea of Kelly Green joining her class. How can there be another person in Amber's class with a colorful name? Let the Color Wars begin!

No wonder **Amber Brown Is Feeling Blue**!

Dayol, Marguerite W. *Papa Alonzo Leatherby: A Collection of Tall Tales From the Best Storyteller in Carroll County.*

Illustrated by Rebecca Leer. Simon & Schuster, 1995, 70pp. Lower Elementary & Up.

■ **FOLKLORE AND HUMOR AND SHORT STORIES.** *Animals; holidays (Halloween, Thanksgiving, Christmas); nature; pioneer life; supernatural.*

■ **RELATED BOOKS: Jack Tales** by Richard Chase; **Paul Bunyan** by Glen Rounds; **Sugarcane House and Other Stories About Mr. Fat** by Adrienne Bond; **Lightning Larry** by Aaron Shepherd; **The Tales of Uncle Remus** series adapted by Julius Lester.

Note: The author wrote nine original tall tales after attending numerous storytelling conferences. Recommended for readers who enjoy humorous tall tales and as a read-aloud, particularly around holidays.

Papa Alonzo Leatherby lived a long time ago. Back in those days, folks in Carroll County didn't have television, Internet, or automobiles. Their favorite pastime was to gather, 'round the pot-belly stove to hear stories from Papa.

Oh, was he a champion storyteller! He could tell the tallest tales you ever heard. All someone had to say was, "I think this is the coldest winter we ever had in Carroll County!" Then off Papa would go! He would tell about the coldest winter years ago when he saw his very own words freeze!

Sometimes Papa would tell how his goat turned blue. Or how he snitched honey from a bear. Or how someone fell into the biggest pumpkin of the county and couldn't get out.

By golly, folks might not believe Papa's tales, but all of them *shore* wish they could spin stories like **Papa Alonzo Leatherby!**

Deary, Terry. *Top Ten Shakespeare Stories.*

Illustrated by Michael Tickner. Scholastic, 1998, 192pp. For all libraries. Children's Books of the Year selection.

■ **CLASSICS.** *Great Britain; love; ethics; problem parents; racism.*

■ **RELATED BOOKS: Shakespeare Stories** by Geraldine McCraughton; **Othello** by Julius Lester; any play or sonnet by William Shakespeare.

Note: Humorous, cartoonist illustrations add to the high interest storytelling style of the author. The book also includes discussions about Shakespeare's plays, authorship, life, and times. Recommended for all libraries and to all types of readers.

Friends, Romans, countrymen! Lend me your ears. I'm here to praise Shakespeare not bury him.

Shakespeare wrote plays to be performed for entertainment. In his day, in the 1500s, he had a tough audience. If they were bored, they would talk among themselves or throw food on the stage. If they became excited, they would cheer their heroes and boo the villains. That's why Shakespeare's plays contained duels, sword fights, witchcraft, blood, and butchery—for entertainment.

Once, the audience became part of the show. During a performance, a fight began in the audience and a person was killed!

Another time, a spectator climbed in a coffin back stage, presumably for the best view in the house. When he stirred inside the coffin, the actors dropped him and fled!

Another time, Queen Elizabeth was sitting on stage (that's where the most important people sat—*on* the stage) and she greeted Shakespeare. He ignored her, probably because he was acting and trying to stay in character. When that didn't work, she dropped a glove. Shakespeare picked it up, added some line about the glove and departed.

How do I know all this? I've read this entertaining book called **Top Ten Shakespeare Stories**. So should you. Get thee to a library.

De Becker, Gavin. *The Gift of Fear: Survival Signals That Protect Us From Violence.*

Little, Brown, 1997, 299pp. High School & Up.

■ **NONFICTION.** *Abuse; crime; death; responsibility; survival.*

■ **RELATED BOOKS: Beauty Bites Beast: Awakening the Warrior with Women & Girls** by Ellen Snortland; **I Know You Really Love Me: A Psychiatrist's Journal of Erotomania, Stalking and Obsessive Love** by Dorren Orion.

Note: *A leading expert, the author intertwines fascinating case histories as well as helpful tips. The text contains seven appendixes for more information. You may wish to read aloud "Signals and Predictive Strategies" in Appendix One. Recommended for nonfiction fans and abused survivors.*

Can you tell when violence is ready to erupt? Your life may depend on it.

Every day 400 Americans suffer from shooting injuries. Each hour 75 American women are raped, and every few seconds a woman is beaten. How can you be sure you aren't the next victim of violence?

All of us have a natural instinct for spotting danger before it occurs. Learning to predict violence is the key to preventing it happening to you. Learn to recognize the signs of danger and learn to value **The Gift of Fear**.

DeFelice, Cynthia. *Ghost of Fossil Glen.*

Farrar, Straus, & Giroux, 1998, 176pp. Upper Elementary & Up. SLJ's Best Books; Children's Books of the Year selection.

■ **MYSTERIES/THRILLERS.** *Hobbies (collecting fossils); peer pressure; Native Americans; school; supernatural; trust.*

■ **RELATED BOOKS: Wait Till Helen Comes** by Mary Downing Hahn; **Stonewords** by Pam Conrad; **Secret, Silent Screams** and **Whispers from the Dead** by Joan Lowry Nixon; **Sharp Horns on the Moon** by Carole Crowe; **The Ghost Belonged to Me** by Richard Peck.

Note: *From the beginning, DeFelice captures the tension and suspense. The heroine's alienation from her friends due to her vivid imagination is portrayed in a realistic manner. Recommended for mystery fans and as a group read-aloud.*

It all began when Allie heard the Voice. It came within her head, but she knew it wasn't her own voice. "The time has come" and "I am L." What did that mean? Even stranger, in her mind Allie saw a young girl whispering, "Help me."

How can Allie convince her friends and family that a ghost is communicating with her? Will they finally believe her story about the **Ghost of Fossil Glen**?

dePaola, Tomie. *26 Fairmount Ave.*

Putnam, 1999, 57pp. Lower Elementary School & Up. Newbery Honor book; ALA Notable Children's Book; Horn Book Fanfare; Cooperative Children's Center Book Choice; Children's Books of the Year selection.

■ **BIOGRAPHY.** *Family; immigrants; moving; school.*

■ **RELATED BOOKS: Nana Upstairs and Nana Downstairs** and **The Art Lesson** by Tomie dePaola; **A Grain of Wheat: A Writer Begins** by Clyde Robert Bulla; **Been to Yesterdays: Poem of a Life** by Lee Bennett Hopkins; **But I'll Be Back Again** by Cynthia Rylant; **Bill Peet** by Bill Peet.

Note: *This is the first installment of Tomie dePaola's autobiography. This acclaimed author and illustrator also portrays his family in the picture books **Nana Upstairs, Nana Downstairs; Now One Foot, Now the Other,** and **The Babysitter.***

In my childhood, I lived in a small town in Connecticut at 26 Fairmount Avenue. My large Italian/Irish family moved there after the hurricane of 1938. Since both of my grandmothers lived in my house, I called my grandmothers "Nana Upstairs" and "Nana Downstairs."

I was a know-it-all kid. I hated the first day of school. All the other kids were crying for their mothers. I thought: What a bunch of crybabies. When I found out that I wouldn't learn to read until the first grade, I told my kindergarten teacher, "Fine. I'll come back next year." Then I walked right out of that school.

Once I learned to read, I read many stories and knew all the fairy tales. I could have told Mr. Walt Disney a thing of two. When I saw the movie *Snow White,* I noticed that Mr. Disney left out of good parts, like the Evil Queen dancing to death in those red-hot iron shoes!

I'm not a kid anymore. I'm a writer and illustrator, but I remember my youth as if it were yesterday. Come visit my house at **26 Fairmount Avenue**.

De Young, C. Coco. *A Letter to Mrs. Roosevelt.*

Delacorte, 1999, 112pp. Upper Elementary & Up. Marguerite De Angeli Award.

■ **HISTORICAL FICTION.** *Family; homeless; school; responsibility; World War 1 (after-effects).*

■ **RELATED BOOKS: Eleanor Roosevelt** by Russell Freedman; **Girls Who Rocked the World: Heroines from Sacagawea to Sheryl Swoopes** by Amelie Welden; **Out of the Dust** by Karen Hesse.

Note: *The story is based on a true incident with the author's family. Its vivid background on the 1930s Depression and New Relief programs is a welcome addition to social studies classes. Recommended for historical fiction fans looking for a strong heroine.*

Johnstown, Pennsylvania
February 5, 1933
Dear Mrs. Eleanor Roosevelt:

Even though you are our First Lady, we students call you "Eleanor Everywhere."

(We don't mean any disrespect, but we always read in the newspapers about your trips to faraway places.) We know that you are traveling in place of your husband President Roosevelt to find out about America's people, especially during this Depression.

Since you seem so kind, I hope you will listen to an 11-year-old girl, because I don't have anyone else to turn to. My family's house is being taken away by the bank, and my family has nowhere to go. Can you help us?

Yours truly,
Margo Bandini

Dickinson, Matt. *The Other Side of Everest: Climbing the North Face Through the Killer Storm.*

Published as **The Death Zone** in Great Britain. Random House, 1999, 233pp. Middle School & Up.

■ **ADVENTURE AND NONFICTION.** *Asia (Tibet); death; nature; sports (mountain climbing); survival.*

■ **RELATED BOOKS: Into Thin Air** by Jon Krakauer; **Ascent and Dissent** by Ken Vernon; **The Climb** by Anatoll Boukreev.

Note: *Well-written, fast-paced account of the infamous disaster on May 10, 1976 is a great companion to Krakauer's modern classic **Into Thin Air.** Highly recommended for all types of readers, especially reluctant readers.*

The Mount Everest observers compile two lists of people: those that reach the top and those that die. The fact that my name is on the first list is a wonder to me.

In the spring of 1996, I was a filmmaker who climbed Mount Everest to film a documentary. I was inexperienced and naïve about *The Death Zone*, a term first coined by a Swiss physician who described the devastating effects of altitude on humans. Mount Everest reaches an altitude where human life cannot sustain.

Unfortunately, on May 10, 1996, 12 names were added to the second list, those that died on Mount Everest. The shock waves of this tragedy reverberated around the world. One climber, Jon Krakauer, wrote a classic book about the disaster called *Into Thin Air.* Both he and I tried to answer these questions: Why did these each of these inexperienced climbers pay $65,000, only to lose their lives? Why did two experienced guides perish? Why does Mount Everest hold such a powerful grip on humans?

Let me be your guide, step by step, on that fateful day, on **The Other Side of Everest**.

Dominick, Andie. *Needles: A Memoir of Growing Up with Diabetes.*

Scribner, 1998, 220pp. Middle School & Up. Alex Award; YALSA Best Books for Young Adults.

■ **NONFICTION.** *Death; illness (diabetes).*

■ **RELATED BOOKS: The Sun, the Rain, and the Insulin: Growing Up With Diabetes** by Joan MacCracken; **When Diabetes Hits Home** by Wendy Satin Rapaport; **Sugar Was My Best Food: Diabetes and Me** by Carol Antoinette Peacock, et.al; **The Autobiography of a Face** by Lucy Greely; **The Dinosaur Tomer** by Marcia Levine Mazur.

Note: *The author is graphically frank about the use of needles in diabetes, which may possibly turn away squeamish readers. However, this story of emotional growth, from denial to acceptance, is presented without didacticism. Recommended for anyone coping with a chronic disease as well as counselors, parents, and anyone interested in a compelling story on a chronic illness.*

I know about needles. My older sister, Denise, was a diabetic.

I idolized my sister. I wanted to look like her, act like her, be her. My wish came true. At nine, I became a diabetic. Now needles belong to me.

Like Denise, I could become reckless. That's when I forgot about diabetes and needles. However, one day I returned from a weekend trip and found Denise on the floor, lifeless and cold. I was shattered, changed forever.

Now I know I must accept my diabetes. Diabetes is a life-altering, chronic illness. For the rest of my life, I must live with **Needles**.

Donnelly, Judy. *The Titanic: Lost . . . And Found.*

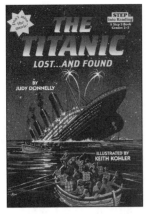

Illustrated by Keith Kohler. Random House, 1987, 48pp. Lower Elementary & Up.

■ **NONFICTION.** *Class conflicts; death; survival; transportation (ships).*

■ **RELATED BOOKS: Inside the Titanic (Giant Cutaway Book)** by Ken Marschall; **On Board the Titanic: What It Was Like When the Great Liner Sank** by Shelley Tanaka; **Exploring the Titanic (Time Quest Book)** by Robert D. Ballard.

> *Note:* Accurate facts and watercolor illustrations convey the high drama of the tragedy, including the 1985 recovery of the shipwreck. Recommended for hard-to-please non-fiction fans and older reluctant readers. You may use this booktalk for other books about the Titanic.

The Titanic was the largest ship built in 1912. It was four city blocks long and as tall as an 11-story building. Best of all, it was thought to be safe because it had two bottoms, one on top of the other—so it could never sink. So everyone thought.

On April 14, 1912, the Titanic hit an iceberg that was a large as a mountain, and the ship sank in two hours. Many of the passengers didn't hurry to the lifeboats because they thought the Titanic was unsinkable. Other passengers in steerage could not find lifeboats in time. Hundreds of passengers were on board when the huge ship sank in the freezing Arctic waters.

Some 80 years later, the Titanic was discovered on the bottom of the ocean. Many unresolved questions were then answered.

Learn the fascinating story of **The Titanic: Lost . . . and Found.**

Draper, Sharon M. *Romiette and Julio.*

Atheneum Books for Young Readers, 1999, 236pp. Middle School & Up.

■ **ROMANCE.** *African Americans; bullies; computers; Hispanic Americans; interracial relations; love; problem parents; racism.*

■ **RELATED BOOKS: The Tragedy of Romeo and Juliet** by William Shakespeare; **If You Come Softly** by Jacqueline Woodson; **A White Romance** by Virginia Hamilton; **Othello** by Julius Lester.

> *Note:* At times Draper's plot seems contrived to parallel Shakespeare's drama **Romeo and Juliet,** but her use of computer chat rooms, gang violence, and contemporary slang make this appealing to young adults. Incidentally, this tale ends happily. Recommended to all romance lovers and anyone else who wants an entertaining read.

My name is Romiette Renee Cappenelle. During online chats, I am known as Afroqueen. That's where I hooked up with Spanishlover, also known as Julio Montague. Then I found out Julio was that new dude that transferred to my school! Talk about coincidences. Julio looks just as fine as he writes, so I'm smitten.

Did you notice that our names—Romiette and Julio—sound like the play *Romeo and Juliet*? Do you think that means something? Are we destined for doom or romance? I guess time will tell—or fate.

Just like the movie *West Side Story,* my school has a gang. They call themselves The Family or Devildogs. They spend their time thinking up ways to intimidate the kids. Like the other day, they threatened Julio and me at lunch. Guess it's 'cause Julio's not black like me. Don't they have more important battles to fight?

We have to be careful. We don't want to end up like those "star-crossed lovers," Romeo and Juliet—dead! We want to make our own history, known forever as **Romiette and Julio.**

D Duncan, Lois (editor). *Trapped! Cages of Mind and Body.*

Simon & Schuster, 1998. Middle School & Up. YALSA Popular Paperbacks selection.

■ **SHORT STORIES.** *Abuse; crime; death; eating disorders; ethics; work; Vietnam War; women's issues.*

■ **RELATED BOOKS: Monster** by Walter Dean Myers; **Rules of the Road** by Joan Bauer; **I Know What You Did Last Summer** and other books by Lois Duncan; **Rats Saw God** by Rob Thomas.

Note: *The eclectic collection contains a wide variety of genres and literary forms, including the traditional short story, play, poetry, and an unusual dual-perspective piece by Walter Dean Myers. Respected authors such as Lois Lowry, Rob Thomas, Francesca Lia Block, Gregory Maguire, Joan Bauer, and Rita Williams-Garcia contribute excellent pieces. Many readers likely may be inspired to read other books by these authors. **Warning:** Mild profanity in Rita Williams-Garcia's play "Cross Over."*

Trapped!

Sometimes, we all feel trapped, don't we? So do the characters from this collection of short pieces, edited by Lois Duncan. (Yes, the Lois Duncan of *I Know What You Did Last Summer.* You Lois Duncan fans will enjoy reading her chronicle poems, each called "Trapped," written from ages 11 to 42.)

Lois Duncan has edited this book of stories, poems and plays, all about entrapment. All the characters become trapped—physically, mentally, and emotionally—in a variety of situations.

In one story you've probably heard before, the Greek hero Theseus is trapped in the labyrinth, a maze that contains the monster Minotaur. Another story tells of an enchanted princess who is trapped inside a block of ice, waiting for her Prince Charming to unthaw her. Try "Pancakes," a funny tale of Jill, a waitress, trapped by her job and hungry, pancake-loving customers. In "The Box," Alicia is trapped within her body, shackled by an eating disorder, anorexia.

Perhaps, you, the reader, will find this book difficult to put down. Maybe you'll have the same experiences as the characters. You'll find yourself **Trapped!**

E Easley, MaryAnn. *I Am the Ice Worm.*

Boyds Mills, 1996, 127pp. Upper Elementary & Up. Junior Literary Guild selection.

■ **ADVENTURE AND HISTORICAL FICTION.** *Disability (deafness); divorce; Native Americans (Inupiats); racism; survival.*

■ **RELATED BOOKS: Frozen Fire** by James Houston; **Hatchet** series and **Dogsong** by Gary Paulsen; **Far North** by Will Hobbs; **Julie of the Wolves** by Jean Craighead George.

Note: *Allison Atwood is a strong heroine based on author's own experiences as a teacher in an Inupiat Alaskan Village. "Ice Worm" means "outsider." Recommended for historical fiction and adventure readers who enjoy survival stories.*

"We're flying awfully low, aren't we?" I tried not to sound anxious, but I was beginning to become frightened when I saw a mountain loom ahead. "Watch out!"

Johnny Skye just laughed. "No problem, hon. I'm totally in charge."

I tried to tell myself that Johnny Skye was a guy who liked to scare girls, but butterflies in my stomach told me the truth. We're going to crash!

As the plane sharply descended, I thought, I'm only 14, too young to die! Suddenly there was blackness and silence. I turned around to face my companion, but Johnny looked odd and strangely waxen.

I had survived the plane crash. Can I survive the snowy wilderness of Alaska?

Edwards, Pamela Duncan. *Barefoot: Escape on the Underground Railroad.*

Illustrated by Henry Cole. HarperCollins, 1997, 32pp. Lower Elementary & Up. Children's Books of the Year selection.

■ **HISTORICAL FICTION.** *African Americans; animals; Civil War; nature; racism, runaways.*

■ **RELATED BOOKS: Allen Jay and the Underground Railroad (On My Own)** by Marlene Targ Bill; **Sweet Clara and the Freedom Quilt** by Deborah Hopkinson; **Aunt Harriet's Underground Railroad in the Sky** by Faith Ringgold; **The Drinking Gourd** by Fernando Mojo.

 Note: Illustrator, Henry Cole, captures the tension and suspense of the text. Excellent for social studies, especially units studying the Civil War or African Americans.

I am running, running, running. I can't stop because I am afraid of what is before me and even more afraid of what lies behind me.

I try to listen for any clue that will guide me to the stop on the Underground Railroad. Like a frog croaking to show me there is freshwater nearby. Like a mouse nibbling on fresh berries for me to share. Like a heron's cry that warns me that Heavy Boots are close behind me.

Of course, these animals don't know they are guiding me to freedom. Or do they?

English, Karen. *Francie.*

Farrar, Straus, & Giroux, 1999, 199pp. Upper Elementary & Up. Coretta Scott King Honor Book; ALA Notable Children's Book; Cooperative Children's Book Center Choice; Children's Books of the Year selection; SLJ's Best Books.

■ **HISTORICAL FICTION.** *African Americans; bullies; crime; hobbies (reading); racism; runaways; secrets; single parents.*

■ **RELATED BOOKS: *To Kill a Mockingbird*** by Harper Lee; ***Roll of Thunder, Hear My Cry*** by Mildred Taylor; ***Spite Fences*** by Trudy Krisher; ***Run Away Home*** by Patricia McKissack.

 Note: Many issues of growing up are presented, from confronting bullies to rebelling against immoral conventions as slavery. Story of post-Civil War Alabama has a suspenseful climax. Recommended for historical fiction fans looking for a strong African-American heroine, for group reads, or as a read-aloud.

That Jesse Pruitt is a strange one. Who ever heard of a 16-year-old boy taking a notion to walk 14 miles a day to go to school? He can't even read or write! What makes him want to learn? My guess is that he probably will do anything to get away from his hard life on a sharecropping farm.

One thing I do know. He didn't beat up any white man, like they're saying.

That's why I'm keeping quiet and sneaking food to him in the woods. Mama says I will get into a lot of trouble, but I don't care.

Like Jesse, I know what it is like to want to run away from Alabama. One day I will leave and make something of myself—or my name isn't **Francie.**

Erdrich, Louise. *The Birchbark House.*

Hyperion Books for Children, 1999, 244pp. Upper Elementary & Up. Publishers Weekly's Best Books; SLJ's Best Books; ALA Notable Children's Book.

■ **HISTORICAL FICTION.** *Death; ecology; illness (smallpox); Native Americans (Ojibwa).*

■ **RELATED BOOKS: Morning Girl** by Michael Dorris; **Sing Down the Moon** by Scott O'Dell; **Sweetgrass** by Jan Hudson.

> *Note:* Through a cycle of four seasons in 1847, Omakayas experiences firsthand the encroachment of whites in northern Minnesota. The author is a member of the Turtle Mountain Band of Ojibwa and wife of children's writer Michael Dorris (who tragically committed suicide). Erdrich infuses life and authenticity into her poetic narrative and pencil drawings. The book includes a glossary and pronunciation guide. Recommended for all types and ages of readers.

She was named Omakayas (Oh-MAH-kay-ahs), or Little Frog, because her first step was a hop.

In 1847, Omakayas lived on an island in Lake Superior and in the summer, a house of birchbark. She was a Native American, from the Ojibwa tribe. She lived with her mother, father, older sister Angeline, younger brother Pinch, and baby Neewo. Life was slow and fine.

One day a visitor came to the lodge, bringing with him an invisible enemy. Smallpox!

Farmer, Penelope. *Penelope.*

McElderry Books, 1996, 192pp. Upper Elementary & Up. Children's Books of the Year selection.

■ **MYSTERIES/THRILLERS.** *Bullies; Great Britain; Native Americans; racism; religion (Hinduism); rivalry; supernatural; time travel.*

■ **RELATED BOOKS: Thicker Than Water** by Penelope Farmer; **Locked in Time** by Lois Duncan; **Melusine** by Lynne Reid Banks; **The Ruby in the Smoke** by Philip Pullman.

> *Note:* In London, Aunt Jo adopts the recently orphaned Flora, but visions and memories that she never experienced haunt Flora. Aunt Jo and Flora's Hindu friend believe in reincarnation and think Flora is the eighteenth-century reincarnation of a lord's daughter, Penelope. Issues such as reincarnation and racism are introduced subtly within the context of a mystery. Recommended as a read-aloud and for all mystery lovers.

"Eat or be eaten."

Flora shuddered when she heard that voice. Only she could hear that voice. That voice would speak deep in her brain and repeated meaningless phrases. Sometimes Flora thought she was losing her mind. The voices would never call her by her name, Flora; instead, they called her by the name her mother gave her: Penelope.

Aunt Jo thought there was a perfectly logical explanation of Flora's voice. She believed that in another lifetime Flora was a girl named Penelope, an 18th-century lord's daughter. Flora didn't want to believe in reincarnation, but what else could it be?

"If I was Penelope in another life, who am I now?" Flora thought. "Am I Flora or **Penelope**?"

Flake, Sharon G. *The Skin I'm In.*

Hyperion Press, 1998, 192pp. Middle School & Up. YASLA Best Books for Young Adults; YASLA Quick Picks for Reluctant Young Adult Readers; Children's Books of the Year selection.

■ **REALISTIC FICTION.** *African Americans; bullies; diaries; disability (skin condition); hobbies (writing); peer pressure; racism; school; self-identity; single parents.*

■ **RELATED BOOKS: I Know Why the Caged Bird Sings** by Maya Angelou; **Jazmin's Notebook** by Nikki Grimes; **Yolanda's Genius** by Carol Fenner.

Note: *Thirteen-year-old Maleeka suffers from low self-esteem due to her classmates' teasing about her dark skin; through her teacher's influence, she discovers her talent for writing and how to stand up for herself against the school bullies. (Another booktalk for this book is in **Keep Talking That Book: Booktalks to Promote Reading, Volume 2**). Recommended for reluctant readers looking for fast-paced realistic fiction and for those with low self-esteem.*

Like me, my teacher is a freak. The kind of person folks can't help but tease. It's bad enough when you're a kid like me, but worse if you're a teacher.

We both got skin problems. Me, I got a black complexion like a Almond-Joy colored girl. But her, with white blotches all over her black face, she looks like someone threw acid on her face.

Not that it bothered her none. She says she learned to live with her face, even to love it. It didn't take overnight, but it came. She learned to see herself in the mirror and like it, though it wasn't nobody's idea of beauty.

My dad told me the same thing once. "Maleeka," he used to say, "You gotta see yourself with your own eyes. That's the only way you know who you are."

It might take me some time, but one day I'm gonna like **The Skin I'm In.**

Fleischman, Paul. *Mind's Eye.*

Henry Holt, 1999, 108pp. Middle School & Up. SLJ's Best Books; YALSA Best Books for Young Adults; Cooperative Children's Book Center Choice; Children's Books of the Year selection.

■ **FANTASY.** *Aging; death; disability (spinal cord injury); Europe (Italy).*

■ **RELATED BOOKS: Peeling the Onion** by Wendy Orr; **Hero of Lesser Causes** by Julie Johnston; **Petey** by Ben Mikaelsen.

Note: *At 88, only her aging body confines Elva. Using the book* **Baedeker's Italy***, Elva teaches Courtney how to fly with the imagination. Written in dialogue, Fleischman's book could be useful as Reader's Theatre or as a student read-aloud. Many literary allusions, including poetry, are included. Recommended for all types of readers, especially reluctant ones.*

Elva:	Courtney, are you awake? Dear girl. It's not healthy to sleep so much.
Courtney:	(*Voice flat.*) Where am I?
Elva:	Don't you remember? You're in a convalescent home, recovering from an accident. I'm Elva. Forgive me, but you seem so young. How old are you?
Courtney:	Sixteen. (*Long pause.*) My spinal cord was severed. I'll never walk again.
Elva:	I'm so very sorry. (*Long pause.*) Forgive me, but

what a blessing that your injuries are strictly below the waist. Your brain was spared. The poet William Blake says, "Five windows light the cavern'd Man . . ." In other words, the five senses light the soul. However, in your case, you'll also need a sixth window to escape from your cavern. You'll need imagination. (*Long pause.*) I have a plan for getting out of this horrible place.

Courtney: Yeah?

Elva: A wonderful plan, but I need your help. I have a book that will take us worlds away from wheelchairs and winters. You can't simply read it. No, indeed. You and I must participate. Get ready. Let's enter the imagination. Let's enter the **Mind's Eye.**

Fleischman, Sid. *Bandit's Moon.*

Illustrated by Jos. A. Smith. Greenwillow, 1998, 144 pp. Upper Elementary & Up. ALA Notable Children's Book; Booklist Editors' Choice; Children's Books of the Year selection.

■ **ADVENTURE AND HISTORICAL FICTION.** *Crime; Hispanic Americans; orphans; racism; secrets; revenge; trust; women's issues.*

■ **RELATED BOOKS: The Midnight Horse** by Sid Fleischman; **Chronicles of Robin Hood** by Rosemary Sutcliff; **I Rode a Horse of Milk White Jade** by Diane Lee Wilson; **Running Freedom** by Pam Muñoz Ryan.

> *Note:* *In the afterword, the Newbery-winning author explains that the story is based on 1850's Mexican legend of Joaquin Murieta, the Robin Hood of the Mountains. The issue of bigotry is presented subtly within high-action adventure. Recommended especially for historical fiction and folklore fans who enjoy spunky heroines.*

"Run for your life, boy! Don't you know who I am? I am the terrible Three-Fingered Jack!" With that, he crossed his eyes and showed me his deformed hand.

I just stood there, waiting, before saying, "I've heard of you, all right. I don't know whether to believe those stories or not."

"Then, adios, Yankee boy. I will shoot you another time after you make up your mind!" He mounted his frisky black stallion and gave me a salute with his fingertips.

"No, wait! Take me with you! Please! I won't be in your way!" I couldn't believe what I heard myself saying. Go off with these Mexican bandits who were enemies of my father? Even worse, what will Three-Fingered Jack think when he finds out that I am not a boy, but a 12-year-old girl?

It was too late to turn back. Like in a trance, I found myself riding with the Mexican bandits under the moonless skies, under the **Bandit's Moon**.

Freedman, Russell. *Babe Didrikson Zaharias: The Making of a Champion.*

Clarion Books, 1999, 192pp. For all libraries. ALA Notable Children's Book; YASLA Best Books for Young Adults; Cooperative Children's Book Center Choice; Bulletin of Center for Children's Book Blue Ribbon; Children's Books of the Year selection; SLJ's Best.

■ **SPORTS AND BIOGRAPHY.** *Sports (golf, track, swimming, tennis, baseball, bowling); illness (cancer); women's issues.*

■ **RELATED BOOKS: Babe Didrikson Zaharias** by Elizabeth A. Lynn; **Up to the Plate: The All-American Girls Professional Baseball League** by Margot Forunato Galt; **Winning Ways: A Photohistory of American Women in Sports** by Sue Macy; **Gutsy Girls: Young Women Who Dare** by Tina Schwager and Michele Schuerger.

> *Note:* *Author's biographies are always informative and entertaining, accompanied by appealing photographs. He only alludes to Babe's homosexuality, stating that Betty Dodd and Babe were "intimate friends." Recommended for purchase in all libraries and useful for readers looking for an engrossing biography of a woman who broke barriers as well as records.*

Who's the best athlete of the 20th century? Some people would say Babe Didrikson Zaharias.

Her given name was Mildred Ella, but her neighbors called her by her nickname "Babe"—not because she was the youngest of her family, but because she could hit homeruns like Babe Ruth.

Babe Didrikson Zaharias wasn't only good at baseball. Born in 1911, when most girls didn't play sports, she also became an All-American basketball player, an Olympic gold medallist in track and field, and a championship golfer. She also mastered tennis, baseball, diving, and bowling.

A reporter once asked, "Is there anything you don't play?"

"Yeah, dolls," Babe answered.

So, who was the best athlete of the 20th century? My vote goes to **Babe Didrikson Zaharias.**

Gallant, Roy A., and Marcia Marshall (editor). *The Day the Sky Split Apart: Investigating a Cosmic Mystery.*

Gale Group, 1995, 147pp. Upper Elementary & Up.

■ **NONFICTION.** *Science (astronomy).*

■ **RELATED BOOKS: Stephen Hawking's Universe: The Cosmos Explained** by David Filkin; **Black Holes and Time Warps: Einstein's Outrageous Legacy** by Kip S. Thorne; **Cosmos** by Carl Sagan.

Note: *The author, who is a former staff member of the American Museum of Natural History, visited the Russian explosion site in 1992. The text is illustrated with drawings and black-and-white photographs. The last two chapters discuss the possibilities of cosmic missiles hitting the earth. Recommended for anyone with a curious mind, especially those who think they don't like science.*

On June 30, 1908, the sky over Siberia exploded. This fireball explosion brought earth tremors, followed by a lit-up night sky for two days, leaving a flattened stretch of wilderness. No one knew what caused this phenomenon and, for 20 years, no one reported it to the Russian authorities.

Now scientists believe an asteroid collided with the earth, bringing the force of 2,000 atomic bombs. If it had hit St. Petersburg, the victims would have numbered in the thousands. Amazingly, only two people died.

The Tunguska meteorite, as it is typically known, provokes many questions. Was it really a meteorite? Why couldn't the phenomenon be caused by a black hole? What are the chances that this could happen again?

Find out the truth behind this unsolved mystery: **The Day the Sky Split Apart.**

Gallo, Donald R. (editor). *No Easy Answers: Short Stories About Teenagers Making Tough Choices.*

Delacorte, 1997, 323pp. Middle School & Up.

■ **SHORT STORIES AND REALISTIC FICTION.** *African Americans; bullies; China; computers; ethics; homosexuality; pregnancy; responsibility; sex and sexuality; sexual abuse; sports.*

■ **RELATED BOOKS: Chicken Soup for the Teenage Soul** series edited by Jack Canfield et al; **Got Issues Much? Celebrities Share their Traumas and Triumphs** by Randy Reisfeld and Marie Morreale; **Stay True: Short Stories for Strong Girls** edited by Marilyn Singer; **Connections: Short Stories** edited by Donald R. Gallo.

Note: *This book includes 16 short stories from acclaimed authors M. E. Kerr, Walter Dean Myers, Rita Williams-Garcia, Alden R. Carter, Lensey Namioka, and others. Some Middle School teachers use this as a discussion book, but teachers should be aware of the controversial issues and mild profanity. Also recommended for all high school collections.*

Got a problem? Take a number, stand in line.

All these teenagers face big problems and they have difficult choices to make. Anthony takes a photograph of a teacher that will certainly lead to her dismissal. Ken writes a lewd note on the computer, never dreaming it could be recovered. Betsy knows what her boyfriend wants, but she isn't willing. Eva is tired of sharing her homework again and again. What will they do? What would you do?

One thing is certain. There are **No Easy Answers.**

Galt, Margot Fortunato. *Up to the Plate: The All-American Girls Professional Baseball League.*

Lerner, 1995, 96pp. For all libraries. Children's Books of the Year selection.

■ **NONFICTION AND SPORTS.** Movies; politics; sports (baseball); responsibility; women's issues; World War II.

■ **RELATED BOOKS: Winning Ways** and **A Whole New Ball Game** by Sue Macy; **Women at Play** by Barbara Gregorich; **A League of Their Own** by Sara Gilbert.

> **Note:** This book is based on the novel by Sara Gilbert that was written for the 1992 film **A League of Their Own**. Sepia photographs add to the text. For sports fans and readers looking for strong heroines.

"Why am I playing baseball in Chicago?" Sophie Kurys thought. "It's too much pressure!"

Sophie wasn't alone with her doubts about playing baseball. In 1943 many persons laughed at the notion of a national baseball league for women. Up to then, there were only "powder puff" women's teams with names like Slapsie Maxie's Curvaceous Cuties or the Num Num Pretzel Girls. However, when men joined the armed services during World War II, women kept baseball alive for America.

In 1998 the Baseball Hall of Fame recognized Sophie Kurys and other women in the first All-American Girls Professional Baseball League. So let's raise our baseball caps to these women and run with them **Up to the Plate**.

Gantos, Jack. *Joey Pigza Swallowed the Key.*

Farrar, Straus, & Giroux, 1998, 192pp. Upper Elementary & Up. Part of a series; **Joey Pigza Loses Control** follows. National Book Award Finalist; ALA Children's Notable Book; National Council for Social Studies Notable; SLJ's Best Books; Children's Books of the Year selection.

■ **REALISTIC FICTION.** Abuse; disabilities (ADD); problem parents; single parent; school (special education); substance abuse (alcohol).

■ **RELATED BOOKS: There's a Boy in the Girl's Bathroom** and **Holes** by Louis Sachar; **Secret Life of Amanda K. Wood** by Cameron Ann; **Dicey's Song** by Besty Byars; **The Great Gilly Hopkins** by Katherine Paterson.

> **Note:** Author Jack Gantos, writer of the **Rotten Ralph** series, presents ADD (attention deficit disorder) from a child's point-of-view in a humorous and compassionate manner. Recommended for realistic fiction readers as well as parents and teachers of ADD and ADHD (attention deficit hyperactivity disorder) children. **Warning:** Text includes "damn" and "hell."

I can't keep still, because I'm wired. I feel like I am in a cartoon nightmare with little red-eyed devils with pitchforks nudging me. I can't help myself. My grandma and dad were born so wired that our family tree looks like a high-voltage tower.

I want to be a good kid. My body just gets ahead of my brain. Like when I swallowed my house key. It seemed like a good idea at the time, but then I had to sit in Mrs. Howard's class with other coma kids.

I know I am special. Everyone says so. I've just got dud meds, a bum diet, and a wired grandma. After I return from this special school, I'm going to announce to everyone at school, "**Joey Pigza Swallowed the Key**, but he's *baaaaack!*"

Garner, Eleanor Ramrath. *Eleanor's Story: An American Girl in Hitler's Germany.*

Peachtree, 1999, 268pp. Middle School & Up. YALSA Best Books for Young Adults.

■ **BIOGRAPHY.** *Death; Europe (Germany); immigrants; rites of passage; World War II.*

■ **RELATED BOOKS: Bad Times, Good Friends** by Ilse-Margret Vogel; **The Diary of a Young Girl: The Definitive Edition** by Anne Frank; **I Have Lived a Thousand Years** by Livia Bitton Jackson; **No Pretty Pictures** by Anita Lobel.

> *Note:* On the eve of World War II, Eleanor's German-born parents emigrated from New Jersey to Germany when Mr. Ramrath accepted a two-year job assignment. Like all innocent victims, they suffered all the horrors and traumas of war. This autobiography tells a different story than most memoirs of World War II, and many readers will sympathize with the family's story of being in the wrong place at the wrong time. Highly recommended as another perspective on World War II.

In 1939, when I was nine, Hitler moved into our neighborhood.

He didn't come in person, but his presence was felt. In Berlin, when we entered a store, we had to raise our arm in a funny salute and say, "Heil, Hitler." I tried to imagine telling our friends in America. I knew they would laugh.

Later, I noticed the Nazi soldiers. When the soldiers strutted by in their shiny black boots, I became uneasy. Meanwhile, Hitler invaded Poland, Holland, Belgium, Luxembourg and France. After that, things didn't seem so funny.

April 20th was Hitler's birthday. Every window in Berlin was covered with bright red swastika flags—except our window. Father had displayed the American flag. I was never so proud of Father.

My mother was furious. "You endangered our family! Someone might report us to the Gestapo! We are American and might be considered enemies."

That time, nothing happened. But, for the next seven years, we faced threats, bombings, and starvation.

I am Eleanor Ramrath. This is my story. I call it **Eleanor's Story: An American Girl in Hitler's Germany.**

Gauthier, Gail. *A Year With Butch and Spike.*

G. P. Putnam, 1998, 216pp. Upper Elementary & Up. Children's Books of the Year selection.

■ **REALISTIC FICTION AND HUMOR.** *Bullies; holidays (Halloween); peer pressure; school; science (project); responsibility.*

■ **RELATED BOOKS: My Life Among the Aliens** by Gail Gauthier; **A Dog on Barkham Street** and **The Bully on Barkham Street** by Mary Stolz; **The Best Christmas Pageant Ever** and **The Best School Year Ever** by Barbara Robinson; **There's a Boy in the Girl's Bathroom** by Louis Sachar.

> *Note:* Teacher's pet Jasper Gordon is placed between two "bad" boys, but learns that the students are not as bad as their reputation. In a realistic manner, the author discusses students coping with an unfair teacher. School topics include ecology, literary terms, pioneer life, and science projects. (Another booktalk for this book is included in **Keep Talking That Book: Booktalks to Promote Reading, Volume 2**). **Warning:** The text contains "damn" and some "gross-out" humor, but should still delight fans of humorous realistic fiction.

Meet Beavis and Butthead: The Cootchers.

Everybody in my town has heard of the Cootchers. Spike and Butch were famous for putting ski wax on the toilets of the girls' room. Last year they shaved an Irish settler's bottom to make Lyddy Daniel's fake beard for the school play. (Was she mad when she found out!) Now here they are, on either side of me in class!

I guess it's true what they say about bad pennies. They just keep turning up. Try as I can, I just can't escape them. I just hope I can survive **A Year with Butch and Spike.**

Gilmore, Kate. *The Exchange Student.*

Houghton Mifflin, 1999, 217pp. Middle School & Up. YASLA Quick Picks for Reluctant Young Adult Readers; YALSA Best Books for Young Adults; Cooperative Children's Book Center Choice;.

■ **SCIENCE FICTION.** *Animals, ecology; science; secrets.*

■ **RELATED BOOKS: Enchantress From the Stars** by Sylvia Louise Engdahl; **Acorna** series by Anne McCaffrey and Margaret Ball; **Alien Secrets** by Annette Curtis Klause.

Note: Note: Set in the year 2094, the author, Kate Gilmore discusses science and ecology within an entertaining plot. Recommended for readers who love to read about animals and think they don't like science fiction. **Warning:** Some profanity.

"Greetings, Earth family," said the seven-foot alien. "I am Fen. In the name of the Republic of Chela, I thank you for your prospective hospitality."

"Hi, Fen. I'm Daria Wells. Welcome to Earth. My family welcomes you as do all my 49 animals."

The alien stumbled over his words: "Did-did you s-say 49 animals?"

Daria laughed. "Yeah. We own a zoo of endangered animals." Daria stopped and stared at Fen. "Fen, look at yourself. You've gone from gray to all pink."

"I am sorry," Fen replied. "I lost control. I am tired now. May I rest?"

As time passed, Fen's behavior seemed, well, alien. He was always asking questions about the animals and refused to talk about his own planet. He obviously was hiding some secret about his mission and his planet.

What gives with Fen? What secret was he hiding? What was the mystery behind **The Exchange Student**?

Gilstrap, John. *Nathan's Run.*

Warner Books, 1996, 368pp. High School & Up. YALSA Popular Paperbacks selection.

■ **MYSTERIES/THRILLERS.** *Abuse; crime; death; orphans; secrets; substance abuse (alcohol).*

■ **RELATED BOOKS: At All Costs** by John Gilstrap; **The Client** by John Grisham; **Hostile Witness: A Novel** by James M. Grippando.

Note: A superior suspense thriller, with well-defined characters in a fast-moving plot. Recommended for mature readers who like John Grisham and other thriller writers. **Warning:** Graphic profanity.

"Lieutenant Michaels, there's been a murder at the Juvenile Detention Center. Please get here right away."

The scene was gruesome. A male guard lay sprawled in his own blood. A child-size bloody footprint pointed out the door. Stabbed five times, the guard was allegedly murdered by Nathan Bailey, a 12-year-old orphan.

When the media was alerted, they, along with the police, began their search for Nathan. Meanwhile, fleeing down the dark highway, Nathan had no where to go. Desperate, Nathan called NewsTalk 900, a local radio station, to plead his case. His honesty won over the talk show host, Denise Carpenter, as well as thousands of listeners.

What is Nathan's story? How innocent is he? What will become of **Nathan's Run**?

Glenn, Mel. *Foreign Exchange: A Mystery in Poems.*

Morrow Junior, 1999, 159pp. Middle School & Up. YASLA Quick Picks for Reluctant Readers.

■ **MYSTERIES/THRILLERS AND POETRY.** *African Americans; crime; death; pregnancy; interracial relations; racism; school; sex and sexuality.*

■ **RELATED BOOKS: Split Image: A Story in Poems; The Taking of Room 114: A Hostage Drama in Poems** and **Who Killed Mr. Chippendale?** books by Mel Glenn; **Making Up Megaboy** by Virginia Walter and Katrina Roeckelin; **Monster** by Walter Dean Myers.

 Note: This riveting mystery is written as free verse poems. Both teens and adults narrate the poems that reveal the prejudices of a small community. For older students, the poems could be used as Reader's Theatre, but there is some mild profanity. Recommended especially for students who think they don't like poetry.

Did you hear the latest news? The headline reads:

Body Found in Lake

Kristen Clarke, 17, was found on Hudson Lake, drowned and possibly strangled. The girl, a senior honor student at Hudson Landing Central High School, had been reported missing the day before.

Allegedly, the last person to see her alive was Kwame Richards from Tower High School. He was participating in a program that paired a Hudson Valley student with a student from the urban area.

The townspeople were shocked at the murder. "It's not supposed to happen here," said Oliver Nesbitt, a town board member. "It's a result of mixing classes and races."

Many agree that that the blending of students from urban Tower High School was an experiment that failed. Shortly after the "Foreign Exchange" dance, Clarke disappeared with Richards.

"We all need to know," continued Oliver Nesbitt, "What really happened during **The Foreign Exchange**?"

Green, Martin I. *Santa, My Life and Times: An Illustrated Autobiography.*

Illustrated by Bill Sienkiewicz. Avon, 1998, 128pp. Upper Elementary & Up.

■ **FANTASY AND FOLKLORE.** *Holidays (Christmas); magic; supernatural.*

■ **RELATED BOOKS: Santa Claus Book** by Alden Perkes; **Letters from Father Christmas** by J.R.R. Tolkien; **Jolly Old Santa Claus** by Sparkle; **Autobiography of Santa Claus** by Jeff Guinn.

 The Illustrations are outstanding, and the text includes poetry as well. Excellent for holiday collections, fantasy lovers, group reading, or as a read-aloud.

My name is Santa Claus. You may have heard of me. During the past years, I have been too busy getting ready for Christmas to write my story, but now the time has come to tell you the truth behind the beard.

I got the idea of doing my autobiography from a 100-year-old woman. "Your story needs telling," she said. Then she began asking me all kinds of questions: Where do you come from? Are there such things as elves? How do reindeer fly?

Here are my answers to the questions that have gone too long unanswered. Here is my story. **Santa, My Life and Times**.

Gregory, Kristiana. *The Great Railroad Race: The Diary of Libby West.*

Scholastic Trade, 1999; 203pp. **Dear America** *series.*

■ **HISTORICAL FICTION.** *Civil War (Reconstruction Era); diaries; love; moving; Native Americans; pioneer life; religion (Mormons); transportation (railroads); work.*

■ **RELATED BOOKS: Across the Wide and Lonesome Prairie** and **Winter of Red Snow** by Kristiana Gregory; **West to a Land of Plenty** by Jim Murphy; **Dragon's Gate** by Laurence Yep.

> *Note:* *Written from the point of view of a 14-year-old girl named Libby, this historical fiction account reads like a primary source. The text contains references to presidential nominee General Grant, Tecumseh, President Andrew Johnson, Brigham Young, and Louisa May Alcott's* **Little Women**. *The appendix contains period photographs, illustrations and historical notes. Recommended for history fans and social studies classes studying The Pacific Railroad Act of 1862.*

Mother told me that it is better to write down my thoughts. That way I don't say them to other people and make people feel bad. I carry my diary with me on our covered wagon throughout this Colorado territory.

Dear Diary, my family is to follow the Union Pacific Railroad as it is being built from Nebraska. Another company called the Central Pacific from California is to meet our company somewhere in the middle of the American desert. All kinds of delays occur, like strikes from the Chinese workers and Indian attacks.

With all these problems, you would think that these two companies would help one another. Instead, each is more interested in holding back the other company. That's why we common folks call it **The Great Railroad Race**.

Grollman, Earl A., and Max Malikow. *Living When a Young Friend Commits Suicide or Even Starts Talking About It.*

Beacon, 1999, 109pp. In all libraries.

■ **NONFICTION.** *Suicide; substance abuse.*

■ **RELATED BOOKS: Words I Never Thought to Speak** by Victoria Alexander; **Straight Talk About Death for Teenagers** by Earl A. Grollman; **Bereaved Children and Teens** by Earl A. Grollman; **When a Friend Dies: A Book for Teens About Grieving and Healing** by Marilyn E. Gootman.

> *Note:* *This valuable resource should be accessible to teachers, students, and counselors. The appendix includes books and audio-visual support materials.*

Every death is painful. No death is more painful than suicide.

If you know a friend who committed suicide (or even talked about it), then this book is a must read. The authors—a grief counselor and a church counselor—will tell you what you can do and what you probably will be feeling.

This book, **Living When a Young Friend Commits Suicide or Even Starts Talking About It**, can save lives. So can you.

Haddix, Margaret Peterson. *Just Ella.*

Simon & Schuster Books for Young Readers, 1999, 185pp. Middle School & Up. VOYA award; YASLA Best Books for Young Adults; YASLA Quick Picks for Reluctant Readers.

■ **FOLKLORE AND ROMANCE.** *Love; women's issues.*

■ **RELATED BOOKS: Ella Enchanted** by Gail Carson Levine; **Spinners** by Donna Napoli; **Silver Woven in My Hair** by Shirley Rousseau Murphy.

Note: In this Cinderella story, Ella decides that love at first sight does not necessarily make a compatible partner. Ella is a feminist with a strong will. Luckily—and predictably—she finds romance on her own terms. Recommended for romance lovers.

I am Ella Brown, also known as Cinders-Ella.

When I danced with the prince, I never imagined what happened after "happily ever after." Just being at the ball was beyond my wildest dreams. Then everything happened so fast. The prince asked my hand in marriage, and I moved into the castle so we could plan our marriage.

We've been married two months. To my disappointment, Prince Charming is a drip, the castle is dark and dank, and the servants think I'm a peasant. I've never felt so alone in my life.

Contrary to rumor, I did not have a fairy godmother. However, I wish a fairy godmother could turn me back into **Just Ella.**

Hall, Donald (editor). *The Oxford Illustrated Book of American Children's Poems.*

Oxford University, 1999, 96pp. Lower Elementary & Up.

■ **POETRY.** *African Americans; animals; family; holidays; Native Americans; self-identity.*

■ **RELATED BOOKS: I, Too, Sing America: Three Centuries of African American Poetry** edited by Catherine Clinton; **In a Sacred Manner I Live: Native American Wisdom** edited by Neil Philip.

Note: This excellent anthology for young readers begins with traditional lullabies, proceeds to poets like Carl Sandburg and Robert Frost, and ends with popular poets like Dr. Seuss and Shel Silverstein. The colorful design adds dimension. Great as a read-aloud during holidays and for related themes.

You know rap music, right? Rap music is poetry set against a steady bass beat.

Some of these poems could fit into a nice beat. Try Eve Merriam's "Catch a Little Rhyme" (page 19). Try the poetry of Nikki Giovanni or Langston Hughes, and see if that doesn't get you a' jumpin'.

Catch all these rappin' rhymes (and more) in **The Oxford Illustrated Book of American Children's Poems.**

Heaney, Seamus (editor), and Rosemary Sutcliff. *Beowulf.*

Farrar, Straus, & Giroux, 2000, 208pp. Middle School & Up. Whitbread Award.

■ **CLASSICS AND POETRY AND FOLKLORE.** *Great Britain; Europe (Sweden); Middle Ages; rites of passage; survival; supernatural.*

■ **RELATED BOOKS: Black Ships Before Troy: The Story of the Iliad** and **The Wanderings of Odysseus: The Story of the Odyssey** by Rosemary Sutcliff. Also, the classics **The Odyssey** and **The Iliad** by Homer.

> *Note:* *This Anglo-Saxon epic poem was anonymously composed during the seventh to 10th centuries. This translation by an Irish Nobel Laureate was a best-seller. Readers may wish to skip the author's introduction, although it contains interesting comments about the symbolism. Along with Homer's poems, Beowulf's odyssey sets the standard for all epic poems. Recommended mainly for mature readers, although the adventure may capture some reluctant readers.*

Before Luke Skywalker from *Star Wars*, there was Beowulf.

Beowulf was a magnificent Scandinavian warrior who fought dragons that were as fierce as Darth Vader. In fact, Beowulf had to face three dragons, each more vicious than the last.

First was Grendel, an outcast who lived in misery among the banished monsters. Then came Grendel's mother who was quite annoyed by the death of her son. Then, 50 years later, came a gold-hoarding dragon breathing fire.

Join Beowulf on his perilous journey to the unknown. May the Force be with **Beowulf**!

Heinlein, Robert A. *The Moon Is a Harsh Mistress.*

First published in 1966. Tom Doherty, 1997, 382pp. High School & Up. Hugo Award winner.

■ **SCIENCE FICTION AND CLASSICS.** *Computers; end-of-the-world; science; war.*

■ **RELATED BOOKS: Stranger in a Strange Land** and **Revolt in 2100: Methuselah's Children** by Robert A. Heinlein; **Childhood's End** and **2001: A Space Odyssey** by Arthur C. Clarke.

> *Note:* *Winner of four Hugo Awards—a record that still stands—Heinlein tells of a Lunar revolution in 2076. A former penal colony on the Moon fights its masters on Earth, using the proclamation TANSTAAFL (There Ain't No Such Thing As A Free Lunch), a slogan of the libertarian movement today. Manuel Garcia O'Kelly, the one-armed technician, narrates the story, with the other characters consisting of a radical blonde bombshell, an aging academic, and an all-knowing computer (preceding "HAL" in* **2001: A Space Odyssey** *by two years). Recommend this classic for older mature readers, since the entire book is written in Lunaspeak, pidgin English that uses few articles, but is easily understood after a few pages.*

"We must get rid of the Authority!"

"Yes—but how?" A peevish voice spoke up during our secret meeting.

"Solidarity. Authority charges too much for water, don't buy. It holds monopoly on export, don't export. It's up to you." Wyoming left the platform, and sat down between Shorty and myself. The audience cheered, maybe more for her lovely face than the content of her speech.

I had my doubts. I had known all my life that we were slaves of Lunar Authority. But what could we do? Lunar Authority was not on the Moon, it was on Earthside—and we had not one ship, not even a small hydrogen bomb. Not even guns. There were three million, unarmed and helpless, among us—and 11 billion of them with bombs and weapons. How long could we Loonies last?

A bull voice boomed: STAY WHERE YOU ARE. YOU ARE UNDER ARREST!

As I ran, I thought, these masters will learn one day that **The Moon Is a Harsh Mistress.**

H

Hemphill, Kris. *A Secret Party in Boston Harbor.*

Illustrated by John Martin & Daniel Van Pelt. Silver Moon, 1998, 88pp. Upper Elementary & Up. **Mysteries in Time** *series, including* **Murder on the Titanic, Murder at Gettysburg,** *and* **Voices From the Titanic** *by James Walker;* **The Hessian's Secret Diary** *by Lisa Banim;* **The Last Village of Central Park** *by Hope Laurie Killcoyne; and many other titles.*

■ **HISTORICAL FICTION.** *American Revolutionary War; family; pioneer life; responsibility; secrets; war.*

■ **RELATED BOOKS:** *Sarah Bishop by Scott O'Dell;* **This Time, Tempe Wick?** *by Patricia Lee Gauch;* **George Midgett's War** *by Sally Edwards.*

Note: Despite contrived plot, the colonial customs and leaders such as Samuel Adams are presented realistically. A map of colonial Boston is included. Good as a read-aloud or for a group read. Also recommended for historical fiction fans looking for strong heroine and for social studies classes.

I saw you that night, March 5, 1770.

Sarah shivered when she read the note. She had hoped that no one saw her at the bloody street riot between the British soldiers and the Boston Minutemen. Later, she was horrified to learn that her best friend Patrick and others were killed, but she still decided to keep silent.

Now someone knew she was a witness. Who could it be?

Whoever it was, that person could also be the spy who was carrying messages to the British soldiers. Sarah knew her father and Samuel Adams were planning a secret mission that would dump the highly taxed British tea in the Boston harbor. Now it was up to Sarah. She knew that, for the mission to be successful, she had to protect the **Secret Party in Boston Harbor**.

Hesse, Karen. *Letters From Rifka.*

With historical notes. Henry Holt, 1992, 148pp. Middle School & Up. National Jewish Book Award; Christopher Award; Sydney Taylor Award; ALA Notable Children's Book.

■ **HISTORICAL FICTION.** *Diaries; family; Europe (Poland, Belgium); immigrants; Jews; racism; religious prejudice; Russia.*

■ **RELATED BOOKS:** *Number the Stars by Lois Lowry;* **The Endless Steppe** *by Esther Hautzig;* **Diary of a Young Girl** *by Anne Frank.*

Note: The award-winning epistolary novel begins in Russia in 1919 and is based on experiences of the author's great-aunt. Twelve-year-old Rifka Nebrot and her family flee the anti-Semitism of post-revolutionary Russia and emigrate to the United States. Upon finally reaching Ellis Island, Rifka is held in quarantine because the ringworm has left her bald. Eventually Rifka is released to begin her new life in America. The author tells an unforgettable story of immigrant courage, ingenuity, and perseverance. Recommended for all types of readers and as a read-aloud.

October 21, 1920
Warsaw, Poland
My Dear Cousin Tovah,

Thanks to your father, we made it to the Poland border. I had a few scary moments, particularly when the Russian soldiers were searching the freight train where we were hiding. I also overheard their cruel remarks about my family, and I think my anger kept up my courage. Why do Russians blame Jews for everything?

Here's the bad news: I caught ringworm during our journey and my head was shaved. Until my hair grows, I can't go with my family to America. Apparently Americans are perfect people who are scared of bald girls. Don't worry. I didn't come all the way from Russia to be refused. I may not be perfect on the outside. I think it is more important to be perfect on the inside.

Pray for your "orphan" cousin,
Rifka

Hill, Pamela Smith. *Ghost Horses.*

Holiday House, 1996, 216 pp. Upper Elementary & Up.

■ **HISTORICAL FICTION AND ADVENTURE.** *Animals (dinosaurs); problem parents; science (paleontology); secrets; self-identity; women's issues; work.*

■ **RELATED BOOKS: A Bone in the Dry Sea** by Peter Dickinson; **Riding Freedom** by Pam Muñoz Ryan; **No Jam Today** by Carole Bolton; **Breaking Rank** by Kristen Randle.

Note: The author provides an accurate and entertaining look at many of the social and scientific issues occurring in the United States during 1899. Tabitha Fortune is a 16-year-old young woman living during a time when women were restricted in their choices and science was being challenged by a maverick named Charles Darwin. Tabitha's preacher-father is against evolution and women's rights. Determined to take part in an expedition digging for dinosaur remains near her hometown in the Badlands, she defies her father and disguises herself as a young man. Recommended for fans of adventure and historical fiction, as well as readers looking for a plucky heroine.

"Look for the bones of the ghost horses," Sally once told me. "They teach you great mysteries."

I remembered those words when Dr. Parker spoke of his expedition for dinosaur fossils in the Rocky Mountains. Despite my yearning to join, I knew I didn't have a chance. In 1899, like women's rights, the study of dinosaurs was discouraged. Even my father quoted Biblical scriptures to remind me I was the weaker sex.

Then I got an idea. I heard myself say to Dr. Parker, "May I volunteer my twin brother Tom Fortune to assist you?"

I hope I can be successful in my masquerade as Tom. I want to search for the **Ghost Horses.**

Hobbs, Will. *Jason's Gold.*

Morrow Junior, 1999, 221pp. Middle School & Up. YALSA Best Books for Young Adults; YASLA Quick Picks for Reluctant Readers; Children's Books of the Year selection.

■ **ADVENTURE.** *Animals (husky dog); survival.*

■ **RELATED BOOKS: Call of the Wild** and **White Fang** by Jack London; **Dog Song** by Gary Paulsen; **Far North** by Will Hobbs.

Note: The story is set during the 1897 Klondike gold rush, with cameo appearances by Jack London and other actual historical figures. Hobbs provides his sources and research in an appended note. Excellent for adventure lovers, especially for Jack London and Gary Paulsen fans.

"Gold!" Jason shouted the newspaper's headlines. "Read all about it! Gold discovered in Alaska!"

All these people discovering gold, Jason thought. That could have been me. Wait a minute. The rush is just beginning. It could still be me.

Jason put down the newspapers. He couldn't afford to waste another minute as a mouthpiece of history while others were making history.

He collected his packsack from the rooming house and set out for Seattle, Washington. From there, he would head north to Alaska.

This gold rush had his name written all over it. It was **Jason's Gold.**

Holm, Jennifer L. *Our Only May Amelia.*

Scholastic, 1999, 251pp. Upper Elementary & Up. Newbery Honor Book; ALA Notable Children's Book; Cooperative Children's Book Center Choice; Children's Books of the Year selection; Publishers Weekly's Best Books.

■ **HISTORICAL FICTION.** *Family; immigrants (Finland); Native Americans (Chinook); pioneer life; pregnancy; women's issues.*

■ **RELATED BOOKS: Caddie Woodlawn** by Carol Brink; **The Little House** series by Laura Ingalls Wilder; **Alice Rose and Sam** by Kathryn Lasky; **Buffalo Woman** by Bill Wallace; **Oh, Those Harper Girls!** by Kathleen Karr.

Note: *May Amelia lives with her strict Finnish father, pregnant mother, and seven brothers in Washington state in 1899. She causes her immigrant parents much grief with her tomboy ways. This is an entertaining read, but the style (present tense, no quotation marks, and capitalized nouns) may be confusing to younger readers.*

Papa is always yelling at me, "Don't Get Into Mischief May Amelia," when I'm just following my brothers. Papa says I am a girl, so I "cannot be doing what the boys are doing." He hollered so loud I'm sure they heard him over at the Petersen farm. Then he shook his finger at me and That Was That. What's worse, he yelled at me on my 12th birthday!

My brother Wilbert tells me that I am the first ever girl born in Nasel, Washington, that I am "A Miracle." I don't want to be a miracle. I just want to do what my seven brothers do. It seems like everyone is conspiring to make me a "Proper Young Lady." I do not think being a Proper Young Lady sounds like fun at all.

My secret birthday wish is to get a sister. That way Mamma and Papa won't be after me all the time, calling me "**Our Only May Amelia.**"

Holt, David, and Bill Mooney. *Spiders in the Hairdo: Modern Urban Legends.*

August House, 1999, 111pp. YALSA Popular Paperbacks selection; YASLA Quick Picks for Reluctant Readers.

■ **FOLKLORE AND SHORT STORIES.** *Crime; death; supernatural.*

■ **RELATED BOOKS: Too Good to Be True: The Colossal Book of Urban Legends** and other books by Jan Harold Brunvand; **Scary Stories to Tell in the Dark** series by Alvin Schwartz.

Note: *Also highly recommended is the Grammy-nominated audio-tape that is narrated by Holt and Mooney, two well-known storytellers. Better purchase multiple copies of this one!*

Some folk call urban legends "modern folktales." They always seem to happen to a "friend of a friend."

Of course, we know urban legends are always true stories, right? As if. Urban legends have only a kernel of truth, enough to make a great story.

Like, have you heard the one about the lady who had her beehive hairdo sprayed so hard that spiders started to nest in it? Of course you have. It happened to a "friend of a friend."

For more urban legends like **Spiders in the Hairdo**, read these stories. They might make your hair stand on end—possibly in the shape of a beehive hairdo!

Holt, Kimberly Willis. *When Zachary Beaver Came to Town.*

Henry Holt, 1999, 227pp. Upper Elementary & Up. National Book Award; VOYA Award; ALA Notable Children's Book; YALSA Best Books for Young Adults; YASLA Top 10 Best Books for Young Adults; SLJ's Best Books, Cooperative Children's Book Center Choice; Publishers Weekly's Best Books.

■ **REALISTIC FICTION.** *Death; problem parents; orphans; Vietnam War.*

■ **RELATED BOOKS: Holes** by Louis Sachar; **Where the Heart Is** by Billie Letts; **To Kill a Mockingbird** by Harper Lee; **My Louisiana Sky** by Kimberly Willis Holt.

Note: *Tobias Wilson, 13, narrates this coming-of-age story of a small Southern town in 1977. Zachary is the focal point, but a secondary plot, which poignantly describes the death of Toby's best friend's brother in Vietnam, also provides interest and insight. Recommended for all types of readers and as a read-aloud, especially for those who loved Louis Sachar's **Holes.***

Nothing ever happens in Antler, Texas. That's why the trailer decorated with Christmas lights caused quite a stir when it pulled into the Dairy Maid parking lot. Folks were lined up with two dollars in hand to see the fattest boy in the world, the 600-pound Zachary Beaver.

What a sorry life Zachary must live, sitting in a cramped trailer while people come to gawk. Still, it's got to be better than my life. I'll bet he doesn't have a mother who left to become a country singer. I'll bet he's not in love with some beautiful girl who never gives him a look. I'll bet his life isn't as awful as mine.

Turned out I was right—and I was wrong. Zachary Beaver's life was both exciting and terrible. All I know is my life was forever changed **When Zachary Beaver Came to Town.**

Hopkinson, Deborah. *A Band of Angels: A Story Inspired by the Jubilee Singers.*

Illustrated by Raul Colon. Atheneum, 1999. 40pp. Lower Elementary & Up. ALA Children's Notable Book; Book Links' Lasting Connection selection; Booklist Editors' Choice; Publishers Weekly's Best Books.

■ **HISTORICAL FICTION.** *African Americans; music; racism; religion*

■ **RELATED BOOKS: Sweet Clara and the Freedom Quilt** by Deborah Hopkinson; **Birdie's Lighthouse** by Deborah Hopkinson; **Barefoot** by Pamela Duncan Edwards.

Note: *This book is based on real events, and Jubilee singer Ella Sheppard was the author's great-grandmother. Fisk University in Nashville, Tennessee, was founded for emancipated slaves in 1866, and the Jubilee Singers still exist today, with revolving members. Recommended for multicultural studies, biography fans, and music lovers.*

My great-great grandmother Ella was born into slavery, but no one could chain her voice. In fact, her pure voice and dynamic piano playing kept Fisk University at Nashville, Tennessee, from closing.

It's true. She joined the Jubilee Singers to help raise money for their school. Not only did the singing group perform popular songs around the world, but they also introduced gospel music to Queen Victoria and President Ulysses Grant. In fact, the Jubilee Singers became so popular that none of them graduated from Fisk University.

If you hear spirituals like *Sweet Low, Sweet Chariot*, remember to thank people like the Jubilee Singers who kept gospel songs alive for the next generation. The Jubilee singers were more than great. They were **A Band of Angels**.

Horvath, Polly. *The Trolls.*

Farrar, Straus, & Giroux, 1999, 144pp. Upper Elementary & Up. ALA Notable Children's Book; Boston Globe/Horn Book Honor book; Horn Book Fanfare; Book Links' Lasting Connection selection; Bulletin of Center for Children's Books Blue Ribbon Award; SLJ's Best Books.

■ **FANTASY AND HUMOR.** *Family; school.*

■ **RELATED BOOKS: Mrs. Coverlet's Magicians** and **While Mrs. Coverlet Is Away** by Mary Nash; **Mary Poppins** series by P.L. Travers; **Ida Early Comes Over the Mountain** by Robert Burch.

Aunt Sally's stories have hidden meanings beyond their humor and provide insight about the family's interactions. Excellent for group read or as a read-aloud. Also recommended for fans of humor and tall tales.

When we first met Aunt Sally, we thought she was a giant. She wore high-heeled shoes and had an enormous beehive hairdo. We kids only heard from her once a year. Each Christmas she sent the same photograph of a moose with Christmas lights dangling from its antlers.

"Where's your moose?" asked Pee-Wee.

"Oh, I didn't bring him, " answered Aunt Sally. "Where would I keep him? In the bathtub?"

"Does she really have a moose, Daddy?" asked Melissa.

"Oh, she was just kidding," said our father. "I think."

Instantly, we decided that Aunt Sally was the most fun grown-up we ever knew. Oh, we did love to hear her tales about our family. Not ordinary stories, but exciting ones that included cougars, bears, and my most favorite of them all, **The Trolls.**

Howard, Ellen *The Gate in the Wall.*

Atheneum, 1999, 128pp. Upper Elementary & Up. Children's Books of the Year selection; Junior Library Guild selection.

■ **HISTORICAL FICTION.** *Abuse; animals (horses and birds); Great Britain (mid-1800s); orphans; substance abuse (alcohol); time travel; transportation (boats); work.*

■ **RELATED BOOKS: Lyddie** by Katherine Paterson; **Switching Well** by Penni R. Griffin; **To Visit the Queen** by Diane Duane; **To Say Nothing of the Dog or How We Found the Bishop's Bird Stump at Last** by Connie Willis.

Emma Deane is a classic Victorian child heroine who experiences sickness, poverty, and labor. Beyond the gate, Emma sees a boat and canal, and eventually she is employed as a canal woman. The foreword provides a history and an illustration of the British Newry Canal. The book also includes a glossary of Victorian and canal talk. Recommended for all types of readers, especially for those who think they don't like historical fiction.

Every day Emma passed by the gate, but she had never noticed it. She was too busy working long hours in a silk factory. She was usually too weak with hunger to notice anything. Today was different.

Locked out of the silk factory for being but a moment late, she spotted the open gate. What Emma saw astonished her. She didn't know it, but she would never be the poor, starving orphan again.

What will Emma find beyond **The Gate in the Wall**?

Howe, Norma. *Adventures of Blue Avenger: A Novel.*

Henry Holt, 1999, 230pp. High School & Up. Part of a series: **Blue Avenger Cracks the Code** *follows. VOYA Award; YALSA Best Books for Young Adults; Bulletin of Center for Children's Books Blue Ribbon.*

■ **REALISTIC FICTION.** *Death; love; men's issues; school; sex and sexuality; single parents.*

■ **RELATED BOOKS: the perks of being a wallflower** by Stephen Chbosky; **Holes** by Louis Sachar; **My Last Night on Earth** by Todd Strasser; **The Man in the Ceiling** by Jules Feiffer.

> *Note:* Howe deals with serious philosophical questions in a humorous way, and this approach elevates the book to a multi-layered and complex novel. The plot is similar to Sachar's **Holes**, but the profanity and frank sexual discussions make this novel for mature readers.

David Bruce Schumacher decided to do it on the morning of his 16th birthday. On that day, he will officially change his name to The Blue Avenger.

David invented his own hero, The Blue Avenger. Week after week, David wrote and illustrated his comic book, expressing his dreams and wishes. It's no accident that The Blue Avenger's main mission is to wipe out handguns after David's father came so close to being killed by a handgun. Now, in his father's honor, David wants to legally assume The Blue Avenger's name and identity.

Like all heroes, The Blue Avenger is not easily understood. Only one person understands The Blue Avenger: fellow classmate, Omaha Nebraska Brown. She knows Blue wants to end all evil on the planet. Like all heroines, Omaha wants to help. However, first she wants to know, "Who is the master of our fate? Are our lives predetermined? Do we have choices in choosing the choices we choose?"

For the answer to these age-old questions, along with lots of action, join in the **Adventures of Blue Avenger.**

Hughes, Andrew. *Van Gogh.*

Barrons, 1994, 31pp. Part of the **Famous Artists** *series, which also includes* **Monet; Cezanne;** *and* **Leonardo Da Vinci**. *Upper Elementary & Up.*

■ **BIOGRAPHY.** *Europe (Netherlands); hobbies (art); mental illness; suicide; work.*

■ **RELATED BOOKS: Van Gogh: Art and Emotion** by David Spence and Tessa Krailing; **The Starry Night** by Neil Waldman; **The First Starry Night** by Joan Shaddox Isom.

> *Note:* The creative layout includes van Gogh's sketches and paintings as well as his artistic project ideas. The book also contains a glossary, list of museums, and an art history dateline. For added effect, teachers may want to play the "Vincent" song by Don McLean. Recommended for art students and biography fans.

The artist Vincent van Gogh was poor and ill throughout his life. When he took his life in 1890, he thought he was a failure. He sold only a small number of paintings, and, due to lack of funds, he often went hungry.

Vincent also suffered from depression. Once he quarreled with friend and famous artist Paul Gauguin. Angry, Gauguin left Vincent's home to spend the night in a nearby hotel. Van Gogh was so upset by his friend's departure that he cut off part of his ear. He laid unconscious in a hospital for three days, but he recovered to paint more vivid, inspired paintings.

In 1990, his painting *Dr. Gachet* sold for $82 million dollars, making it the most expensive painting ever sold to date. At last, people recognized the genius of one of the world's greatest artists: **Van Gogh**.

Hurwitz, Johanna. *Llama in the Library.*

Illustrated by Mark Graham. Morrow, 1999, 113pp. Upper Elementary & Up. Part of a series; A Llama in the Family precedes.

■ **REALISTIC FICTION AND HUMOR.** *Animals (llamas); friendship; love; pregnancy; school; supernatural (ghosts).*

■ **RELATED BOOKS: A Llama in the Family** by Johanna Hurwitz; **The Burning Questions of Bingo Brown** by Betsy Byars; the **Fudge** series by Judy Blume, including **Tales of a Fourth Grade Nothing; Aldo Applesauce** and others in the **Aldo** series by Johanna Hurwitz.

Note: *In this sequel to **A Llama in the Family**, 10-year-old Adam faces life-altering situations, including his mother's pregnancy and his love for new girl, Alana Brow. The story is told with good-natured humor, and problems are resolved realistically and humorously. A former librarian, Hurwitz creates a good portrayal of the librarian;. Recommended for realistic fiction readers who like a humorous slant, as well as for a group read or read-aloud.*

I'm just like any other guy in the fifth grade. Pretty ordinary, really. I enjoy doing things like hunting for ghosts or joking with my best buddy during Sex Education.

Yet I'm famous in my town. That's because my Mom raises llamas. In fact, if it weren't for llamas, my picture wouldn't be in the newspaper. It all came about when I had this brainstorm: Why not have a **Llama in the Library**?

Jackson, Shirley. *The Haunting of Hill House.*

First published in 1959. Penguin Books, 1987, 246pp. High School & Up.

■ **CLASSICS AND HORROR.** *Mental illness; movies; supernatural.*

■ **RELATED BOOKS: The House of Usher and Other Stories** by Edgar Allan Poe; **The Shining** by Stephen King; **We Have Always Lived in the Castle** by Shirley Jackson.

Note: *First published in 1959, this classic of psychological terror is a template for other horror books about haunted houses. The main character, Eleanor Vance, receives an unusual invitation from Dr. John Montague, to attend a ghost watch in Hill House, an infamous estate in New England. In spite of the terrifying incidents, Eleanor cannot seem to flee the haunted house. Ending is a shocker. Two movies titled **The Haunting** are based on this book. Recommended for Stephen King lovers, and horror and mystery fans.*

Hill House is neither safe nor sane. It is a dwelling of contained ill will. The Hill House has 80 years of unexplained accidents, suicides, and insanity. It broods and stalks its victims. It dislikes letting its guests leave. The last person who tried to leave was killed at the turn of the driveway.

This very evening, four people will arrive at the Hill House. Tonight the house will select one more victim.

Come, join them for **The Haunting of Hill House**.

Johnson, Scott. *Safe at Second.*

Philomel, 1999, 245pp. Middle School & Up. YASLA Best Books for Young Adults; YASLA Quick Picks for Reluctant Readers; SLJ's Best Books.

■ **REALISTIC FICTION AND SPORTS.** *Disability (glass eye); friendship; peer pressure; self-identity.*

■ **RELATED BOOKS: Tangerine** by Edward Bloor; **One of the Boys** and **Overnight Sensation** by Scott Johnson; **The Moves Make the Man** by Bruce Brooks; **The Kid From Tomkinsville** by John Tunis; **Brian's Song** by William Blinn.

> *Note:* *The main character, Paulie, tells of his friend's tragic consequences and recovery after Todd loses an eye playing baseball; other conflicts including facing SATs and choosing a college are also presented. Recommended for sports fans and readers who enjoy realistic fiction. **Warning:** Profanity.*

I'm an expert on baseball. I know every Big League batting average for the last seven years. My trouble is, I can't play baseball. I'm always sitting on the bench during a game.

I don't have to be good. That's been the job of my best friend, Todd.

He had all the scouts wanting to sign him up, with enough trophies to fill the Baseball Hall of Fame. Plus, he had enough charm and good looks to fill a stadium. He had Hall of Fame tattooed over all his forehead—until a baseball hit him in his face, and all of that changed.

With his glass eye, his golden life has become darker. Now he hangs with the wild kids and avoids his girlfriend, Melissa.

Now it's my turn to help him. After all, where would I be without Todd's friendship? For the two of us, he has to recover.

Jordan, Sherryl. *The Raging Quiet.*

Simon & Schuster for Young People, 1999, 266pp. Middle School & Up. ALA Notable Children's Book; YASLA Top 10 Best Books for Young Adults; YALSA Best Books for Young Adults; Children's Books of the Year selection; SLJ's Best Books.

■ **HISTORICAL FICTION AND ROMANCE.** *Disability (deafness); love; Middle Ages.*

■ **RELATED BOOKS: The Witch of Blackbird Pond** by Elizabeth George Speare; **The Primrose Way** by Jackie French Koller; **Jackaroo** series by Cynthia Voight; **Tess of the D'Urbervilles** by Thomas Hardy.

> *Note:* *New Zealand author Sherryl Jordan has written a riveting Middle Age romance between a young widow and a deaf boy. Recommended for romance and historical fiction lovers.*

"You, she-devil! We all know what you did to your husband. You cursed him and he died. Now, get out of our village! Out, a'fore we hang you!"

Marnie jerked upright. She had been sleeping fitfully, rocking in her chair, and recalling what had happened that very day. It was alarming to think that her townspeople had turned against her. True, she was a widow who lived alone and, true, she had befriended a beggar boy who turned out to be deaf. People thought it strange that she and the boy talked with their hands. But, 'twas dangerous during these times to be called a she-devil.

Then, she heard it, rumbling like thunder. That noise was no dream. That rumbling was a wagon to take her to her hanging!

J | Juster, Norton. *The Phantom Tollbooth.*

Illustrations by Jules Feiffer with an appreciation by Maurice Sendak. First published in 1961. Special 35th Anniversary Edition. Random House, 1996, 256pp. Upper Elementary & Up.

■ **FANTASY AND HUMOR AND CLASSICS.** *Magic; time travel.*

■ **RELATED BOOKS: Alice's Adventures in Wonderland** by Lewis Carroll; **The Wizard of Oz** series by Frank Baum; **Mary Poppins** series by P. L. Travers; **The Pirates' Mixed-Up Voyage** by Margaret Mahy.

 Note: *First published in 1961, this classic still continues to delight readers of all ages. Jules Feiffer's illustrations are as vital as Tennial's were to* **Alice's Adventures in Wonderland.** *Also great as a read-aloud for younger children.*

FOR MILO, WHO HAS PLENTY OF TIME

Next to the note was an enormous package. Inside the package were instructions for building a turnpike tollbooth. Not just any old, boring tollbooth. No, this tollbooth was magical— it was a phantom tollbooth. Included were tickets and a map to magical lands like Dictionopolis (where spelling is required).

After Dictionopolis, Milo traveled the Lands Beyond on a quest for Rhyme and Reason. He sailed the Sea of Knowledge, climbed Mountains of Ignorance, and visited the Valley of Sound. Accompanied by his watchdog Tock (who ticks), Milo found excitement in the Land of the Imagination, where language takes on a life of its own.

Join him. Buy your ticket to illogical insanity at **The Phantom Tollbooth.**

K | Karr, Kathleen. *Phoebe's Folly.*

HarperCollins, 1996, 199pp. Upper Elementary & Up. Book two of the **Petticoat Party** *series:* **Go West, Young Women!** *precedes;* **Oregon, Sweet Oregon** *follows.*

■ **ADVENTURE, HISTORICAL FICTION, AND HUMOR.** *Native Americans; pioneer life; rivalry; survival; women's issues.*

■ **RELATED BOOKS: Go West, Young Women!, Oregon, Sweet Oregon** and **Gold-Rush Phoebe** by Kathleen Karr; **Across the Wide and Lonesome Prairie** by Kristiana Gregory; **Buffalo Woman** by Bill Wallace.

 Note: *Karr studied journals of pioneers and then traveled the Oregon Trail to add to the story's authenticity; an Oregon Trail map is included. Recommended for adventure, western, and historical fiction fans who like a humorous slant.*

My name is Phoebe Brown. I'm a member of Miss Simpson's Petticoat Party. I am mighty proud of that. After all, our group made it to Laramie all alone in a covered wagon. What's really amazing is that we couldn't even shoot a rifle!

Of course, some men folks thought they should teach us gals how to shoot. Men can be right useful when they set their minds to it. After we got the hang of shooting rifles, we were swollen with pride. Some people might even call us cocky.

(Sorry, I just can't resist a pun.)

Still, I wish I hadn't opened my big mouth and challenged the Snake Indians to a shooting contest. This might be my biggest folly!

Kaysen, Susanna. *Girl, Interrupted.*

Turtle Bay Books, 1993, 169pp. High School & Up.

■ **BIOGRAPHY.** *Mental illness; movies; runaways; suicide.*

■ **RELATED BOOKS: Postcards From the Edge** by Carrie Fisher; **I Never Promised You a Rose Garden** by Joanne Greenberg (Hannah Green); **One Flew Over the Cuckoo's Nest** by Ken Kesey.

> *Note:* This book of brief essays is deftly rendered, and often darkly funny. In 1967, the author, then 18, spent nearly two years on the ward for teenage girls at McLean Hospital, a renowned psychiatric facility. Recommended for mature readers, especially for reluctant readers because of the short book length and its compelling topic.

People always ask me, "How did you end up in the booby hatch?"

Booby hatch. Now that's a strange name for mental institution, but I guess it's better than *cuckoo's nest.* My answer? "It's easy."

It's easy to slip into a parallel universe. Once you are in it, you can still see the world from where you came. It still has a grip on you, yet you are still apart from it.

In fact, it's almost fun to see which one of us loonies is the craziest. I have a borderline personality disorder. Polly and Georgina are schizophrenic. Lisa is a sociopath.

Yet, in a strange way, we are free. We have nothing more to lose. My old life is on hold. My institutionalized life is that of a **Girl, Interrupted.**

Kilborne, Sarah S. *Leaving Vietnam: The Journey of Tuan Ngo, a Boat Boy. (Ready-to-Read: Level 3, Reading Alone).*

Illustrated by Melissa Sweet. Simon & Schuster, 1999, 48pp. Lower Elementary & Up. Children's Books of the Year selection; Junior Library Guild Selection.

■ **HISTORICAL FICTION.** *Immigrants (Vietnam); survival; Vietnam War.*

■ **RELATED BOOKS: The New Americans: Vietnamese Boat People (Finding Out Books)** by James Haskins; **Angkat: The Cambodian Cinderella** by Jewell Reinhart Coburn; **Goodbye Vietnam** by Gloria Whelan (for older readers); **The Clay Marble** by Minfong Ho (for older readers).

> *Note:* Ten-year-old Tuan's journey from Vietnam is based on a true story. An author's note provides additional information about the Vietnam War and the fate of Tuan's family. The fine watercolor illustrations include a map of Vietnam. Good for a read-aloud, particularly when celebrating different cultures. Also, recommended for beginning readers as an introduction to historical fiction.

It is a moonless night in Vietnam. We all wear black. That's so the Viet Cong soldiers won't see us escape. A boat is waiting for us to take us to America.

None of us want to leave our home and family, but we don't have enough food. The Viet Cong soldiers have eaten all of our rice and destroyed our hut. Tonight my father and I leave behind my mother and family. We will send them money from America, so one day they can join us.

As we sail away, we hear gunshots from the soldiers. I duck and close my ears, because I am afraid. At last, we are on our way, **Leaving Vietnam.**

King, Stephen. *The Girl Who Loved Tom Gordon.*

Scribner, 1999, 224pp. High School & Up. YALSA Best Books for Young Adults.

■ **HORROR AND ADVENTURE.** *Divorce; supernatural; survival (Appalachian Trail); sports (baseball).*

■ **RELATED BOOKS: The Lord of the Flies** by William Golding; **Cujo** and **Bag of Bones** by Stephen King; **The Haunting of Hill House** by Shirley Jackson; **Jurassic Park** by Michael Crighton.

Note: *Beginning with **Bag of Bones**, Stephen King began evolving from a writer of horror to a master of psychological thrillers. Here the author presents a twisted fairy tale within a coming-of-age story. Trish idolizes Tom Gordon, a real-life relief pitcher of the Boston Red Sox. During her odyssey through the Appalachian Trail, she hallucinates about her life, including her crush on Tom Gordon, whose exploits she listens to on her Walkman.*
***Warning:** Contains graphic profanity.*

"I'm not scared," Trish McFarland said, speaking out loud in her most authoritative nine-year-old voice. "I'm not lost. The trail's right over there. Somewhere. I'm not lost."

Trish tried to stay calm. Suddenly, something moved under her. She saw a fat black snake slithering through the leaves. She shrieked and ran, panic-stricken.

Then she stopped running and started thinking. This was no time to panic. The Appalachian Trail was long and winding. The vast woods were filled with everything fearful, anything that could overwhelm a person into a nasty, no-brain panic.

Why had she agreed to go on this stupid hike with her mother and brother? Why had she strayed off the Trail? What would happen to her?

King-Smith, Dick. *Mr. Ape.*

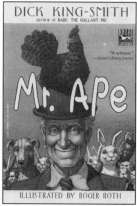

Illustrated by Roger Roth. Crown, 1998, 128pp. Lower Elementary & Up.

■ **FANTASY AND HUMOR.** *Animals; friendship; homeless.*

■ **RELATED BOOKS: Babe: The Gallant Pig** and **Ace: The Very Important Pig** by Dick King-Smith; **Mr. Popper's Penguins** by Richard and Florence Atwater; the **Freddy** series by Walter R. Brooks; **Charlotte's Web** and **Stuart Little** by E. B. White; **Dr. Doolittle** series by High Lofting; **The Cricket in Times Square** by George Seldon.

Note: *King-Smith's book **Babe: The Gallant Pig** was made into 1995 film that was nominated for an Oscar. Roth's illustrations add to the chapter book's hilarity. Recommended for animal lovers and reluctant readers who enjoy humorous fantasies.*

Dear school children:

My name is Archibald Peregrine Edmund Spring-Russell of Penny Royal. You can call me Mr. Ape. Everyone does. Although I live alone in a 15 bedroom house, I always have plenty of company.

I have hens, rabbits, and guinea pigs in my living room. I have canaries in my music room. I even keep a talking parrot in the kitchen where I sleep. For human company, I have gypsies, Jack and his son Joe. They help with all my animals. Jack has really great ideas like stringing up a trapeze set with twine or making golf clubs for my birds.

Right now I'm running out of room in my house, so if any of you want a rabbit, guinea pig or canary, write me to say how you will care for your new pet.

Sincerely yours,
Mr. Ape

Klise, Kate. *Regarding the Fountain: A Tale, in Letters, of Liars and Leaks.*

Avon Books, 1998, 138pp. Upper Elementary & Up.

■ **FANTASY AND HUMOR.** *Ecology (pollution); ethics; school.*

■ **RELATED BOOKS: The Landry News** by Andrew Clements; **Letters From Camp** by Kate Klise; **Nothing but the Truth** by Avi; **The Ink Drinker** by Eric Sanvosin.

Note: Hilarious story and visual elements (memos, headlines and faxes) will appeal to the reluctant reader. Recommended for a group read or a read-aloud.

Dry Creek School Bulletin: Yesterday Principal Walter Russ slipped in the puddle by the water fountain and made a bid for its replacement to Flowing Water Fountains Company.

Memo to Fifth Grade from Florence, Flowing Water Fountains: Thank you for your lovely suggestions regarding the new water fountain. I agree that it should contain tropical fish and chocolate shakes.

TV Newscaster: Here's our latest leak about Dry Creek's water fountain scandal. Ms. Sally Manders, President of the School Board, is organizing a campaign to Save Our Old Water Fountain. Is there something fishy going on in Dry Creek? Stay tuned for more leaks!

Komaiko, Leah. *Annie Bananie Moves to Barry Avenue.*

Illustrated by Abby Carter. Delacorte, 1996, 85pp. Lower Elementary & Up. Second in the series: **Annie Bananie** *precedes; followed by* **Annie Bananie: Best Friends to the End; Annie Bananie and the People's Court; Annie Bananie and the Pain Sisters.**

■ **HUMOR AND REALISTIC FICTION.** *Animals (dogs); friendship; rivalry; moving.*

■ **RELATED BOOKS: Annie Bananie** series by Leah Komaiko; the **Al** series by Constance C. Greene, including **A Girl Called Al; I Know You, Al; Your Old Pal, Al; The Pink Motel** by Carol Ryrie Brink; **The Egypt Game** by Zilpha Keatley Snyder.

Note: Young readers will enjoy this humorous slant of real-life situations. Use this episodic chapter book as a group read or read-aloud. Also recommended as a step up from Beverly Cleary's **Ramona** series and as a companion to the **Al** series by Constance C. Green, an underrated series that should be rediscovered.

My name is Libby and I live on Barry Avenue. For a long time I thought Barry Avenue should be called Boring Avenue. Then Annie Bananie moved to Barry Avenue. Barry Avenue, boring? Never again.

Annie is so cool. She can do perfect cartwheels, one after another. She likes to search through garbage cans for undiscovered treasures. Not long ago, she started a club called the Barry Avenue Beauties. (We thought about calling ourselves Barry Avenue Bowwows 'cause we like dogs so much. On the other hand, we don't want to be identified as dogs, know what I mean?)

Now, so many things are happening on Barry Avenue, I'm having trouble finding time to write! Life just isn't the same when a girl named **Annie Bananie Moves to Barry Avenue.**

Koss, Amy Goldman. *The Ashwater Experiment.*

Dial, 1999, 153pp. Upper Elementary & Up. Society of School Librarians International Honor Book; Bulletin of Center for Children's Books Blue Ribbon; Children's Books of the Year selection; SLJ's Best Books.

■ **REALISTIC FICTION.** *Diaries; friendship; hobbies (gardening); moving.*

■ **RELATED BOOKS: The Landry News** by Andrew Clements; **One Hundred Dresses** by Eleanor Estes; **Nothing About the Truth** by Avi ; **The Trouble With Zinny Weston** by Amy Goldman Koss.

Note: Sensitive theme of alienation is handled creatively through the main character's diary entries and stream-of-consciousness style. This book will challenge good readers who like realistic fiction.

What if I was the only REAL person on Earth? What if the whole world was set up for the purpose of testing my reaction to events? What if these Watchers (as I call them) keep observing me, Hiliary Siegal, to see what I would do next?

If I am the only real person on Earth, then I must open a door to make something appear behind it. That's a pretty powerful thought. Of course, that could make the reverse true. When I close a door, I could be totally forgotten, like I never existed. Maybe those 17 schools I attended never existed either.

So far, Ashwater seems like all the other 17 schools. There's always a class clown, a smart kid, and a queen. My role is always the same, a new kid trying to blend in with all the other sleepwalkers.

Wait a minute. Why am I worrying? How can people hurt me when they aren't real? Hold that thought and join me in **The Ashwater Experiment**.

Koss, Amy Goldman. *How I Saved Hanukkah.*

Illustrated by Diane DeGroat. Dial, 1998, 88pp. Lower Elementary & Up. Children's Books of the Year selection.

■ **REALISTIC FICTION.** *Family; friendship; holidays (Hanukkah); Jews; religious prejudice.*

■ **RELATED BOOKS: Let the Celebration Begin!** by Margaret Wild; **The Flying Latke** by Arthur Yorinks; **While the Candles Burn** by Elaine Greenstein.

Note: Koss wrote the story for her Jewish daughter to explain the importance of dreidels, latkes, and other holiday traditions. Main character Marla Feinstein's curiosity leads her to discover her Jewish heritage and to educate others. Recommended for holiday collections and readers looking for books on Jewish customs; also, good for a group read or as a read-aloud.

My teacher says variety is the spice of life. She says everyone is different and that's good.

Well, around Christmas time, it seems like everyone isn't different—just me. I really feel different when everyone in class makes red-and-green candles for Christmas, I make blue-and-white candles for Hanukkah. That's because I'm the only Jewish kid in my fourth-grade class.

I just had to know why I was different. My parents couldn't really help because my family doesn't really make a big deal over Hanukkah. So I asked, read, and learned. I learned that for religious reasons, the Jews fought against King Antiochus 2,000 years ago. When they finally won, they lit a lamp to celebrate and discovered that, instead of burning one night, their lamp oil lasted eight nights. That's why today, during Hanukkah, the Jews light candles for eight nights.

The more I learn about Hanukkah, the more interesting the celebration becomes. My family even got the spirit. This year my family is planning a big Hanukkah celebration and inviting all our friends, Jewish and non-Jewish. My mother is even making latkes! (That's like a potato pancake.)

I've renewed a tradition in my family! That's **How I Saved Hanukkah** for myself and for others.

Levine, Gail Carson. *Dave at Night.*

HarperCollins Juvenile Books, 1999, 281pp. Middle School & Up. ALA Notable Children's Book; VOYA Award; YALSA Best Books for Young Adults; Children's Books of the Year selection; Cooperative Children's Book Center Choice; SLJ's Best; Publishers Weekly's Best.

■ **HISTORICAL FICTION.** *African Americans; bullies; homeless; interracial relations; Jews; orphans.*

■ **RELATED BOOKS: Jazz Country** by Nat Hentoff; **Bud, Not Buddy** by Christopher Paul Curtis; **Having Our Say** by Sarah L. Delany and A. Elizabeth Delany with Amy Hill Hearth.

Note: This Newbery Honor author **(Ella Enchanted)** introduces the Harlem Renaissance with people like Langston Hughes and Countee Cullen. The story is based on the Levine's father and his life in New York City during the 1920s. The author's afterword provides a detailed biography of her father. Recommended for music lovers and historical fiction readers.

I'm Dave. Right from the start, I've always caused trouble. My mama died of complications from having me. It only got worse. When Papa died, I was sent to the Hebrew House for Boys. We orphans called it the Hell Hole for Brats.

Sometimes I need an escape from the bullies and the beatings. In Harlem at night, I can blend in with the city rhythms. And what rhythms! Trumpets wailing so recklessly that they seemed to be laughing. Wide-awake music beatin' with bright colors and short straight lines. Jazz music, they call it. This music doesn't have locks or fences. It can blast through anything, even my orphan's blues.

Join me, **Dave at Night**. It's a trip you'll never forget.

Lossiah, Lynn King. *Cherokee Little People: Secrets and Mysteries of the Yun Tsunsdi.*

Illustrated by Ernie Lossiah. Cherokee Publications, 1998, 175pp. Upper Elementary & Up.

■ **FOLKLORE.** *Animals; Native Americans (Cherokee); nature; religion; supernatural.*

■ **RELATED BOOKS: Between Earth and Sky: Legends of Native American Sacred Places** by Joseph Bruchac; **In a Sacred Manner I Live: Native American Wisdom** edited by Neil Philip; **Dancing Drum: A Cherokee Legend (Native American Legends)** by Terri Cohlene.

Note: James Mooney collected stories when he lived among the Cherokees from 1887-90, and these stories are now contained in the Smithsonian. The Cherokee author believes the Little People were real and not folklore. Her detailed sketches add to the text, and the book also contains a glossary of Native American terms. Recommended for readers who enjoy multicultural folklore and as a read-aloud.

Many years ago, the Cherokee knew many things about the Earth and its creatures. They knew the earth was round before Columbus sailed to their land. How? Through the Little-People-Who-Wore-White.

The Little People were mystical creatures from above. Many moons ago, they appeared to the Cherokee in a gleaming realm of light. They told the tribe about a special man who lived many oceans away and had taught people a better way to live. Because of his enemies, this man would die. As they talked, the sky darkened. The tribe began to cry and mourn his death.

On the road lay a crystal. A woman picked up the crystal. As her tears fell on the crystal, it transformed into a cross. Others picked up crystals and all the crystals turned to crosses. These crosses of stone were passed on to future generations. Today, some Cherokee people still have these crosses.

Did Little People really exist or were they just imaginary? Recently, archeologists have found burial sites that have skeletons of adults less than three feet tall. You decide if you believe in the **Cherokee Little People**.

Lowry, Lois. *Stay! Keeper's Story.*

Illustrated by True Kelley. Houghton Mifflin, 1997, 127pp. Middle School & Up. Children's Books of the Year selection.

■ **FANTASY AND HUMOR.** *Animals (dogs); homeless; orphans.*

■ **RELATED BOOKS:** The **Bunnicula** series by James and Deborah Howe, including **Bunnicula: A Rabbit-Tale of Mystery**; **Shiloh** series by Phyllis Reynolds Naylor; **The Incredible Journey** by Sheila Burnford; **Look Back Moss** by Betty Levin.

Note: *Lowry has written a hilarious yet heartwarming book about a stray dog. As the narrator, Keeper is an intelligent, observant dog with a penchant for poetry. Recommended for dog fans as well as readers of fantasy and humor. Also, this book sits up and begs to be read aloud. However, in the text the word "bitch" may need to be defined to listeners as a female dog.*

I do not like to be referred to as The Dog. I find that title insulting. I have a name, although, to be sure, I had many names bestowed upon me until my final name of Keeper.

Like many dogs, my background is sordid. I was born in the gutter, abandoned by my mother. I resorted to stealing for a living. (It sounds like a politician's background but, unfortunately, I was unable to run for office.) Due to my cleverness and talents, I became a celebrity who appeared on TV commercials, flirted with Cybil Shephard on Jay Leno's show, and was interviewed by Oprah Winfrey. Putting on the dog, so to speak.

Alas, fame and fortune mean nothing without a family. It wasn't until I found a home and my long-lost sister that I found my name, Keeper.

Therefore, in order to remain top dog, I immodestly call my tale **Stay! Keeper's Story**.

Luft, Lorna. *Me and My Shadows: A Family Memoir.*

Pocket, 1998, 417pp. High School & Up.

■ **BIOGRAPHY.** *Substance abuse (drugs and alcohol); eating disorders (anorexia); homosexuality; mental illness; movies; music; problem parents (addicts, mental illness); rivalry; show business; suicide.*

■ *Related books:* **Get Happy: The Life of Judy Garland** by Gerald Clarke; **Under the Rainbow: The Real Liza Minnelli** by George Mair; **Dream Lovers: Bobby Darin and Sandra Dee** by Dodd Darin; **Child Bride: Untold Story of Priscilla Presley** by Susanne Finstad.

Note: *In this controversial book, Luft talks frankly about her family's addictions; although some readers claim that her account is not completely accurate. Nevertheless, young readers may identify with Luft's identity crisis. Contains previously unpublished photographs of Judy Garland. Recommended for biography fans and readers who enjoy tell-all stories.*

Judy Garland is a Hollywood legend. She was only 15 when she made the movie *The Wizard of Oz*, and the movie is still watched long after her death in 1969. Judy Garland was also my mother.

My sister, Liza Minnelli, is also a legend. Yet both of them were addicted to drugs and alcohol. In that sense, these two legends were very human, like you and I.

I was bound by these shadows of my past. Living with two Hollywood legends did not spare me the pain of having someone you love addicted to drugs and alcohol. For a time I was bound by my own addictions. With professional help, I learned to forsake my fast living and reliance on drugs. I learned to step out in the sun and be myself. No longer am I bound to **Me and My Shadows**.

Lynch, Chris. *Extreme Elvin.*

HarperCollins, 1999, 240pp. High School & Up. Part of a series: Slot Machine precedes. Children's Books of the Year selection.

■ **REALISTIC FICTION.** *Bullies; eating disorders (obesity); friendship; illness (hemorrhoids); love; religion (Catholic); school (Catholic); self-identity; sex and sexuality (masturbation); single parents.*

■ **RELATED BOOKS: Slot Machine** by Chris Lynch; **The Catcher in the Rye** by J. D. Salinger; **the perks of being a wallflower** by Stephen Chbosky; **Lord of the Fries** by Tim Wynne-Jones; **One Fat Summer** by Robert Lipsyte.

> *Note:* *Overweight antihero Elvin Bishop continues his adolescent saga, this time afflicted with hemorrhoids. Lynch makes such a dreaded condition funny. Recommended for mature readers who like humorous realistic fiction and for reluctant readers looking for frank books about adolescence.* **Warning:** *Text contains profanity as well as a masturbation scene.*

Now that I am 14 years old, I am a TEEN. (That's T-E-E-N, in big capital letters.) I'm also A Young Adult. (That phrase had to be dreamed up by an old adult.) Now I am supposed to have Relationships. (You'd better capitalize that word, too.)

Of course, Fat Persons cannot have Relationships, even if they are "Teens." Not that I consider myself a Fat Person, just a guy who has some fat on him. No pun intended, but there's a big difference.

Fat or not, I'm still one of Them. You know, a person who gets picked on, no matter what. Like being accused of catching VD from Sally whom I barely touched. Like protecting my best girl from the school bully called Darth. (His nickname is self-explanatory.)

Okay, I am super-dramatic. I accept that. Just call me **Extreme Elvin**.

Macaulay, David. *Ship.*

Houghton Mifflin, 1995, 95pp. For all libraries.

■ **NONFICTION.** *Diaries; Europe (Spain); Hispanic Americans; transportation; work.*

■ **RELATED BOOKS:** *Other books by David Macaulay:* **Castle; Underground; Unbuilding.** *Also,* **A Night to Remember** *by Walter Lord;* **James Cameron's Titanic** *by Ed W. Marsh.*

> *Note:* *Although the ship Magdalena is fictional, fascinating details about maritime archeology, boat building, and artifact restorations are accurate and enhance the plot. The award-winning illustrations contain a variety of artistic styles, including detailed architectural drawings, sepia-toned journal entries, and bluish overtones that make the reader feel like he or she is underwater. Recommended for history buffs and Titanic fans of all ages.*

Try to think of ancient wooden ships as the space shuttles of the 15th-century. They also explored unknown territory.

Maria Sousa and her archaeologist friend Jack Stevens realized this when they discovered an ancient ship's anchor at the bottom of the ocean. After many detailed plans and underwater excursions, they discovered the fragments of a Spanish ship called Magdalena. More important, they found the diary of the ship owner's family, and it gave important clues about the ship's beginnings and its tragic end.

How was a ship as magnificent as Magdalena built? What cargo was the ship carrying? What caused its final fate? Did the crew survive?

Book an imaginary passage on the voyage of the doomed **Ship**.

McCourt, Frank. 'Tis: A Memoir.

*Scribner, 1999, 367pp. Sequel to **Angela's Ashes**. High School & Up.*

■ **BIOGRAPHY.** *Class conflict; immigrants (Ireland); Ireland; religion (Catholic); rites of passage; self-identity; substance abuse (alcohol).*

■ **RELATED BOOKS: Angela's Ashes** by Frank McCourt; **A Star Called Henry** by Roddy Doyle; **The Great Shame: And the Triumph of the Irish in the English-speaking World** by Thomas Keneally.

> *Note:* Author of **Angela's Ashes**, McCourt continues his story, beginning in October 1949, upon his arrival in America. McCourt is a brilliant storyteller, with his voice in every sentence, revealing a wry humor. **Warning:** Some profanity and sexual situations.

'Tis odd being Irish in America.

An immigrant without an education, I work many jobs, one as a houseman in the lobby of an expensive New York hotel. I sweep floors and empty ashtrays. I'm told, "You, Irish, come 'ere, clean up, take garbage, let's go." I wouldn't mind that if it weren't in front of those college girls who are golden. That's when I wish I was invisible, and sometimes I am.

One day my presence becomes known. There's a yelp from a college girl and the maitre d' rushes over. She's crying, and he's barking, "McCourt, boy, get over here right now. Did you remove a paper napkin?"

"I cleaned up. I emptied the ashtrays."

"Lemme tell you something, McCourt. This young lady here is the daughter of an important man, and she had a paper napkin with a phone number from a Princeton boy. Find that paper."

I go the kitchen, red-faced and humiliated. I find a clean paper napkin, write a made-up phone number on it, stain it with coffee, then hand it to the maitre d', who hands it to the girl. Her friends loudly cheer. My only sorrow is that I won't be there when she calls that number.

McDaniel, Lurlene. *The Girl Death Left Behind.*

Mass Market Paperback, 1999, 176pp. Middle School & Up. YASLA Quick Picks for Reluctant Readers.

■ **REALISTIC FICTION.** *Abuse; death; moving; orphans; rivalry; school; survival.*

■ **RELATED BOOKS: Goodbye Doesn't Mean Forever; Angel of Mercy;** and **Reach for Tomorrow (One Last Wish)** by Lurlene McDaniel; **Daddy Long Legs** by Jean Webster.

> *Note:* The author is a favorite among many young adults because she writes inspirational stories about teenagers facing life-altering situations. One of her best novels, this story expresses the shock a 14-year-old girl faces when her family is killed in a car accident. Beth's courage and strength of character should appeal to many young adults.

"Is my family all right?" Beth asked the doctor. "I didn't go to the picnic with them because I had the flu."

"According to the police," the doctor said, "The van rolled over a hill and smashed into a tree. The impact was severe."

Beth shuddered. "They're all right, aren't they?"

"No, Beth. They arrived at the emergency room, DOA. Dead on arrival."

That's when Beth's world fell apart. Her Aunt Camille insisted that Beth move to Florida with them. Beth intensely disliked her cousin Terri and she missed all of her old friends.

How would Beth cope? Especially now that she was **The Girl Death Left Behind.**

McKee, Tim (editor). *No More Strangers Now: Young Voices From a New South Africa.*

Photographs by Anne Blackshaw. DK, 1998, 107pp. Middle School & Up. Jane Addams Honor Book; YASLA Best Books for Young Adults; ALA Notable Children's Book; Book Links' Lasting Connections list.

■ **BIOGRAPHY.** *Africa (South Africa); politics; racism.*

■ **RELATED BOOKS: Miriam's Song: A Memoir** by Mark Mathabane; **Voices of South Africa** by Carolyn Meyer; **South Africa: Coming of Age Under Apartheid** by Jason and Ettagale Laur.

Note: *The book includes a foreword by Archbishop Desmond Tutu. Compelling photographs accompany readable first-person text. Introduction gives an excellent history of South Africa; however, it may be necessary to explain that apartheid is a Dutch word that means "separateness." Due to its pleasing format, this book could appeal to reluctant readers. Also recommended as a history primary source; select one of the biographies for a read-aloud.*

In South Africa, the question used to be "What are you? Are you Black, White, or Colored?" (In South Africa, "Colored" is considered a mixture of the Black and White races.)

Luckily, things are different now. South Africa used to have a racist government that separated the races by a policy called *apartheid.* Since democracy appeared in 1994, the question is, "How can we be rebuild South Africa for all the people?"

The young adults in South Africa have experienced a fascinating change in their lives, from a repressive government to a democracy. Twelve young adults, from ages 13 to 19, share their experiences with us.

Leandra is a white Afrikaner who was taught to fear Blacks until she attended a weekend camp that changed her viewpoint. Nonhlanhla's brother was a Black activist in the Soweto uprising; unfortunately, he gave his life for South Africa's freedom. Nithaninia is Colored, always stuck in the middle of a race war, until democracy changed her status.

All tell of their freedom from the chains of racism. They all share a hope that there are **No More Strangers Now.**

McKinley, Robin. *The Stone Fey.*

Illustrated by John Clapp. Harcourt Brace, 1985. Illustrations, 1998. Middle School & Up. Children's Books of the Year selection.

■ **FANTASY.** *Love; nature; supernatural.*

■ **RELATED BOOKS: Sirena** by Donna Jo Napoli; **A Knot in the Grain and Other Stories** by Robin McKinley; **Imaginary Lands** edited by Robin McKinley.

Note: *The text was first published in **Imaginary Lands**, a short story collection edited by McKinley. In this picture book edition, John Clapp adds lovely watercolors that perfectly capture the mood of this romantic tale. Although the short text looks appropriate for elementary students, the text is too complex.*

Maddy caught her breath. There he was again. This time the magical creature was sitting on a rock. He seemed to have materialized out of rock—or perhaps out of air. She recognized him from one of her grandmother's stories—he was a Stone Fey.

Now and again, the Stone Fey would leave messages for her. Once he left a pile of rocks in a beautiful mosaic of shimmering grays, that formed the letter M.

Now the Hills had a different meaning to Maddy. No longer was herding sheep a boring and useless task. She waited impatiently for each day to arrive. She even wondered if she was in love with this supernatural creature, this stone fey.

What happens to a mere mortal girl when she loves **The Stone Fey**?

McKissack, Patricia. *Run Away Home.*

Scholastic, 1997, 128pp. Upper Elementary & Up. Teachers Choice Award; Children's Books of the Year selection.

■ **HISTORICAL FICTION.** *African Americans; animals (dogs); Civil War (Reconstruction); family; interracial relations; Native Americans (Apaches); racism; runaways; secrets.*

■ **RELATED BOOKS: Christmas in the Quarters** and **Sojourner Truth: Ain't I a Woman?** by Patricia McKissack; **To Be a Slave** by Julius Lester; **Barefoot: Escape on the Underground Railroad** by Pamela Duncan Edwards; **Cezanne Pinto: A Memoir** by Mary Stolz.

> *Note:* This fascinating story is based on the author's family history. A young African-American girl (Sarah Jane) befriends an Apache boy who has escaped from the train transporting Geronimo and his companions-in-exile from Florida to Alabama in 1888. The story contains references to Geronimo, Booker T. Washington, Harriet Tubman, and Andrew Jackson. Recommended for all readers.

I had to hide that Apache boy called Sky from the authorities. My great-grandparents were runaway slaves so I can understand his fright.

Not that Sky appreciates my help. He is the most un-person I have ever met: ungrateful, unpleasant, uneverything. So what if he fought with Geronimo? Does that give him the right to be so snippity?

Still, I understand his anger. A few years ago the Civil War was fought so we black people could be free. I think it should have included Indians too.

Today I saw a white man on a horse approach our house. I just know he's come for Sky. I whispered to myself, "Sky, run away. Be free."

Sky's story is called **Run Away Home**.

MacLaine, Shirley. *The Camino: A Journey of the Spirit.*

Pocket Books, 2000, 307pp. Middle School & Up.

■ **BIOGRAPHY.** *Ethics; Europe (Spain); religion; supernatural.*

■ **RELATED BOOKS: Out on a Limb; Dancing in the Light; It's All in the Playing; Going Within;** and **Dance While You Can;** all by Shirley MacLaine; **Soul Stories** by Gary Zukav; **Chicken Soup for the Teenage Soul** series edited by Jack Canfield et al.

>
> *Note:* Santiago de Compostela Camino is a famous pilgrimage that has been undertaken by people for centuries across Northern Spain. MacLaine, in her 60s, completed the grueling walk in 30 days. She discusses the history of the trail, beginning in the days of Charlemagne, and, typically, speculates on her "past lives" at Atlantis and Lemuria. She also identifies "Gerry" her politician/lover from her book **Out on a Limb** as Swedish Prime Minister Olaf Palme who was later assassinated. Recommended for readers who enjoy reading pop philosophy and otherworldly adventures.

"The Camino"—which means "a road" or "the way"—is a pilgrimage that lies in Northern Spain. According to many mystics, The Camino lies directly under the Milky Way. By walking this 500-mile path, we can align with the stars to become more psychic.

Some think I'm too psychic for my own good. I'm Shirley MacLaine: actress, writer and, some would say, spokeswoman for the New Age. Some might say I'm crazy. I call myself a Seeker of Truth.

With my celebrity baggage, I began my pilgrimage. On a pilgrimage, a story is a critical element. Fortunately, I have lots of stories to share. I endured stalking paparazzi, worshiping fans, and many fellow pilgrims. Somewhere in that madness, I found myself.

Join me. Walk **The Camino** with me.

McLaren, Clemence. *Waiting for Odysseus.*

Atheneum, 2000, 160pp. Middle School & Up.

■ **FOLKLORE AND ROMANCE.** *Love; war; women's issues.*

■ **RELATED BOOKS: Inside the Walls of Troy** by Clemence McClaren; **Black Ships Before Troy: The Story of the Iliad** and **The Wanderings of Odysseus: The Story of the Odyssey** by Rosemary Sutcliff; **The Odyssey** and **The Iliad** by Homer.

> *Note:* Explain to students the background of Homer's epic poem, **The Odyssey**. Discuss Odysseus' participation in the Trojan War and his 10 year voyage through the islands of the Aegean Sea. This story is a fascinating page-turner from the viewpoints of four women in Odysseus' life: Penelope, his wife; the witch, Circe; the goddess, Athena; and a trusted family servant, Eurycleia. Highly recommended to all students, especially those studying Ancient Greece, folklore or women's studies.

I loved him the first moment. The Greeks believe love can strike like that, like an arrow shooting sweet poison in your veins. I felt like this when I saw Odysseus.

I am Penelope, cousin to Helen, the most beautiful woman in the world. According to gossip, Helen was the daughter of Zeus. All the Greek kings wanted her. For the first time, I felt jealous of Helen.

One day I saw Odysseus in the olive grove. He took my hand and said, "For years I've tried to envision my wife. No picture came to mind. Until I met you . . ."

I was speechless.

"Zeus Thunderer, woman! End my agony! Do you want me or not?"

I nodded. "More than life itself."

At that time I didn't know that Helen would take my Odysseus away to fight in the Trojan War. Then, on his return to me, the sorceress Circe kept him on an island. Now he has been gone for more than 20 years.

Meanwhile, I am bothered by suitors wanting my hand in marriage. I want nothing to do with any of them. So, here I sit, **Waiting for Odysseus.**

M

McNeal, Laura, and Tom McNeal. *Crooked.*

Knopf, 1999, 224pp. High School & Up. YASLA Best Books for Young Adults; YASLA Top Ten Young Adult Books; Children's Books of the Year selection.

■ **REALISTIC FICTION.** *Abuse; bullies; crime; death; divorce; illness (cancer); love; peer pressure; secrets; sex and sexuality.*

■ **RELATED BOOKS: Armageddon Summer** by Jane Yolen and Bruce Coville; **The Falcon** by Jackie French Koller; **The Dog Who Lost His Bob** by Laura and Tom McNeal; **When Jeff Comes Home** by Catherine Atkins; **The Outsiders** by S. E. Hinton.

> *Note:* *Ninth-graders Amos and Clara suffer from the physical abuse of bullies, and, in alternating chapters with two points-of-view narration, discover romance. Many issues are discussed: divorce, cancer, and death of a parent as well as confrontation with delinquents. Recommended for mature readers who enjoy realistic fiction with uncompromising issues. **Warning:** Some profanity with issues of sexuality discussed, including condoms and attempted rape.*

Amos' head hurt. He vaguely remembered watching the Tripp brothers vandalizing his neighbor's yard and after that, he saw a baseball bat swing toward his head.

Now that he was in the hospital recovering from a concussion, he tried to piece together his life. He thought about his father who pretended to be healthy when he was actually dying from cancer. He thought about his attempt to fit in with the other students. Most of all, he thought about Clara.

Clara made him happy. It was a weird kind of happy. Before he met her, things that made him happy came from the outside—like getting an A on a test. Now happiness seemed to come within him. Now it worked from the inside out.

He needed all the happiness he could find. Especially since he knew the Tripp brothers would do all they could to stop him from talking to the police.

How could he keep his head on straight when life seemed so **Crooked**?

Macy, Sue. *Winning Ways: A Photohistory of American Women in Sports.*

Henry Holt, 1996, 188pp. Upper Elementary & Up.

■ **NONFICTION AND SPORTS.** *Sports (women); women's issues.*

■ **RELATED BOOKS: A Whole New Ball Game** by Sue Macy; **Up to the Plate** by Margot Fortunato; **Locker Room Mirror** by Nathan Aaseng; **Little Girls in Pretty Boxes** by Joan Ryan.

> *Note:* *The text includes excellent photographs, timelines, and a bibliography of related books and organizations. For sports and nonfiction fans as well as readers looking for strong heroines. Also recommended for book reports.*

Until recently, women were discouraged from entering sports competitions. Even bicycling or walking was considered dangerous for women. Physicians claimed that exercise caused small tumors on ankle joints and prevented women from bearing healthy children.

The first Olympic games in 1896 excluded women. Even 35 years later, the head of the Olympics Committee announced, "The ancient Greeks kept women out of their athletic games. They didn't even let them on the sidelines. I'm not sure that they're not right."

Of course, there were always a few women who refused to listen. These women dared to go over Niagara Falls in a barrel, swim the English Channel and fly airplanes.

Read all about their **Winning Ways.**

Mah, Adeline Yen. *Chinese Cinderella: The True Story of an Unwanted Daughter.*

Delacorte, 1999, 205pp. Middle School & Up. YALSA Best Books for Young Adults; Children's Books of the Year selection; Publishers Weekly's Best Books;.

■ **BIOGRAPHY.** *Abuse; Asia; China; friendship; problem parents; stepparents.*

■ **RELATED BOOKS: Falling Leaves: The True Story of an Unwanted Chinese Daughter** by Adeline Yen Mah; **Ties That Bind, Ties That Break: A Novel** by Lensey Namioka; **Bound Feet and Western Dress** by Pang-Mei Natasha Chang; **Daughter of the River** by Hong Ying.

> *Note:* This is a fascinating account of an abused and unloved Chinese girl who becomes a respected medical doctor, due to her intelligence and integrity. Recommended for all types of readers, especially for those looking for an unforgettable biography.

This is the true story of my childhood in China. My family considered me bad luck because my mother died giving birth to me. They made me feel unloved and unwanted. I didn't even know my own birthday! No one told me and certainly no one celebrated it.

At least my bird loved me. I called her Pretty Young Thing or PYT. One day my father wanted to see if our dog was cured of his illness. He ordered Oldest Brother to fetch PYT. My stomach rolled over as I watched our dog pounce on my beloved bird. I wondered how I would get over this heartbreak, but somehow I learned to survive, to endure, and, yes, triumph.

Do you remember the story of Cinderella? The Chinese were the first to tell of the orphaned girl, abused by her stepmother and stepsisters, who lived happily ever after. That story was my story. Truly, I was a **Chinese Cinderella.**

Manheim, Camryn. *Wake Up, I'm Fat!*

Foreword by Rosie O'Donnell. Doubleday, 1999, 289pp. High School & Up.

■ **BIOGRAPHY.** *Self-identity; show business; substance abuse (speed, LSD, marijuana).*

■ **RELATED BOOKS: FAT!SO?: Because You Don't Have to Apologize for Your Size** by Marilyn Wann; **Life in the Fat Lane** by Cherie Bennett; **Well Rounded: Eight Simple Steps for Changing Your Life . . . Not Your Size** by Catherine Lippincott.

> *Note:* Because the text discusses drug use and includes profanity, recommend this joyous celebration of being overweight (but healthy) to a mature middle school student.

When I accepted my Emmy award for Best Supporting Actress for the TV show *The Practice*, I proclaimed, "This is for all the fat girls!"

I got a lot of mail on that statement, mostly from other fat girls who said, "You go, fat girl!"

I'm Camryn Manheim. Most agents and casting directors tell me, "You're too fat." Tell me, how many Emmys have they won?

Not only am I an award-winning actress, but I'm also a writer. Guess what the title of my book and Broadway show is? You're right: **Wake Up, I'm Fat!**

Marshall, James (author and illustrator). *Rats on the Roof and Other Stories.*

*First published in 1991. Econo-Clad Books, 1999, 80 pp. First in a series; **Rats on the Range and Other Stories** follows. Lower Elementary & Up.*

■ **HUMOR AND FANTASY.** *Animals; rivalry.*

■ **RELATED BOOKS: A Toad for Tuesday** by Russell E. Erickson; **Winnie the Pooh** by A.A. Milne; **The Cricket in Times Square** series by George Selden; **Animal Fare** by Jane Yolen; the **Freddie** series by Walter Brooks; other books by James Marshall: **Rats on the Range and Other Stories, The Cut-Ups, The Stupids.**

Note: *The seven short stories included are humorous with unexpected plot twists. Black-and-white illustrations by author, cartoonist, and Caldecott winner Marshall are a perfect complement. Highly recommended as a read-aloud because each chapter is a self-contained plot.*

"We have a very serious problem," explained Otis Dog. "We've got rats on the roof and they are keeping us awake at night. That's why we decided to call you."

Tomcat looked at him in horror. "Rats, you say? Why didn't you say so earlier? How disgusting! Somebody call 911! Ugh!"

Still shuddering, Tomcat scurried out the door. Rats on the roof are not the only problem in this wacky neighborhood. No, no, no. There are cranky dogs, vain frogs, a bossy brontosaurus, and a crafty goose that almost got cooked. Everyone is trying to outsmart the other one.

Find out who becomes top dog in **Rats on the Roof and Other Stories.**

Mathabane, Miriam, as told to Mark Mathabane. *Miriam's Song: A Memoir.*

Simon & Schuster, 2000, 315pp. Middle School & Up.

■ **BIOGRAPHY.** *Africa (South Africa); pregnancy; racism; school; sexual abuse; substance abuse (alcohol).*

■ **RELATED BOOKS: Kaffir Boy: The True Story of a Black Youth's Coming of Age in Apartheid South Africa; Kaffir Boy in America** and **African Women: Three Generations** by Mark Mathabane; **Voices of South Africa** by Carolyn Meyer.

Note: *Miriam's brother, Mark Mathabane, is a renowned writer and expatriate of South Africa; his book **Kaffir Boy** became a best-seller that discusses the horrors of living in a South African township. Today South Africa is a democracy, thanks to the courage of Nelson Mandela, Mark Mathabane, and so many others who fought the racist regime. This book integrates important South African political events within the context of Miriam's story. Highly recommended as a resource in African history, as a biography, and as an inspiring read.*

I am Miriam Mathabane. I am a black South African, considered to be inferior in my own country. I was born during *apartheid*, the government's system of separating the races. I was educated under what was called Bantu Education.

Bantu Education was nothing more than slave education. Until I came to America when I was 23, I had never heard of Hitler, the Holocaust, or American slavery. My teacher was responsible for more than 100 students. The teacher punished the students for wearing the wrong uniform, not paying our school fees, or failing the cleanliness inspection.

I dreamed of being a nurse. Yet, I knew under this racist system, I would never achieve my goal. I would always be restricted in my township, at school, and in South Africa.

Hear me sing my song of endurance, **Miriam's Song.**

Matas, Carol. *Greater Than Angels.*

M

Simon & Schuster, 1998, 133pp; Aladdin Paperbacks, 1999, 176pp. Middle School & Up. 1999-2000 Battle of the Books.

■ **HISTORICAL FICTION.** *Europe (France); France; Holocaust; Jews; religion; religious prejudice; racism; World War II.*

■ **RELATED BOOKS: After the War** and **Daniel's Story** by Carol Matas; **The Devil's Arithmetic** by Jane Yolen; **I Have Lived a Thousand Years** by Livia Bitton Jackson; **No Pretty Pictures** by Anita Lobel.

Note: This historical novel tells the story of Anne Hirsch and her Jewish family who are deported in 1940 from Germany into France; they escape with the help of various French organizations. Issues of religion during adversity are handled well. The book also provides information about international organizations that helped Jews during the Holocaust. A map of occupied France and Germany is included. Recommended for classes studying the Holocaust and World War II as well as historical fiction readers.

Sneaking around when you choose to do it is exciting and fun. You know, like going to the theater without your mother knowing about it. Hiding in a woodpile fearing your life, however, is quite another thing.

My nightmare began in October 1940 when the German soldiers transported my family and me to a French concentration camp. Hunger and death surrounded us. It made all of us question God's lack of involvement in our suffering.

Should we allow evil to overtake us? Is it true that if humans retain the spirit of God, they are **Greater Than Angels**?

Meyer, Carolyn. *Mary, Bloody Mary.*

Harcourt Brace, 1999, 227pp. Middle School & Up. YASLA Top 10 Best Books for Young Adults; YALSA Best Books for Young Adults; Children's Books of the Year selection.

■ **HISTORICAL FICTION.** *Death; divorce; Great Britain; love; politics; religious prejudice.*

■ **RELATED BOOKS: Isabel: Jewel of Castilla (Royal Diaries)** by Carolyn Meyer; **Marie Antoinette: Princess of Versailles Austria-France (Royal Diaries)** by Kathryn Lasky.

Note: This meticulously researched book describes the teen years of Mary Tudor, half-sister to Queen Elizabeth, The Virgin Queen. By the time Anne Boleyn is beheaded by Mary and Elizabeth's father, King Henry VIII, Mary has become a bitter woman, known as Bloody Queen Mary for her savage religious genocide. Because of its readable style, this novel is highly recommended for all readers as well as all teachers of European history classes.

What if you began life as a Princess and, as you grew older, became a servant in your own home? That happened to me.

I'm Mary Tudor, first born daughter to King Henry VIII of England. My father loved my mother, Queen Catherine—until the witch possessed him. My father divorced my mother and forbade me to see my mother again. Then, still under the witch's spell, my father called me to court to wait on my half-sister, Elizabeth—as a servant!

Anne Boleyn was a witch; I never doubted it. She had a birthmark and an extra finger to prove it. Because of this evil witch who called herself queen, I lost everything: my mother's presence, my father's affection, and my chances of a fruitful marriage. And I came close—very close—to losing my life.

I command you, hear my story, the story of **Mary, Bloody Mary**.

Mikaelsen, Ben. *Petey.*

Hyperion Books for Children, 1998, 280pp. Middle School & Up. YASLA Teens Top Ten Best Books; Alex Award; YASLA Best Books for Young Adults.

■ **REALISTIC FICTION.** *Bullies; disability (cerebral palsy); friendship; mental illness.*

■ **RELATED BOOKS: Flowers for Algernon** by Daniel Keyes; **The Heart Is the Lonely Hunter** by Carson McCullers; **Matthew Unstrung** by Kate Seago; **Mind's Eye** by Paul Fleischman; **Holes** by Louis Sachar.

Note: This book tells two stories within one. It begins with the tragic youth and adulthood of Petey, who is born in 1922. Then with a switch in point of view, the story becomes Trevor's, focusing on his gradual acceptance of Petey. The underlying message of this heartwarming story (which has a "happy ending" when Trevor reunites Petey with his friend Calvin) is that everyone deserves care, respect, and a chance to make a difference. Recommended for all, especially for special education teachers and their classes as a read-aloud.

In 1924, when Petey was two, he was admitted into the Warm Springs Insane Asylum.

Petey wasn't insane. Petey had cerebral palsy. His body acted crazy from time to time, but Petey couldn't help that. He was as sane as they come. Not just sane, but wise. You see, Petey lived each moment as if it were his last, taking childlike delight in peering through a window or feeling the wind blow across his face.

It had been many years since Petey had a friend. He had watched his friends disappear over the years—Esteban, Joe, Cassie, and Owen. Petey wondered if he would shut down like his patient friend, Calvin, who sat in a wheelchair in a catatonic trance. One day Calvin was taken away. Petey promised himself that he would never love anyone again.

Then Petey met Trevor, a troubled teen. Should Petey open his heart one last time?

Mollel, Tololwa M. *Subira Subira.*

Illustrated by Linda Saport. Houghton Mifflin, 2000, 32pp. Lower Elementary & Up. Children's Books of the Year selection.

■ **FOLKLORE.** *Africa (Tanzania); rites of passage; rivalry; supernatural.*

■ **RELATED BOOKS: Chinye** by Obi Onyefulu and illustrated by Evie Safarewicz; **A Story a Story** retold and illustrated by Gail E. Haley; **Fly-Away Girl** by Ann Grifalcon.

Note: The acclaimed Tanzanian storyteller tells this traditional African folktale with the setting in contemporary Tanzania. Mollel includes lyrics to a traditional Tanzanian song, along with a pronunciation guide and glossary of African words. Pastel illustrations beautifully express the supernatural qualities. Readers will identify with Tatu's sibling problem. Recommended as a read-aloud.

Tatu had a problem: She had to take care of her little brother. Some of you may have had the same problem as Tatu, even though Tatu lives far away in a small African village.

Tatu was tired of her brother's tantrums. She decided to teach him a lesson that he would never forget. So she went to a mysterious spirit woman who lived in the dark forest. The sorceress ordered Tatu to pluck three whiskers from a lion.

With only a song on her lips, Tatu approached the giant anthill, singing, "**Subira, Subira.**" Will her song keep the lion sleeping so her wish can be granted?

Morgenstern, Mindy. *The Real Rules for Girls.*

Designed by Amy Inouye; creative concept by Mari Florence. Girls Press, 1999, 111pp. Middle School & Up.

■ **NONFICTION.** *Love; peer pressure; rites of passage; self-identity; women's issues; work.*

■ **RELATED BOOKS: Girls in America: Their Stories, Their Words** edited by Carol Cassidy; **Beyond Beauty** edited by Jane Pratt; **Wake Up, I'm Fat!** by Camryn Manheim; **Got Issues Much?** edited by Randi Reisfeld and Marie Morreale.

 Morgenstern's witty one-liners reveal a compassionate look at girls and adolescence, like dating, getting along with people and accepting yourself. Uses quotes from famous women and photos from the 1950s and 1960s. Highly recommended for all adolescent girls.

Girls, it's a tough world out there.

Not to worry. You're ahead of the game when you follow this author's advice: "Your first boyfriend should be like the first pancake. Just a tester to see if the griddle is hot enough." Another piece of wisdom: "The football captains of today are the burger jockeys of tomorrow." Also, I'll bet you didn't know that everybody's family is as freaky as yours. This book is filled with all kinds of truths.

As TV's **Friends'** co-star Courteney Cox Arquette says, "Let's break the silence and tell **The Real Rules for Girls.**"

Morris, Gerald. *The Squire, His Knight, & His Lady.*

*Houghton Mifflin, 1999, 240pp. Part of a series; **The Squire's Tale** follows. Middle School & Up. YALSA Best Books for Young Adults; Children's Books of the Year selection.*

■ **ADVENTURE AND FOLKLORE.** *Great Britain (Wales); love; Middle Ages; supernatural; survival.*

■ **RELATED BOOKS: The Squire's Tale** by Gerald Morris; **Sir Gawain and the Green Knight** by Geoffrey Chaucer; **Gawain and Lady Green** by Anne Eliot Crompton; **World of King Arthur and His Court** by Kevin Crossley-Holland.

Readers do not need to read the first book to appreciate this traditional folktale from King Arthur. This story also includes the romantic subplot of King Arthur, Lancelot, and Queen Guinevere. Recommended for literature and social science classes, as well as readers interested in the Middle Ages, folklore, and adventure.

"I am the Knight of Green Chapel, and I know that your name is Sir Gawain. Here is my warning: After you behead me, in one year you will return to me for the answering blow!"

With that prophecy, the Green Knight bowed his head to take the blows from Sir Gawain's axe. The ladies at King Arthur's Court moaned and fainted as they witnessed bright red blood flowing from the Green Knight's severed head. Then astonishingly, the Green Knight's severed body picked up his bloody head and placed it back on his neck!

"Remember, Sir Gawain," said the Green Knight's severed head. "Next year your neck shall receive my blow. Your fate will not be a kind as mine."

Are you up for Sir Gawain's quest to find the Green Knight in **The Squire, His Knight, & His Lady**?

Mosier, Elizabeth. *My Life as a Girl.*

Random House, 1999, 192pp. High School & Up.

■ **ROMANCE.** *Love; sex and sexuality.*

■ **RELATED BOOKS: Summer Sisters** by Judy Blume; **The Wind Blows Backward** by Mary Downing Hahn; **Someone Like You** by Sarah Dessen; **How Far Would You Have Gotten If I Hadn't Called You Back** by Valerie Hobbs.

> *Note:* This introspective, witty, debut novel pivots around Jaime Cody's narration with the tantalizing good-girl-falls-for-bad-boy theme. Recommended for mature readers who love a fiery romance and strong characters.

"Oh no," I said, dropping my book. "It's Buddy."

From my college dormitory window, I spotted Buddy climbing out of his blood-colored Mustang. He was wild-haired and wide-eyed, looking as if he'd driven the 3,000 miles from Phoenix to my preppy college campus.

Elaine leaned over my shoulder, "Wow, he's hot. Who's Buddy?"

"It's Jaime's boyfriend," Amanda answered.

"He's not my boyfriend. He's not even supposed to know where I am."

"Should I call Campus Security?" asked Elaine.

"Oh, Elaine, don't overreact! He's not dangerous," I said, less certain now.

We watched Buddy walk slowly to the dormitory, begin knocking, then pounding, on the door. "Jaime!" Buddy bellowed. "Open up!"

I faced my colleagues, open-mouthed and disapproving. I realized, if I let Buddy in, that I would have to face my past—**My Life as a Girl**. Last summer's memories were hot and hazy, a wonderful blur. Summer was over. I thought. I had no time for romance. I thought.

Slowly and deliberately, I walked to the front door and unlatched the lock.

Most, Bernard. *Catbirds and Dogfish.*

Harcourt Brace, 1995, 30pp. Lower Elementary & Up.

■ **NONFICTION AND HUMOR.** *Animals (rare); nature; science (zoology).*

■ **RELATED BOOKS: Whatever Happened to Dinosaurs? And Zoodles** by Bernard Most; **Amazing Animals: The Fastest, Heaviest, Smallest, Largest, Fiercest, and Funniest** by Mario Gomboli; **Amazing Animals (Ranger Rick's Naturescope, Part 1, 2, 3)** by National Wildlife Federation and Sandra Stotsky.

> *Note:* The author's imaginative illustrations portray animals humorously, then factually. Scientific facts are included for older readers. Recommended for animal and science fans as well as readers who appreciate humor.

Can catbirds meow? (Yes, they can.) Can dogfish swim the dog paddle? (Absolutely not.) Can you ride a horsefly? (Are you nuts?)

Sometimes animals are named after other animals, because they remind us of other animals. For instance, a catbird has a song that sounds like "meow." A dogfish is a shark with a keen sense of smell like dogs. A mousebird is a bird from South Africa that climbs trees and eats berries like mice.

Read on to find out more about rabbitfish, elephant seals, pig frogs, and, of course, **Catbirds and Dogfish.** Happy hunting!

Murray, Bill, with George Peper. *Cinderella Story: My Life in Golf.*

Doubleday, 1999, 211pp. Middle School & Up.

■ **SPORTS AND HUMOR.** *Hobbies (golf); sports (golf).*

■ **RELATED BOOKS: I'm Not Really Here** and **Don't Stand Next to a Naked Man** by Tim Allen; **Pure Drivel** by Steve Martin; books by Dave Barry.

 This light-hearted book should appeal to a reluctant reader who enjoys golf.

I'm Bill X, also known as Bill Murray, comedian and actor. I'm a golf addict.

As a child, I became hooked when I caddied for 60 cents a half-hour. Once my brothers and I got busted for giving a blind golfer three hole-in-one trophies.

Later, as an adult, I starred in a movie about golf, *Caddyshack.* As the character Carl Spackler, I uttered the infamous lines, "Cinderella Story outta nowhere. Former greenskeeper and now about to become the Master's champion!"

Unfortunately, the real Bill Murray never became a Master's champion. I only became a friend to some golf champions, like Arnold Palmer and Jack Nicklaus. Knowing them only makes my golf addiction worse. But, boy, do I have some great stories.

Tee off with me in my **Cinderella Story: My Life in Golf.**

Myers, Walter Dean. *145th Street: Short Stories.*

Delacorte, 2000, 151pp. Middle School & Up. Boston Globe/Horn Book Award; Children's Books of the Year selection.

■ **SHORT STORIES.** *African Americans; aging; bullies; death; holidays (Christmas); sports (boxing, basketball); supernatural.*

■ **RELATED BOOKS: Monster** and **Darnell Rock Reporting** by Walter Dean Myers; **Jazmin's Notebook** by Nikki Grimes.

 Myers uses the backdrop of Harlem to tell 10 stories of laughter and tragedy, good and bad choices, and love and violence. Versatile vignettes stress the importance of a united community, especially to fight crime and gangs. The author switches viewpoints, from teen to adult, subtly presenting the contribution that all members make in a community. "A Christmas Story" might make a good read-aloud during the holidays. Recommended for all readers.

Come to the block party at 145th Street.

Meet Big Joe who gave himself a funeral before he died. Then there's Angela: she can forecast deaths through her dreams. Jamie isn't concerned about Angela's dreams; he's too worried about blowing last night's basketball game. Meanwhile, hoods are taking over the 'hood.

Good or bad, there's something for everyone on **145th Street.**

Namioka, Lensey. *Ties That Bind, Ties That Break: A Novel.*

Delacorte, 1999, 160pp. Middle School & Up. YASLA Top 10 Best Books for Young Adults; YALSA Best Books for Young Adults; Children's Books of the Year selection.

■ **HISTORICAL FICTION.** *Asia (China); China; rites of passage; women's issues.*

■ **RELATED BOOKS: Chinese Cinderella: The True Story of an Unwanted Daughter** by Adeline Yen Mah; **Bound Feet and Western Dress** by Pan-Meil Natasha Chang; **Women of the Silk** by Gail Tsukiyama; **Ribbons** by Laurence Yep.

> *Note:* *In lyrical, descriptive prose, Namioka compassionately tells of Ailin Tao's life in China in 1911, a time of transition from the old traditions. Ailin finally comes to America as a nanny. An author's note discusses the history of foot binding and other painful customs women have endured. Recommended for any multicultural project.*

I was five when Mother told Father that my feet were to be bound: "If Third Sister is to marry, she must be controlled and kept from running around, like a boy. Mrs. Liu might change her mind about her marriage."

That's when I first discovered that life is hard on women in China. We must marry whomever our parents select. We must obey all our parents' wishes, like binding our feet.

Then I saw Second Sister's bound feet. The sight made me sick. Her toes had been forced under the soles of her feet, like a piece of bread folded over. It must have been agony, lasting for years.

I vowed to myself: I'll never let them do this to me. Never, never, never!

I didn't know it then, but that decision changed my life forever.

Napoli, Donna Jo, and Richard Tchen. *Spinners.*

Dutton Children's Books, 1999, 197pp. High School & Up. Children's Books of the Year selection.

■ **FOLKLORE.** *Disability (physical); love; sex and sexuality.*

■ **RELATED BOOKS: The Prince of the Pond: Otherwise Known as De Fawg Pin; The Magic Circle** and **Zel** by Donna Jo Napoli; **Beauty** and **Rose Daughter** by Robin McKinley; **Ella Enchanted** by Gail Carson Levine.

> *Note:* *The text skillfully draws us into the plot before we readers recognize the original source in folklore. For another twist on the Rumpelstiltskin story, read Vivian Vande Velde's story, "Straw into Gold" found in* **Tales From the Brothers Grim and Sisters Weird.** *Warning: Contains some subtle sexual scenes, making this a book for a mature reader.*

In a time long ago, there lived two spinners, as different from each other as could be. One was a beautiful girl; the other, a lonely, deformed man. She was beautiful and pure; he was wrecked with bitterness.

One unfortunate day they were brought together when a greedy king demanded that the beauty spin straw into gold. The deformed man promised to secretly help her in exchange for her first child. To save her baby, the beautiful spinner must guess her unknown father's secret name.

Does this plot sound like some folk tale you've heard before? Remember *Rumpelstiltskin*? Find out the "true" story behind the two **Spinners.**

Napoli, Donna Jo, and S. November (editor). *Stones in Water.*

Dutton, 1997, 154pp. Middle School & Up. Sydney Taylor Jewish Award; ALA Notable Children's Book; YASLA Best Books for Young Adults; Children's Books of the Year selection.

■ **HISTORICAL FICTION.** *Europe (Italy and Germany); friendship; Holocaust; Jews; religion prejudice; secrets; survival; World War II.*

■ **RELATED BOOKS: Daniel's Story** and **Greater Than Angels** by Carol Matas; **Thanks to My Mother** by Schoschana Rabinovici; **Jacob's Rescue: A Holocaust Story** by Malka Drucker; **The Devil's Arithmetic** by Jane Yolen.

Note: *Based on a true story, Robert and Samuele are deported from Venice by Nazi soldiers to a Munich work camp; after Samuele's death, Roberto escapes the work camp, only to confront wild animals and a cold Russian winter. After surviving those harsh conditions, Roberto participates in the Partigiano, an underground group that works to hide endangered Jews. In realistic progression, Roberto changes from passive victim to hero. Recommended for all types of readers, especially those interested in the Holocaust. However, be aware that the horror of war is graphically presented.*

The nightmare began when Roberto accompanied his Jewish friend Samuele to the movies. Suddenly, Roberto heard angry shouts as German soldiers burst in the theater and rounded up all the boys. Deported to Germany by train, the bewildered boys watched their Venice homeland disappear as they began a new life in a work camp.

At first, Roberto didn't understand what was happening. Boys were shot while trying to escape. In the freezing climate, clothes and food were a luxury. Then Roberto felt overwhelmed and helpless.

However, Samuele never lost his survival skills. He quickly changed his name to Enzo to hide his Jewish heritage. Then he devised several plans of escape, no matter how outlandish they seemed. More important, he gave Roberto hope.

"You have to fight this," said Samuele. "Not with fists, but inside. Don't let them win over the inside of you. Remember who you are."

Roberto never forgot Samuele's words, even when he no longer had Samuele to guide him. Roberto devised a plan to escape the work camp. He vowed to make a path of **Stones in Water**, so he could escape to freedom.

Naylor, Phyllis Reynolds. *Jade Green: A Ghost Story.*

Atheneum, 2000, 168pp. Upper Elementary & Up.

■ **MYSTERIES/THRILLERS.** *Orphans; suicide; supernatural.*

■ **RELATED BOOKS: Under the Cat's Eye: A Tale of Morph and Mystery** by Gillian Rubinstein; **Down a Dark Hall** by Lois Duncan; **Wait Till Helen Comes** by Mary Downing Hahn; **Ghost of Fossil Glen** by Cynthia De Felice; **The Haunting of Hill House** by Shirley Jackson.

Note: *This Newbery award-winning author sets this ghost story in Charleston, South Carolina. Recently orphaned, the main character Judith discovers the ghost of Jade Green, a young teenager who recently committed suicide in the mansion. Good as a read-aloud because of cliff-hanging chapters. Also, recommended for fans of gothic tales with resourceful heroines.*

As I stepped from the carriage, the old Southern home seemed to be watching me. The curtains in the windows were half opened, looking like cat's eyes spying on an intruder.

I reassured myself: Be brave, Judith. Now that I've lost my family, I am lucky to have someone like Uncle Geoffrey. Yes, he's strange. So what? Maybe he has good reasons for forbidding anything green in his house. He doesn't need to know I brought my beloved mother's photograph enclosed in a green frame.

One day I may learn the secret behind the power of **Jade Green.** Until then, only the house knows its darkest secrets.

Naylor, Phyllis Reynolds. *Sang Spell.*

Atheneum, 1998, 192pp. Middle School & Up. Children's Books of the Year selection.

■ **FANTASY.** *Asian Americans; death; Hispanic Americans (Melungeons); interracial relations; Native Americans (Melungeons); runaways; supernatural; survival; work*

■ **RELATED BOOKS: *Daughter of the Legend*** by Jesse Stuart et al; ***The Melungeons*** by Bonnie Ball; ***Going Through the Gate*** by Janet Anderson; ***The Giver*** by Lois Lowry.

Note: Naylor researched the Melungeons in Virginia, finding them to be of mixed ethnicity. Various nature symbols give the story several subtexts about grief and survival. Recommended for reluctant readers looking for a supernatural read; also recommended as a read-aloud.

The way to Sang Hollow is not the same way out. No one gets in or leaves the same way. Sang Hollow's aura is misty gray, sealed forever in fog.

After a stranger robbed him and left him on a deserted road, Josh found himself in Sang Hollow. There he began digging along with the other Melungeons for the plant ginseng (called "sang") in the Appalachian area. If he wasn't thinking about escaping, he was thinking about his mother's sudden death.

Once Josh tried to escape, but the path led him back to Sang Hollow. His feet just seemed to return to the starting point. When he asked Mavis questions about Sang Hollow, she only talked in riddles. Maybe she, too, was a part of this witches' spell, this sang spell.

Would he ever be able to escape the **Sang Spell?**

Nixon, Joan Lowery. *The Other Side of Dark.*

Econo-Clad, 1986, 185pp. Middle School & Up. Edgar Allan Poe Award.

■ **MYSTERIES/THRILLERS.** *Crime; death; illness (coma); revenge.*

■ **RELATED BOOKS: *The Séance; The Stalker;*** and **Secret, Silent Screams:** all by Joan Lowery Nixon; **Stranger With My Face** by Lois Duncan; **Eva** by Peter Dickinson.

Note: The suspenseful plot contains Stacey's reoccurring memory flashes of the killer as she tries to adjust to her new life. Recommended for mystery fans and reluctant readers.

My eyelids were heavy. My body was not my own. I wanted to drift back to sleep, so I could make my memories disappear. The doctor wouldn't let me.

"Stacy, don't fall asleep again. Wake up and listen to me," he urged. "You must understand that you are coming out of a four-year coma. You were 13 when you came to this hospital, but now you are 17."

"You're lying!" I gasped. "When my mother comes, she'll tell you that you are wrong."

He spoke more gently. "Your mother is dead. She was shot. You were also shot, but you survived. You were lucky."

Lucky? I didn't feel lucky. No wonder I wanted to sleep for four years. I must have tried to block it all out. Nevertheless, I knew that time would bring back memories of the day of my mother's murder and of her killer. Once the killer knew I was awake, what would happen to me?

I would only be safe if I remained on **The Other Side of Dark.**

Nixon, Joan Lowery. *Who Are You?*

Delacorte, 1999, 192pp. Middle School & Up. YASLA Quick Picks for Reluctant Readers.

■ **MYSTERIES/THRILLERS.** *Crime; science.*

■ **RELATED BOOKS: A Candidate for Murder; The Haunting;** and **Whispers From the Dead;** all by Joan Lowery Nixon; **Down a Dark Hall** by Lois Duncan; **Close to a Killer** by Marsha Qualey.

> **Note:** Four-time Edgar winner (for Best Mystery of the Year) Nixon gives mystery lovers another suspenseful book, this time into the high-powered art gallery world. As for the secret file, Merson believed Kristi was his grand-daughter via in vitro fertilization. This topic is handled tastefully, so it can be recommended to all mystery lovers.

The doorbell rang and I got the shock of my life.

"I'm Sergeant Janice Nims, homicide detective. This is my partner Sergeant Jerry Balker. We're here to ask Kristi Evans if she knows Douglas Merson."

"I'm Kristi," I answered. "I don't know Douglas Merson."

"Unfortunately, he may know you. You see, he was shot twice, but it looks like he'll survive. We found a file that interested us. There are newspaper clippings of a birth announcement, school awards, an honorable mention in a citywide art show, and art awards in high school."

My parents and I took a look. To our horror, the file was labeled "Kristin Anne Evans." The skin of my back prickled. I had been targeted and didn't know it.

Sergeant Balker continued, "There's a possibility Kristi was being stalked."

Stalked? I'm so shocked I'm speechless. I never heard of this guy before, but he's obviously heard of me.

My first question to my stalker: **"Who Are You?"**

O'Dell, Scott. *Sarah Bishop.*

Houghton Mifflin, 1980, 184pp. Upper Elementary & Up. Winner of Hans Christian Anderson Award.

■ **HISTORICAL FICTION.** *American Revolutionary War; family; pioneer life; survival; war.*

■ **RELATED BOOKS: My Brother Sam Is Dead** by James Lincoln Collier and Christopher Collier; **The Fighting Ground** by Avi; **Witch of Blackbird Pond** by Elizabeth George Speare; **War Comes to Willy Freeman** by James Lincoln Collier and Christopher Collier; **Johnny Tremain** by Esther Forbes.

> **Note:** The plot describes Sarah Bishop's life after the deaths of her father and brother (who take opposite sides during the American Revolution). She escapes to the wilderness of Westchester County and lives in a cave. Because of Sarah's unusual behavior, some Quakers accuse her of being a witch. The fast-paced novel presents an accurate overview of colonial life and presents both sides of the American Revolution. Real-life historical figures such as Ben Franklin and Thomas Paine briefly appear. Recommended for all readers, especially reluctant readers who think they don't like historical fiction.

"Why are they shooting at us?" I asked my father.

"Sarah, 'tis only one person shooting at us, and that's Purdy," my father answered. "He's not really shooting at us. Just in our direction to remind us."

"Remind us? Of what?"

"That he is a Patriot for the revolution. That he knows we are for King George and against the revolution."

It isn't easy being a Tory in a New England town of patriots. Mr. Purdy's shooting is only the beginning of my family's hardships. My brother Chad has taken the patriot side too!

Regardless of misfortunes brought upon my family, I will survive or my name isn't **Sarah Bishop.**

O

O'Neill, Jennifer. *Surviving Myself.*

William Morrow, 1999, 238 pp. High School & Up

■ **BIOGRAPHY.** *Problem parents; self-identity; sexual abuse; show business; suicide.*

■ **RELATED BOOKS: *Me and My Shadows*** by Lorna Luft; ***Get Happy: The Life of Judy Garland*** by Gerald Clarke; ***Little Girl Lost*** by Drew Barrymore and Todd Gold.

 Note: O'Neill concludes by citing "Born Again" Christian philosophy, but until then she poignantly touches upon acquiring self-esteem and avoiding abusive relationships. Recommended for biography fans as well as readers from abusive situations.

I was similar to Dorothy from *The Wizard of Oz*. I'd been in black-and-white Kansas, then whisked away to the colorful land of Oz and found it wasn't what it was cracked up to be. After the film *Summer of '42*, my Oz was Hollywood and stardom. I was an accident waiting to happen.

On the way to Oz, I was chased by flying monkeys and wicked witches. At 14, I tried to commit suicide, I married at 17, and had a daughter at 19. I wanted to get through childhood as fast as possible, because it was so unpleasant. One trait I liked about myself is that I never gave up. This trait saved my life, because the hardest task I had was **Surviving Myself.**

P

Panzer, Nora (editor). *Celebrate America: In Poetry and Art.*

Hyperion, 1994, 96pp. For all libraries.

■ **POETRY.** *African Americans; American Revolutionary War; Civil War; Hispanic Americans; holidays (Martin Luther King Jr. Day); immigrants; interracial relations; pioneer life; politics.*

■ **RELATED BOOKS: Hand in Hand: An American History Through Poetry** by Lee Bennett Hopkins; **The Scrambled States of America** by Laurie Ketter; **I, Too, Sing America** by Catherine Clinton; **Ballad of the Civil War** by Mary Stolz.

Note: This thoughtfully conceived volume includes paintings, sculpture, drawings, and photographs from the National Museum of American Art at the Smithsonian. Panzer has divided the book into five sections: the country's landscape, its melting pot make-up, city and rural life, American history, and American pastimes. More than 100 poets celebrate multiculturalism, including Maya Angelou, Robert Frost, Winslow Homer, and Thomas Hart Benton. Recommended for purchase in all libraries, and as a group read or read-aloud.

"These United States are essentially the greatest poem," proclaimed poet Walt Whitman. "I hear America singing (with) the varied carols I hear."

Other poets such as Stephen Vincent Benet and Langston Hughes also shared Whitman's fascination with America. From the harshness of the Wild West to the love of baseball, they wrote about the grandeur and complexities of the United States.

Come join these poets on this tour from sea to shining sea. Come, **Celebrate America.**

Paterson, Katherine. *Marvin's Best Christmas Present Ever, Level 3, I Can Read Book.*

Illustrated by Jane Clark Brown. HarperCollins, 1997, 48pp. Lower Elementary & Up. Sequel to **The Smallest Cow in the World.** *ALA Children's Notable Book; American Booksellers Association Pick of the Lists; SLJ's Best Books.*

■ **REALISTIC FICTION.** *Animals (birds); family; holidays (Christmas).*

■ **RELATED BOOKS: The Smallest Cow in the World** by Katherine Paterson; **The Polar Express** by Chris Van Allsburg; **How the Grinch Stole Christmas** by Dr. Seuss.

 Note: *Marvin decides to make a wreath for his family's trailer. When the wreath is placed outside the trailer and taken down the next spring, a family of birds have nested, so the wreath remains. Brown's pencil illustrations match the story's charm. Recommended for beginning readers and as a read-aloud. Great selection for holiday collections.*

No matter how hard Marvin tried, he never seemed to pick the perfect Christmas gift for his Mom and Dad. Last year he gave his Mom a macaroni necklace that she never wore and gave his Dad an ashtray right before he quit smoking.

This year was different—his gift kept on giving all year long.

Help his parents unwrap their perfect gift: **Marvin's Best Christmas Present Ever.**

Paterson, Katherine. *Preacher's Boy.*

Clarion, 1999, 160pp. Upper Elementary & Up. Parents' Choice Gold Award; Cooperative Children's Book Center Choice; Children's Books of the Year selection; Booklist's Books for the Middle Readers.

■ **HISTORICAL FICTION.** *Family; homeless; mental illness; religion; men's issues; self-identity.*

■ **RELATED BOOKS: The Adventures of Tom Sawyer** and **The Adventures of Huckleberry Finn** by Mark Twain; **The Great Brain** series by John D. Fitzgerald; the **Soup and Me** series and **A Day No Pigs Would Die** by Robert Newton Peck.

 Note: *The Newbery award-winning author sets the story during late-1890s in Vermont and skillfully interweaves historical figures such as Charles Darwin. Ten-year-old Robbie decides to become an atheist to escape the label of "preacher's boy." Robbie identifies with Huckleberry Finn, so this novel could be read in conjunction with* **The Adventures of Huckleberry Finn** *and* **The Adventures of Tom Sawyer.** *Other issues portrayed are religion, self-identity, and masculinity. Recommended for reluctant readers who enjoy reading about mischievous boys and their adventures.*

Don't get me wrong. I wouldn't trade my Pa for anyone else's. But land o' Goshen, why do I have to be a preacher's son?

People expect too much of me because of my Pa. They think they can tell me how to behave. They expect me to be good and even worse, clean. (NOT just on Sundays!) That's asking a lot of a free spirit like me.

I said it once, and I'll say it again: Why, oh why, did I have to be born a **Preacher's Boy?**

Peck, Ira (editor). *Nellie Bly's Book: Around the World in 72 Days.*

Twenty-First Century Books, 1998, 127pp. For all libraries.

■ **BIOGRAPHY.** *Work; women's issues.*

■ **RELATED BOOKS: Around the World in 80 Days** by Jules Verne; **Gutsy Girls: Young Women Who Dare** by Tina Schwager and Michele Schuerger; **Cool Women** edited by Pam Nelson.

> *Note:* Show the book cover, which has a picture of Nellie modeling her outfit that took her around the world in 72 days. (Jules Verne's earlier fictional character, Phileas Fogg, accomplished it in 80 days; during the trip, Nellie would meet the admiring Verne.) Bly's journalistic account is intriguing, and rich with details, but it also reveals her ignorance about other cultures. Recommended for all types of readers, especially reluctant ones looking for an entertaining biography.

In 1889 she was the most famous young woman in the world. She had songs written about her. Clothes, games, and toys were named after her.

Who was she? Nellie Bly was her name. She was the first American female journalist. She became a legend by traveling around the world in 72 days. Of course, in those days there were no airplanes so Nellie traveled by train, boat, or carriage. No one, man or woman, had ever attempted it before.

In the late-1800s, it was unthinkable that a 25-year-old woman could travel around the world and do it alone. Nellie Bly proved that a woman could be adventurous and independent.

To top it off, Nellie Bly traveled with only one dress, a coat, and a small bag!

Read more about this admirable woman's travels in **Nellie Bly's Book: Around the World in 72 Days**.

Peck, Richard. *The Ghost Belonged to Me.*

*First published in 1975. Puffin, 1997, 192pp. Upper Elementary & Up. First of **Blossom Culp** series; **Ghosts I Have Been; The Dreadful Future of Blossom Culp;** and **Blossom Culp and the Sleep of Death** follow.*

■ **MYSTERIES/THRILLERS.** *Animals (dogs); friendship; love; supernatural.*

■ **RELATED BOOKS: Blossom Culp** series by Richard Peck; **Ghost of Fossil Cave** by Cynthia DeFelice; **Wait Till Helen Comes** by Mary Downing Hahn; **Stonewords** by Pam Conrad.

> *Note:* First published in 1975, the plot contains interesting social aspects of St. Louis, Missouri in the 1900s. Disney's film, **Child of Glass** is based on this story. Recommended for mystery lovers, particularly reluctant readers.

Many people don't take to the notion of ghosts in Missouri. But I'm a' telling you that I had a girl ghost hiding in our barn loft.

My friend, Blossom Culp, first told me all about ghosts 'cause her Mom sees the Unseen. Her Mom says I have the Gift to see the Unseen too. I wasn't right sure I wanted that kind of Gift, but there it is.

The first I time I saw the ghost, she cried out to me. "The dead and the dying! The dead are robbed and cannot forestall it!" Not a right pleasant message, I can tell you.

I don't blame you if you think I'm fibbin'. After all, as the ghost told me, a boy is hard to believe. Still, I'll always be proud that *The Ghost Belonged to Me*.

Pernoud, Regine, and Marie-Veronique Clin. *Joan of Arc: Her Story.*

*Originally published as **Jeanne d'Arc** in 1986. Translated and revised by Jeremy duQuesnay Adams. St. Martin's Press, 1998, 304pp. High School & Up.*

■ **BIOGRAPHY.** *France; religion; religious prejudice; war; women's issues.*

■ **RELATED BOOKS: Joan of Arc: In Her Own Words** compiled by Willard R. Trask; **Joan of Arc: By Herself and Her Witnesses** by Regine Pernoud; **Saint Joan** by George Bernard Shaw; for younger readers, **Joan of Arc** by Diane Stanley.

Note: This best-selling French edition, expertly translated by Jeremy duQuesnay Adams, clears away myths about Joan of Arc, but recommended this only to mature readers who enjoy long biographies. Try other versions for a briefer look at Joan of Arc; this booktalk can be used with other books about Joan of Arc, including Diane Stanley's award-winning **Joan of Arc.**

Joan of Arc took command of an army at age 17. Two years later, in 1431, she was burned alive at the stake. Later, she was recognized as a saint by the Catholic Church.

Who was the real Joan of Arc? Why would a French peasant girl don a man's armor and fight for the French throne? How was she captured? Why did Charles the VII, the French king who owed his crown to her, refuse to pay her ransom?

Luckily, because of the records of her infamous trial, we know more of her short life than we do of any other human being before her time (including Plato and Jesus).

Discover the truth. There is no one in history like **Joan of Arc**. This is her story.

Peske, Nancy, and Beverly West. *Cinematherapy: Girl's Guide to Movies for Every Mood.*

Dell, 1999, 243pp. High school & Up.

■ **NONFICTION.** *Abuse; love; movie novels; rites of passages; sex and sexuality; show business; women's issues.*

■ **RELATED BOOKS: A Woman's View** and **Silent Stars** by Jeanine Basinger; **Flesh and Fantasy** by Penny Stallings.

Note: Films are categorized according to cathartic pleasures, with added quotes and cartoon drawings. Film buffs as well as reluctant female readers should enjoy this visually attractive book. *Warning:* Some quotes include "bitch" in the text.

Having a bad hair day? Cheer yourself up by watching some films with women who have hair blues and still end up catching the leading man.

Maybe you're stuck in a dysfunctional romance. Tune in to some really sick film romances so you can recognize the signs of a nowhere romance.

Got the Mommie Dearest blues? Check out Movie Monster Moms in a couple flicks, and your Mom might look better to you. (Sometimes it helps to remind yourself that other people have it worse.)

Movies are more than entertainment—sometimes they are self-medication. That's why this book is entitled **Cinematherapy: Girl's Guide to Movies for Every Mood**.

Pilkey, Dav. *The Adventures of Captain Underpants: An Epic Novel.*

*Scholastic, 1997, 128pp. Lower & Upper Elementary. First book of the **Captain Underwear** series, which includes **Captain Underpants &
The Attack of the Talking Toilets; Captain Underpants & the Invasion of the Incredibly Naughty Cafeteria Ladies From
Outer Space; Captain Underpants and the Perilous Plot of Professor Poopypants.***

■ **HUMOR AND SCIENCE FICTION.** *Magic; school; time travel.*

■ **RELATED BOOKS: Captain Underpants** series by Dav Pilkey; **The Man in the Ceiling** by Jules Feiffer; **The Cut-Ups** by
James Marshall; **The Brain and Me** series by John D. Fitzgerald.

Note: *Author introduces George Beard and Harold Hutchins, two fourth-grade pranksters, who are nabbed by Mr. Krupp, the principal, whom they hypnotize into believing he is Captain Underpants. Pilkey admits that the main characters' pranks are based on his own adventures. The author's drawings and comic book layout will appeal to beginning reluctant readers. Also recommended, if you dare, as a read-aloud.*	Look in the sky! It's a plane! It's an egg-salad sandwich! No, it's Captain Underpants! He is a mighty super-hero who fights for truth, justice, and all that is preshrunk and cottony. There is nothing too big for Captain Underpants! In just one day, he smashes robots, outsmarts evil Dr. Diaper, and destroys the Laser-Matic 2000! Don't miss **Captain Underpants** and his exciting adventures. Warning: Some materials may be offensive to people who don't wear underwear!

Pinkney, Andrea Davis. *Duke Ellington: The Piano Prince and His Orchestra.*

*Illustrated by J. Brian Pinkney. Disney, 1998, 32pp. Lower Elementary & Up. Caldecott Honor Book; Coretta Scott King Honor Book; ALA
Children's Notable Book; Children's Books of the Year selection; Booklist Editors' Choice; SLJ's Best Books.*

■ **BIOGRAPHY.** *African Americans; music.*

■ **RELATED BOOKS: I See the Rhythm** by Toyomi Igus; **Snowflake Bentley** by Jacqueline Briggs Martin; **Beethoven Lives
Upstairs** by Barbara Nicol.

Pinkney's jive writing style complements her husband's illustrations, which visually present Ellington's music as colors of a paint box. Recommended for music and art fans as well as those looking for an inspiring biography about an African-American legend.

Believe it, man. Duke Ellington could jive those pearlies like nobody else. He could write songs that were as smooth as a 'do sleeked with pomade and as jumpy as a kite tail in the wind.

Dig this. Duke didn't want to take piano lessons when he was a kid because he wanted to hang out with the other cats playing baseball. He got tired of making "umpty-dum" sounds on the keys with the same old songs, so he invented his own kind of jive.

By the end of his life, he had written more than 1,000 songs from hot-buttered bop to sweet orchestral suites. No wonder everyone called him the King of the Keys.

Plath, Sylvia. *The Bell Jar.*

First published in 1963. Harper Perennial Library, 2000, 264pp. High School & Up.

■ **CLASSICS AND REALISTIC FICTION.** *Mental illness; peer pressure; self-identity; suicide; women's issues.*

■ **RELATED BOOKS: The Journals of Sylvia Plath** by Sylvia Plath et al; **Girl, Interrupted** by Susanna Kaysen; **I Never Promised You a Rose Garden** by Joanne Greenberg (Hannah Green); **One Flew Over the Cuckoo's Nest** by Ken Kesey.

Note: *This fictional account narrated by the character Esther is based on Plath's 1953 experiences as a college student with her suicide attempts, institutionalization in a mental hospital, and experiences with shock therapy. It was so autobiographical that she elected to publish it in 1963 in London under a pen name. A month after the book's publication, she committed suicide. She was then married to poet Ted Hughes. This sad, honest, and perfectly written classic is recommended for older students.*

I feel like the eye of a tornado: very still and empty, slowly moving along in the surrounding hullabaloo. Like a tornado's center, I look at other people in critical situations. Even if the events surprise me or make me sick, I never react. I just pretend things are normal.

I can even look at my own critical situations with a tornado's eye. When I'm in a scalding hot tub, I can dissolve all my problems in one swoosh. All of them. That lying lover Buddy, that two-faced Doreen, all of them. I feel pure again.

It's quite amazing to me that I lived most of my life in the rarified atmosphere of a Bell Jar, stewing in my own sour air. How am I any different from the other gossiping bridge-playing college students? Those girls, too, sat under a bell jar of a sort. At least, unlike them, I can recognize my own **Bell Jar.**

Poitier, Sidney. *The Measure of a Man: A Spiritual Autobiography.*

Harper San Francisco, 2000, 255pp. Middle School & Up.

■ **BIOGRAPHY.** *African Americans; Caribbean and Latin America (Cat Island); ethics; immigrants (Caribbean); movies; racism; religion; responsibility; show business.*

■ **RELATED BOOKS: My Life** by Sidney Poitier; **Soul Stories** by Gary Zukav; **Walden** by Henry David Thoreau; **Chicken Soup for the Teenage Soul** edited by Jack Canfield.

Note: *Poitier's words are conversationally self-critical as he discusses values such as integrity, commitment, faith, forgiveness, and simplicity. Highly recommended for all types of readers and should be owned in all high school libraries.* **Warning:** *Some profanity.*

I was born on Cat Island, a small island in the Caribbean. Somehow, through luck, determination, and a strong sense of self, I became a movie star. I even won an Academy Award, being the first African American to win as best actor. However, as I grow older, my years in Hollywood interested me far less than my years on Cat Island.

On Cat Island I was stimulated, but I wasn't bombarded. There was no electricity, no automobiles, and no books. Only my strong, disciplined family guided me, and their words and actions still speak to me today.

I never saw a mirror until I was 10 so I had no idea how I looked. Consequently, I had no idea that my dark skin would cast me in an inferior position. As I entered the modern world, I would leave behind the nurturing of my family, but I would take their protection with me. My self worth would be my cloak and I would try to wear it with dignity.

Still, I always question the mysteries of life. Why are we here? Is my life a random toss of the dice or is it my destiny? I have no wish to play the pontificating fool, pretending I know the answers to life's questions. This is an exploration of how well I've done at measuring up to the values I've learned.

Join me, Sidney Poitier, on my journey, **The Measure of a Man.**

Porter, Connie. *Imani All Mine.*

Houghton Mifflin, 1999, 224pp. High School & Up. YASLA Top 10 Best Books for Young Adults; YASLA Best Books for Young Adults.

■ **REALISTIC FICTION.** *African Americans; death; interracial relations; pregnancy; sex and sexuality; sexual abuse.*

■ **RELATED BOOKS: The Amazing "True" Story of a Teenage Single Mom** by Katherine Arnoldi; **The Hip Mama Survival Guide** by Ariel Gore; **Annie's Baby: The Diary of Anonymous, a Pregnant Teenager** by Beatrice Sparks; **Speak** by Laurie Halse Anderson.

 *Porter wrote the **Addy** books in the **American Girls** series. In this novel, 15-year-old Tasha tells her story in a matter-of-fact voice, using street lingo. Eventually, she reveals she is a rape victim. Tasha's struggle to be a good mother to Imani, in spite of her mother and society's disapproval, is heroic. The ending is a shocker. Because of the profanity and subject content, recommend this unforgettable book to mature readers.*

Mama say I'm grown now. She say Imani all mine. I like not having to share my baby with no one.

Imani so little she be crying when I be getting up to go to school. I be 15, so I be in high school. I don't be mad at Imani when she cry. I look in her face and see me. I be smiling.

Now I got Peanut too. Imani let Peanut hold her, and he say, maybe people think this my baby.

I told him they'd be thinking wrong because **Imani All Mine.**

Powell, Randy. *Tribute to Another Dead Rock Star.*

Farrar, Straus, & Giroux, 1999, 215pp. Middle School & Up. YALSA Best Books for Young Adults; Children's Books of the Year selection.

■ **REALISTIC FICTION.** *Death; disability (mental retardation); music; show business; stepparents.*

■ **RELATED BOOKS: Turn It Up!** by Todd Strasser; **Chartbreak** by Gillian Cross; **Don't Blame the Music** by Caroline B. Cooney.

 *Grady Grennan narrates the story of his mom, Debbie Grennan, a fictional rock star. Grady's mildly retarded half-brother, Louie, is being raised by a "born again" Christian family. Grady gradually accepts his dysfunctional family history, the death of his mother, and his stepmother. Highly recommended as a quick read for all sorts of readers—cynics, liberals, slackers, and rock star lovers. **Warning:** Some profanity.*

My mom was a rock star. She recorded five CDs in five years, each better than the last. Mom was 36 when, at the height of her career, she died.

Mom's death from a drug overdose really messed up my life. I'm now staying with my half-brother's family. Louie is cool, but my stepmom is the Wicked Witch of the East. But it's my real Mom I blame. She threw her life away, like it was something on the bargain rack.

Still, she was my mother and we had some good times. I did love her. I still do.

Mom, this is for you. Here's my **Tribute to Another Dead Rock Star.**

Pressler, Mirjam. *Halinka.*

Translated from German by Elizabeth D. Crawford. Henry Holt, 1998, 192pp. High School & Up. National Council for Social Studies Notable Book; Children's Books of the Year selection.

■ **HISTORICAL FICTION.** *Abuse; Europe (Germany); Jews; homosexuality; orphans; problem parents; racism; secrets; self-identity.*

■ **RELATED BOOKS: I Was a Teenage Fairy** by Francesca Lia Block; **Caucasia** by Danzy Senna; **The Broken Bridge** by Philip Pullman; **From the Notebooks of Melanin Sun** by Jacqueline Woodson.

Note: *Set in 1952, fictional character Halinka, 12, shares a dormitory room with six girls in Germany. The first-person account discusses racist bullies, her obsession with food, and her mother's abuse. Pressler was a recipient of the German Literature Prize in 1994.* **Warning:** *For mature readers; contains a sexual scene between lesbians.*

I live by a set of rules. First, I don't smile at anyone I've never seen smile. After all, I don't want to force myself on anyone. Ever. That protects me from getting hurt.

Another rule: Don't dream of palaces, or you may lose your place in the hut. That means that if I am daydreaming about my future, I might lose focus on preventing my next disaster.

Most important, I don't let my feelings show or say what I really think. That way I can be sure that my words won't be used against me. I never underestimate people, especially myself.

Of course, these are hard rules to follow, but it's the only way to remain safe. I answer only when someone calls my name: **Halinka.**

Prince, Maggie. *The House of Hound Hill.*

Houghton Mifflin, 1998, 256pp. Middle School & Up.

■ **HISTORICAL FICTION AND MYSTERIES/THRILLERS.** *Class conflicts; Great Britain; Middle Ages; illness; supernatural; time travel.*

■ **RELATED BOOKS: King of Shadows** by Susan Cooper; **Switching Well** by Penni Griffin; **The Ruby and the Smoke** by Philip Pullman; **The Shakespeare Stealer** by Gary Blackwood; **In a Dark Wood** by Michael Cadnum.

Note: *The Black Plague of London killed one-fourth of the city's population. In the author's notes, Prince provides informative details about everyday life during 17th-century England. Recommended for horror fans and readers looking for a spunky heroine.* **Warning:** *Not for the faint-hearted. Descriptions of disease-carrying rats and effects of the Plague are horrifyingly vivid.*

Mad Emily of Hound Hill.

Maybe that will be my next name. How else can I explain my crazy hallucinations?

My family just moved to London. Our house appeared to be haunted, with its crooked stairs and the mysterious man looking for his cat at midnight. The house's forbidden past seemed embedded in its very stone, enclosed within the misty air.

Suddenly, I was transported into 17th-century London. I was helplessly trapped during the bubonic plague, engulfed in its foul stench. On the cobblestone streets, bloody infected rats lay dying.

Have I now become infected with a disease more than four centuries old? Am I now trapped in time and space? Am I doomed never to leave **The House on Hound Hill?**

P

Propp, Vera W. *When the Soldiers Were Gone.*

Putnam, 1999, 112pp. Upper Elementary & Up. Booklist Books for the Middle Readers; Children's Books of the Year selection.

■ **HISTORICAL FICTION.** *Adoption; bullies; Europe (Holland); Holocaust; Jews; moving; religion prejudice; school; World War II.*

■ **RELATED BOOKS: Hide and Seek** by Ida Vos; **Daniel's Story** by Carol Matas; **Devil's Arithmetic** by Jane Yolen; **How I Saved Hanukkah** by Amy Koss; **Letters From Rifka** by Karen Hesse.

> **Note:** An immigrant from Germany, Propp includes the factual story in the afterword. Narrated through a young child's eyes and based on a true story, this novel is a good introduction to the Holocaust. Eight-year-old Benjamin learns he must leave the loving foster family that hid him for three years during World War II and return to his Jewish family. Recommended by acclaimed author Jim Trelease, especially for historical fiction fans.

"Come in, Henk, and meet your parents," said Papa.

Henk was confused. His parents? What did Papa mean? Weren't he and Mama his family? Who were these pale-looking people?

"It's okay, Benjamin," said the pale man. "When you meet your brother and go to school, you'll feel better."

His brother? He had no brother. There must be a mistake. His name was Henk, not Benjamin. Furthermore, although he was eight, he had never been to school. Papa never told him why. Papa only told him to hide when the bad soldiers came to their house.

Yesterday Uncle Jan said the war was over and the Allied troops were in Holland. Papa said Henk didn't need to hide from the soldiers anymore.

Now, everything has changed. Henk must leave his family, change his name to Benjamin, and live with people who said they were his parents. Why? Why were things different **When the Soldiers Were Gone?**

Q

Qualey, Marsha. *Close to a Killer.*

Delacorte, 1999, 224pp. Middle School & Up. YASLA Best Books for Young Adults; YASLA Quick Picks for Reluctant Readers; Children's Books of the Year selection.

■ **MYSTERIES/THRILLERS.** *Crime; death.*

■ **RELATED BOOKS: Thin Ice** by Marsha Qualey; **The Killer's Cousin** by Nancy Werlin; **For Mike** by Shelley Sykes; books by Mary Higgins Clark.

> **Note:** This riveting mystery with an original plot offers strong characters and lots of suspense. Recommended for all mystery lovers.

"So, Barrie, how are the Killers?"

Oh no, not again. People always want to know about the Killers. My mother owns a beauty shop, Killer's Cut. All the beauticians, including my mother, had committed murder. All had served jail time and were now rehabilitated. The Killers were the talk of the town—so was the recent murder of Paul Worthington. I knew him too. I got five dollars every week for delivering a message to Cindy, another Killer beautician.

Then another murder happened. I know Mrs. Liston was a lousy tipper, but come on! I'm worried. Am I **Close to a Killer?**

Rabinovici, Schoschana. *Thanks to My Mother.*

Translated by James Skofield. Dial, 1998, 256pp. High School & Up. ALA Batchelder Award; ALA Children's Notable Book; Children's Books of the Year selection; National Council for Social Studies Notable Book.

■ **BIOGRAPHY.** *Diaries; death; Europe (Lithuania); hobbies (writing); Holocaust; Jews; poetry; racism; religion prejudice; single parents; World War II; survival; war.*

■ **RELATED BOOKS: The Diary of a Young Girl** by Anne Frank; **Letters From Rifka** by Karen Hesse; **No Pretty Pictures** by Anita Lobel; **The Seamstress** by Sara Tuvel Bernstein.

 Note: *The author's account of the 1941 German invasion of Lithuania was published in 1994 and is required reading in some German classrooms. The text also includes poems and personal photographs by Rabinovici. The translation includes footnotes to explain Jewish terms and historical events. Recommended for history buffs as well as readers interested in Jewish history or the Holocaust. **Warning:** Very grim with vivid details of concentration camp conditions.*

"Zyd! Zyd!"

My mother and I could hear them crying "Jews! Jews!" on the streets as they pulled two men into the police truck. We both remained hidden because we feared the *chappers,* or catchers, who were Lithuanian students who volunteered to capture Jews for the Nazi Party. Before the war, my town had 60,000 Jews. A year later, in 1942, thanks to the *chappers*, there were only 1,800 Jews. More than 50,000 Jews had disappeared!

One day the *chappers* came for us. They banged loudly on our door, crying, "Zyd! Zyd!" That was the day my family was sent to the ghetto with the other Polish Jews.

Before we were separated, my grandfather said, "Who among us can say how we will die or what we must endure?" How right he was.

I was one of the lucky ones. I survived, **Thanks to My Mother.**

Ray, Mary Lyn. *Basket Moon.*

Illustrated by Barbara Cooney. Little, Brown, and Co., 1999, 32pp. Lower Elementary & Up. Publishers Weekly's Best Books; Children's Books of the Year selection.

■ **HISTORICAL FICTION.** *Class conflict; family; nature; rites of passage; self-identity; work.*

■ **RELATED BOOKS: Shaker Boy** by Mary Lyn Ray, illustrated by Jeanette Winter; **When I Was Young in the Mountains** by Cynthia Rylant; **Miss Rumphius** by Barbara Cooney.

 Note: *Ray's poetic coming-of-age story is beautifully complemented by Caldecott award-winner Barbara Cooney's oil pastels depicting seasonal changes. Children will understand the boy's longing to join Pa, his pride in his father's work, and his hurt when they are ridiculed. The author includes an afterword describing the history of basket-weaving in the Hudson Valley during the 19th century. Recommended as a read-aloud, and for historical fiction fans and nature lovers.*

I couldn't wait to grow up so I could join Pa when he went down the mountain to sell our baskets. He went when the moon was almost full; we called it Basket Moon. As I waited, I helped weave some baskets and listened to the snow fall on our lonesome mountain. If I listened carefully, I could even hear the trees talk.

Finally the day came when I was nine, and Pa said I could go with him. I don't know what to think about the people in Hudson Valley. Although I didn't know what it meant, I didn't like being called a "bushwhacker." The men's laughter about Pa and me seemed to circle like crows around my head. Caw. Caw. Caw.

I wanted to go back home, where the trees bent as the wind watches—back to the land of **Basket Moon.**

Regan, Dian Curtis. *Monsters in the Attic.*

Illustrated by Laura Cornell. Henry Holt, 1995, 178pp. Upper Elementary & Up. Part of the **Monster of the Month Club Quartet** *series that include* **Monster of the Month Club; Monsters in Cyberspace;** *and* **Monsters & My One True Love.**

■ **FANTASY AND HUMOR.** *Animals (cats); hobbies (collecting dolls); love; school; single parents; supernatural.*

■ **RELATED BOOKS:** The **Monster** series by Dian Curtis Regan; **Diary of a Monster's Son** by Ellen Conford; **Ma and Pa Dracula** by Ann M. Martin; **Vampire in the Bathtub** by Brenda Seabrooke.

 Note: *The title suggests that this is a "scary" book, but the content actually covers many adolescent issues. Thirteen-year-old Rilla Harmony Earth is given a gift membership in Monster of the Month club and the collectible dolls come to life in her attic bedroom. Rilla's imaginary world is obviously tonic for her loneliness, and her dream world diminishes when she finds a boyfriend. Issues like New Age medicine and Rillas's search for her father are skillfully interwoven into the plot. Herbal remedies for common ailments are included. Recommended for readers who enjoy mixing humorous fantasy with realism.*

There is a monster mermaid in Rilla's bathtub. A "mer-monster," if you will. It was one of those monsters that Rilla received from the Monster of the Month Club. People may have thought they were only stuffed toys, but Rilla knew better.

Legends warn that cozy collectibles like the mer-monster become real monsters when heavenly stars line up in angled shapes like lightening. Look it up. It's all right there in the Funky Facts About Stars.

Unfortunately, monsters are allergic to adults—particularly mothers. That's just why Rilla is hiding her **Monsters in the Attic.** Wouldn't you?

Reisfeld, Randi, and Marie Morreale. *Got Issues Much? Celebrities Share Their Traumas and Triumphs.*

Scholastic, 1999, 227pp. Middle School & Up. Quick Picks for Reluctant Young Adult Readers.

■ **NONFICTION.** *Abuse; African Americans; disability (dyslexia); eating disorders (anorexia, obesity); ethics; friendship; homosexuality; music; self-identity; show business.*

■ **RELATED BOOKS: Girl Gets Real: A Teenager's Guide to Life** by Danielle Fishel and Monica Rizzo; **The Real Rules for Girls** by Mindy Morgenstern; **Beyond Beauty** edited by Jane Pratt; **Wake Up! I'm Fat!** by Camryn Manheim.

 Note: *The authors do an excellent job of helping teens realize that everyone has serious problems, even their favorite celebrities. Recommended for all types of readers, as well as for guidance counselors.*

Issues. Nobody likes 'em. Everybody's got 'em—even celebrities. Celebrities have issues about weight, broken hearts, self-esteem, and, well, *stuff.*

For example, Leonardo DiCaprio was such a loser in high school that he was called "Leonardo Retardo." Kate Winslet's nickname was "Blubber." Jim Carrey's father lost his job and his family was homeless. James Van Der Beek of Dawson's Creek is dyslexic. Sean "Puffy" Combs lost his best friend in a shoot out. Drew Barrymore? She's been there, done that—again and again.

Got Issues Much? Well, duh. Who doesn't? Hear it from the people who have it all—including issues.

Rinaldi, Ann. *The Coffin Quilt: The Feud Between the Hatfields and the McCoys.*

Harcourt Brace, 1999, 160pp. Middle School & Up.

■ **HISTORICAL FICTION.** *Ethics; family; revenge; rivalry; love; secrets.*

■ **RELATED BOOKS: Soldier's Heart** by Gary Paulsen; **Cast Two Shadows: The American Revolution in the South** by Ann Rinaldi; **Across Five Aprils** by Irene Hunt; **Romeo and Juliet** by William Shakespeare.

> *Note:* *Rinaldi closely follows the real events of the Hatfield-McCoy feud that occurred during 1889 in West Virginia-Kentucky community. In the author's note she writes that "the Civil War conditioned men who fought in it to kill and to hate,"—a profound statement about the after-effects of war. Recommended especially for romance lovers who think they don't like historical fiction.*

Today they hanged Elliot Mounts.

He was just a half-wit and dirt poor, but he didn't deserve to die. A'fore the hangin', the sheriff asked Elliot Mounts if he had any last words.

"I never kilt her," he said.

Sick and disgusted, I turned away. The McCoys were all over the place, making sure the hanging went on as scheduled. Folks said the Hatfields might come any minute to stop the hanging. I wish they had.

I'm Fanny McCoy. This here hanging was the result of my sister, Roseanna McCoy running off with Johnse Hatfield. For years there's been bad blood 'tween the Hatfields and the McCoys. But when hearing of this romance, some folks got in a hanging mood.

I reckon I'm supposed to take up sides with my kinfolk, the McCoys. Not likely. There's too much dying around these parts. Maybe writing this down will help. I call my scribbles: **The Coffin Quilt: The Feud Between the Hatfields and the McCoys.**

Roberts, Monty. *Shy Boy: The Horse That Came in From the Wild.*

Photographs by Christopher Dydyk. HarperCollins, 1999, 241pp. Middle School & Up.

■ **NONFICTION AND BIOGRAPHY.** *Animals (horses); ethics.*

■ **RELATED BOOKS: The Man Who Listens to Horses** by Monty Roberts; **The Horse Whisperer** by Nicholas Evans; **Horse Sense and the Human Heart** by Adele Von Rust McCormick; **Wild Horses I Have Known** by Hope Ryden.

> *Note:* *Roberts is the prototype for the horse trainer in Nicholas Evans' movie **The Horse Whisperer,** although he disclaims the film's portrayal of his training techniques. A PBS documentary was also produced about Shy Boy. The appendix includes Web sites on horses. Recommended for all animal lovers.*

Do you want to know my philosophy? We should make the world better for horses—all horses, even the ones without names and who run free. We don't have as many wild horses as we used to have. Long ago we had millions of horses that roamed the North American Plains. Now we have only 30,000 horses.

Shy Boy was such a horse, a wild mustang that I had my eye on for 45 years. I knew we would be friends one day. How did I know? You see, I used patience to create a trust between a horse and me. I also used *Equus,* a language that any horse understands. Eventually, after 45 patient years, Shy Boy did indeed become my friend.

Maybe he will become your friend, too.

Rocklin, Joanne. *Strudel Stories.*

Delacorte, 1997, 131pp. Upper Elementary & Up. ALA Children's Notable Book; SLJ's Best Books; Children's Books of the Year selection.

■ **SHORT STORIES.** *Death; Jews; immigrants (Russia); Russia; sports (baseball).*

■ **RELATED BOOKS: Dreams in the Golden Country** by Kathryn Lasky; **Journey to America** and **Silver Days** by Sonia Levitin; **The All-of-a-Kind Family** by Sydney Taylor.

> *Note:* The short stories follow a Jewish family through seven generations and more than 100 years as they brave war and immigration. The book includes a family tree, strudel recipe, and eloquent author's note. This is an excellent choice for oral history, intergenerational projects, and immigration units.

I couldn't believe my eyes. Standing at the kitchen counter and stirring something in a bowl was Grandpa Willy's ghost!

"Peel those apples for me," Jessica said.

"Oh, it's you," I said, sitting down. "From the back, in that baseball cap and green apron, I thought . . ."

"You thought I was Grandpa, right?"

"Don't be a dork," I said. "Grandpa's dead." Then I began to cry. Finally.

"Hey, don't cry. I'm making Grandpa's strudel. That means I have to tell all the stories he used to tell. I'll start with the one about the boy who danced with ghosts and then tell the one about the apple that turned to gold."

"Don't forget the one about the greatest baseball moment ever," I sniffed, still blinking back my tears.

"I won't," Jessica promised.

That day I was sure I could hear and feel Grandpa Willy, as Jessica told all the **Strudel Stories.**

Rostkowski, Margaret I. *After the Dancing Days.*

HarperTrophy, 1986, 217pp. Middle School & Up. IRA Children's Book Award.

■ **HISTORICAL FICTION.** *Disability (burns, blindness, amputations); Europe (France); France; friendship; World War I.*

■ **RELATED BOOKS: Phoenix Rising** by Karen Hesse; **Heroes: A Novel** by Robert Cormier; **The Eternal Spring of Mr. Ito** by Sheila Garrigue; **Soldier's Heart** by Gary Paulsen.

> *Note:* This book deservedly is still in print, due to readers' recommendations. Annie, 13, begins a forbidden friendship with a badly disfigured soldier in the aftermath of World War I. Eventually her mother accepts the horrors that war brings. The novel could work well in an integrated study of literature and history of the time period, but don't just limit it to that. Recommend this book often to all types of readers.

"Mother, yesterday at the train station, those men . . ."

"What about those men, Annie?"

"That man on the stretcher with his face gone. Will he and the others be all right?"

"Of course they'll be all right. The war is over. Now, don't think about them any more."

I continued to think about those soldiers. That's why I joined Father at St. John's hospital. That's where I met Andrew, the man who had no lips. At first I was horrified at his appearance, but eventually we became friends.

Andrew told me everything about himself: how he was gassed in France, how his father refused to see him and his disfigurement, why he hated winning the Purple Heart. He even tried to find out what happened to my Uncle Paul who was also killed in France.

This time I don't care what my mother says. Andrew needs me. He reminds me of the Irish folk song: "Where are your legs that used to run/When first you went to carry a gun? I fear your dancing days are done."

I want to help Andrew face his new life *After the Dancing Days.*

100   Keep Talking that Book! Booktalks to Promote Reading, Grades 2-12, Volume III

Rylant, Cynthia. *Henry and Mudge: The First Book.*

Illustrated by Sucie Stevenson. Bradbury, 1987. Lower Elementary & Up. First of **Henry and Mudge** *series; 17 books follow.*

- ■ **REALISTIC FICTION.** *Animals (dogs); responsibility.*
- ■ **RELATED BOOKS:** Books by Cynthia Rylant: **Henry and Mudge in Puddle Trouble; Henry and Mudge in the Green Time; Henry and Mudge Under the Yellow Moon.**

Note: *This is the first book in the acclaimed, humorous, easy-to-read series featuring Henry and his lovable 180-pound dog, Mudge. Recommended for beginning readers, especially for dog lovers.*

My name is Henry. I wanted a dog. Not just any dog. I didn't want a short dog or a curly one. I definitely didn't want one with pointed ears.

Then I found Mudge. He was perfect. He didn't have pointed ears, and he definitely wasn't short. He weighed 180 pounds and stood three feet tall.

Now I am not alone anymore. We're a team: **Henry and Mudge.**

Rylant, Cynthia. *Poppleton and Friends.*

Illustrated by Mark Teague. Econo-Clad Books, 1999, 48pp. Lower Elementary & Up. Second book in the **Poppleton** *series;* **Poppleton** *precedes. Other series titles are* **Poppleton Everyday; Poppleton Forever; Poppleton in Spring; Poppleton in Fall;** *and* **Poppleton Through and Through.**

- ■ **FANTASY AND HUMOR.** *Animals; friendship.*
- ■ **RELATED BOOKS: Poppleton** series by Cynthia Rylant; **George and Martha** series by James Marshall; **Frog and Toad** series by Arnold Lobel.

Note: *This book contains three stories about friendship between Poppleton, a pig; Hudson, a mouse; and Cherry Sue, a llama. Excellent for beginning readers, and as a read-aloud. Recommended to animal lovers and fans of humorous fantasy.*

Poppleton the Pig wanted to live until he was 100. One day he heard a man on TV say that eating grapefruit leads to a longer life. Even though Poppleton hated grapefruit, he decided to give it a try. Everyday he ate grapefruit even though it turned his face green and his lips inside-out.

"Why would anyone want to live to be 100 years old with no lips?" asked his friend, Hudson the Mouse.

"Besides," added Uncle Bill the Mouse, "I'm 100 years old and never touched a grapefruit. The secret to living a longer life is having a lot of friends."

"Thank Goodness," said Poppleton. "I can get my lips back."

St. George, Judith. *Sacagawea.*

With maps and bibliography. Philomel Books, 1997, 128pp. Upper Elementary & Up.

■ **BIOGRAPHY AND ADVENTURE.** *Abuse; interracial relations; Native Americans; pioneer life; racism; women's issues.*

■ **RELATED BOOKS: Girl of the Shining Mountains: Sacagawea's Story** by Connie Roop and Peter Geiger Roop; **Streams to the River, River to the Sea** by Scott O' Dell; **Double Life of Pocahontas** by Jean Fritz; **Girls Who Rocked the World: Heroines From Sacagawea to Sheryl Swoopes** by Amelie Welden.

Note: St. George recreates Sacagawea's 5,000 mile trip with Lewis and Clark from the Missouri River and Rocky Mountains to the Pacific Ocean. The story is based on the author's extensive research and personal reenacted journey. Maps and an extensive bibliography are included. Because Sacagawea has more memorials dedicated to her than any other American woman does, her life could be included during Women's History Month. Also recommended for historical fiction readers looking for a resourceful heroine and for adventure fans.

My name is Sacagawea, which means Bird Woman. I don't feel anything like a bird. I'm 16 years old, pregnant, and married to a French-Canadian trapper and trader. Right now I feel heavy and earthbound.

Today, all of that is going to change. Two soldiers told my husband that they want to be the first white men to cross the western frontier. They call themselves Captain Lewis and Captain Clark. They will be mapping out rivers and mountains at President Jefferson's request. They are going past my old Shoshone home and need me to be an interpreter.

Home! I will finally see again my people and the Great Waters! At last, I, **Sacagawea**, have been given wings.

Schwager, Tina, and Michele Schuerger. *Gutsy Girls: Young Women Who Dare.*

Free Spirit, 1999, 260pp. Upper Elementary & Up. YASLA Quick Picks for Reluctant Young Adult Readers; Children's Books of the Years selection.

■ **BIOGRAPHY AND ADVENTURE.** *Disability (physical); rites of passage; self-identity; survival; women's issues.*

■ **RELATED BOOKS: Girls Who Rocked the World: Heroines from Sacajawea to Sheryl Swoopes** by Amelie Welden; **Girls Like Us: 40 Extraordinary Women Celebrating Girlhood in Story, Poem, and Song** edited by Gina Misiroglu; **Cool Women: The Thinking Girl's Guide to the Hippest Women in History** edited by Pam Nelson.

Note: Part One features 25 first-person interviews with young women discussing their daring feats. Part Two tells readers how they can set goals and follow their dreams. Valuable information is contained about each sport, including addresses, Web sites, and recommended books. Highly recommended for most libraries.

Meet 25 gutsy girls. Find out what it takes to climb a mountain, free-fall out of an airplane, walk a circus high wire, or explore the remote wilderness. These women live life to the extreme.

As these women reveal, each of them set personal goals. Nahara was paralyzed from a car accident, but she eventually learned to swim and received the Courage Award. She set each goal within reach and after obtaining it set another goal. So can you.

These gutsy girls followed their dreams. As a toddler, Melissa Buhl would tip her training wheels sideways, sometimes crashing to the ground. That excitement never left her. Eventually she became a BMX and mountain bike racer, winning several championships.

So, here's to the **Gutsy Girls**. You go, girls!

Schwartz, Ted. *Kids and Guns: The History, the Present, the Dangers, and the Remedies.*

Franklin Watts, 1999, 128pp. For all libraries.

■ **NONFICTION.** *Crime; death; ethics; men's issues; politics; school.*

■ **RELATED BOOKS: Making Up Megaboy** by Virginia Walker and Katrina Roeckelin; **Monster** by Walter Dean Myers; **The Taking of Room 114: A Hostage Drama in Poems** by Mel Glenn.

Note: This book was published before the Columbine incident, but unfortunately the problem of school violence continues. The text offers valuable information on history and laws concerning guns, including background on the Second Amendment of the Constitution and gun safety. Recommended for both teachers and students, this book is certain to produce thought-provoking discussions.

On March 24, 1998, two students from Jonesboro, Arkansas, 11-year-old Drew Golden and 13-year-old Michael Johnson, pulled the fire alarm at the Westside Elementary School. They hid among nearby trees with three rifles and seven handguns. Twenty-two rounds of ammunition were fired in four minutes, leaving four children and one teacher dead.

Again and again, from Paducah, Kentucky, to Columbine, Colorado, this scenario has reoccurred, ending in multiple deaths. How are kids getting guns? How safe are our schools? What can you do if someone talks about violence? Discover the ugly truth about the deadliest of combinations: **Kids and Guns.**

Scieszka, Jon. *It's All Greek to Me.*

*Illustrated by Lane Smith. Viking Children's Books, 1999, 80pp. Lower Elementary & Up. Eighth book of **Time Warp** series. Preceded by **Knights of the Kitchen Table; Not-So-Jolly Roger; Good, Bad, and Goofy; Your Mother Was a Neanderthal; 2095; Tut, Tut; Summer Reading Is Killing Me!** Children's Books of the Year selection.*

■ **FOLKLORE AND HUMOR.** *Europe (ancient Greece); magic; time travel.*

■ **RELATED BOOKS: Top 10 Greek Legends** by Terry Deary; the **Time Warp** series and **Squids Will be Squids** by Jon Scieszka and Lane Smith.

*Note: Another humorous addition to the **Time Warp** series with a short glossary of Greek gods and monsters along with a pronunciation guide. Fun addition to any study of ancient history (including Greek mythology), but reluctant readers will enjoy this one anytime. Also, great read-aloud.*

Don't ask me how my friends and I got here to Ancient Greece. Fred, Sam, and I were innocently performing a school play about Greek mythology. Suddenly the fake thunderbolt hit "The Book," and we were whisked away to Mount Olympus.

You know about "The Book," don't you? This book is magical and has the power to transport us back through time. We're already been to the Stone Age, Ancient Egypt, Camelot, and a bunch of other places. Now we're at the gate of Hades confronted by a three-headed dog named Cerberus. Great Zeus!

How will we get safely home? Don't ask me. **It's All Greek to Me!**

Scieszka, Jon. *Summer Reading Is Killing Me!*

Illustrated by Lane Smith. Viking, 1998, 73pp. Lower Elementary & Up. Title in **Time Warp** *series (see Booktalk entry for* **It's All Greek to Me!** *for other series titles). Children's Books of the Year selection.*

■ **FANTASY AND ADVENTURE.** *Friendship; hobbies (reading); school (library); time travel.*

■ **RELATED BOOKS: The Twits** by Roald Dahl; **Hoboken Chicken Emergency** by Daniel Pinkwater; **Nate the Great** by Marjorie Sharmat; **Book of Three** by Lloyd Alexander; and 60 other books mentioned in text.

Note: *The humorous* **Time Warp** *series can be read in any order. The premise of series is that Sam, Fred, and Joe use "The Book"—a time-warping, green-mist-expelling book that triggers time travel. This seventh* **Time Warp** *series title includes a bibliography of literary characters that is separated for early, middle, and older readers. Recommended for fantasy and humor fans as well as book lovers. Great as a summer read.*

Sam, Fred, and I did not want to spend our summer vacation in a library—at least, not in an ordinary one. Nevertheless, when we entered the time-warp, we found ourselves transported to scenes from books on our summer reading list. That's when things got pretty hairy.

Like our meeting Teddy Bear who claimed he was sick of his sweet image. He decided to wipe out all good characters and make his own reading list: Teddy Bear and the Magic Pebble, Green-Eggs-and-Dracula, and Headless-Horseman-the-Pooh.

After hiding from a 266-pound chicken and watching Homer Price being carried off by the Headless Horseman, we were relieved to return home. Adventures like these made me realize that **Summer Reading Is Killing Me!**

Seabrooke, Brenda. *The Vampire in My Bathtub.*

Holiday House, 1999, 128pp. Upper Elementary & Up.

■ **HUMOR.** *Moving; supernatural (vampires).*

■ **RELATED BOOKS: Ma and Pa Dracula** by Ann M. Martin; **Bunnicula** series by James and Deborah Howe; **Diary of a Monster's Son** by Ellen Conford.

Note: *In this hilarious account of a vampire who is kindhearted, overweight, and loves TV, the narrator, Jeff, must protect Eugene from his evil bloodsucking cousin, Vennard. Jeff meets his nosy neighbor, who he calls "Bat Ears," and together they resolve to protect Eugene. Recommended to any reader who enjoys humor.*

What do you do when your worst nightmare comes true? You scream, right?

Wrong. I was too scared to scream. I was alone in the house anyway, so no one would hear. I had opened up in this old trunk in a locked closet in our house. Something was in there. Something furry and big. It was moving. It could talk too!

"Grrrreetings. I am Eugene Aloysius Pierre Phillippe Carondelet, at your service." He made a funny bow. "I have been in this country and trunk for 117 years."

"How do you explain that?" I asked.

"It is quite simple. I am a vampire."

Of course, I made Eugene prove it. He tried his best, but he was a bit out of practice. He was so out of shape that he couldn't even crawl back into the trunk.

So, I put him in the bathtub. Hey, it was cozy with a quilt and pillow. My next problem was, what would my mom say when she saw **The Vampire in My Bathtub**?

Seidler, Tor. *Mean Margaret.*

Illustrated by Jon Agee. HarperCollins, 1997, 167pp. Upper Elementary & Up. National Book Award Finalist; ALA Children's Notable Book.
- ■ **FANTASY AND HUMOR.** *Abuse; animals; bullies; eating disorders (obesity); love; problem parents (alcoholism, obesity).*
- ■ **RELATED BOOKS: Poppleton** series by Cynthia Rylant; **Wainscott Weasel** and **A Rat's Tale** by Tor Seidler.

Note: *A tyrannical three-year-old child, Margaret is adopted by a pair of newlywed woodchucks. She terrorizes animals in the forest, including a squirrel, a testy snake, a skunk, and a couple of bats. Margaret eventually realizes that there is more to life than being nasty. Themes of sibling rivalry, alcoholism, obesity, and unconditional love are interwoven into the text. Sketches give childlike flavor to themes that might otherwise verge on adultlike. Recommended for beginning readers as an introduction to fantasy and humor; also great as a read-aloud.*

Every night Fred the woodchuck had the same dream. In the dream he was a married woodchuck with a wife leaning on his shoulder.

"What an awful dream!" he thought. "Who wants a wife? Forget it! I'll just have a chilly shoulder!"

Nevertheless, he found himself looking for such a female. However, all he saw were woodchucks with filthy paws or pea-green teeth. It was enough to rub his fur the wrong way.

Then he met Phoebe. She was the perfect wife until she decided to adopt a noisy and demanding human child, **Mean Margaret**.

Shaik, Fatima. *Melitte.*

Dial, 1997, 147pp. Upper Elementary & Up. American Booksellers Association Pick of the List; Children's Books of the Year selection.
- ■ **HISTORICAL FICTION.** *Abuse; African Americans; interracial relations; orphans; racism; religion; runaways; secrets; trust; woman's issues; work.*
- ■ **RELATED BOOKS: Jump Ship to Freedom** by James Lincoln Collier and Christopher Collier; **Anthony Burns: Defeat & Triumph of a Fugitive Slave** by Virginia Hamilton; **To Be a Slave** by Julius Lester.

Note: *The story is set in Louisiana, spanning the years 1765-72, when the colony was changing from French to Spanish rule. Melitte, a mulatto slave, eventually escapes with the help of Marie, the young daughter of Melitte's owners. Shaik is a recipient of a National Endowment for Humanities Fellowship Award. Recommended for all readers, especially those looking for story from slave's point of view.*

My slave name is Melitte. Sometimes I feel as strange as my name. I find it hard to live under the cruel thumb of my French owners.

At night I dream of my mother whom I never really knew. During the day I work on sewing little pieces so I can buy my freedom. Each stitch I sew and every book I read helps me get closer to my dream.

One day I promise that I will be able to walk proudly down New Orleans streets as a free black woman, or my name isn't **Melitte**.

Shapiro, Marc. *J. K. Rowling: The Wizard Behind Harry Potter.*

St. Martin's Griffin, 2000, 107pp. Upper Elementary & Up.

■ **BIOGRAPHY.** *Great Britain; hobbies (writing); self-identity; single parents; work.*

■ **RELATED BOOKS: Harry Potter** series: **Harry Potter and the Sorcerer's Stone; Harry Potter and the Chamber of Secrets; Harry Potter and the Prisoner of Azkaban; Harry Potter and the Goblet of Fire;** three more follow, all by J. K. Rowling.

 *This fascinating biography on the author of the **Harry Potter** series will keep those fans reading. Born July 31, 1966, Joanne Kathleen Rowling was always a closet writer who was too shy to submit her work to publishers. However, when she became a single mother on welfare, she found the courage to submit her story about the wizard Harry Potter. No one was more amazed than Rowling at the **Harry Potter** series' success. Rowling is an inspirational story for those who struggle with adversity and low self-esteem. Recommended for purchase—duplicate copies would be an asset!*

Joanne Kathleen Rowling, better known as J. K. Rowling, is a true wizard. Through her magical **Harry Potter** series, she was able to enchant readers of all ages. For the first time in publishing history, Rowling's books were number one, two, and three on *The New York Times* best-seller list. What's more amazing is that these books are considered children's books!

This book answers all the questions Harry Potter fans want to know. From where did the idea for the **Harry Potter** series come? From where did the name Harry Potter come? How did a single mother on welfare become a best-selling author?

After reading this biography, you will know the real **J. K. Rowling: The Wizard Behind Harry Potter.**

Shatner, William, with Chris Kreski. *Get a Life!*

Pocket Books, 1999, 320pp. Middle School & Up.

■ **BIOGRAPHY.** *Movies; show business; time travel.*

■ **RELATED BOOKS: Star Trek Movie Memories** by William Shatner; **Dark Victory (Star Trek)** by William Shatner; **I Am Not Spock** by Leonard Nimroy.

 *The **Star Trek** TV series is a forerunner to **Star Wars,** which invites comparisons between the two philosophies and slogans. Shatner also includes Trekkie Web sites, such as "If Dr. Seuss Wrote Star Trek." Recommended for movie and science fiction buffs.*

Hello, Trekkies. (Or Trekkers, Trekoo, Trekonovich, and all other *Star Trek* fans.)

Beam down another goodie from me, Captain Kirk. Even though I died in the film *Star Trek VIII,* I've risen again to talk about my death scene.

First, the writers wanted Captain Kirk to be shot in the back. Come on. Get real. The Captain deserves to be killed heroically, don't you agree?

Finally, the writers gave the character a death scene that I could accept, but you know what? I discovered that I didn't want Captain Kirk to die. Could it be that I am a Trekkie fan and want *Star Trek* to continue? Go figure. I guess I need to **Get a Life!**

Sheehy, Gail. *Hillary's Choice.*

Random House, 1999, 389pp. High School & Up.

■ **BIOGRAPHY.** *Abuse; ethics; love; politics; problem parents; sex and sexuality; sexual abuse; substance abuse (alcohol); women's issues.*

■ **RELATED BOOKS: Bill and Hillary: The Marriage** by Christopher P. Anderson; **Hell to Pay: The Unfolding Story of Hillary Rodham Clinton** by Barbara Olson; **The Case Against Hillary Clinton** by Peggy Noonan; **Passages** by Gail Sheehy.

Note: This engrossing, well-researched biography is both sympathetic and direct. Author suggests Bill Clinton has "dissociative identities"— what used to be called "multiple personalities," or many identities that have been split into separate entities. The author considers Hillary a love addict who denies the reality of her husband's philandering. The book could be helpful to teenagers who are in dysfunctional relationships. Also recommended as a group read for mature readers.

"I think we're all addicted to something," former President Bill Clinton said. "Some people are addicted to drugs. Some to power. Some to food. Some to sex. We're all addicted to something."

Hillary Clinton's addiction is her husband. So addicted did Hillary become to Bill Clinton that she gave up the chance for a prominent career of her own, moved to Arkansas, and stayed there for 18 years.

Later, Hillary would pay a price for her choice. When Bill Clinton became the second President to be impeached, many people wondered why Hillary selected such a man.

The answers are complicated because the Clintons are complicated. Their story is both an American love story and an American tragedy. Find out the fascinating story behind **Hillary's Choice.**

Shelley, Mary. *Frankenstein.*

First published in 1818. Revised and updated bibliography. Signet, 1965, 150pp. Middle School & Up.

■ **CLASSICS AND HORROR.** *Death; ethics; supernatural.*

■ **RELATED BOOKS: Dracula** by Bram Stoker; **Dr. Jekyll and Mr. Hyde** by Robert Louis Stevenson; books by Stephen King, especially **Bag of Bones; Interview With the Vampire** by Anne Rice.

Note: In 1818, wife of Romantic poet Percy Shelley, Mary Shelley (who was also the daughter of the intellectual rebels William Godwin and Mary Wollstonecraft), wrote a story to satisfy a dare made by poet Lord William Byron. To most of us, "Frankenstein" is the name of a monster, not the creator. Perhaps instinctively we know the monster and creator are halves of a single being. The narration may be confusing since three different narrators tell the story: the ship's captain, Dr. Frankenstein, and the monster. The archaic style may be too slow for reluctant readers, so recommend this one to mature readers who love horror. This edition includes an afterword by Harold Bloom, as well as a revised and updated bibliography. Adapted versions can be recommended; this booktalk can be used for these adaptations.

On a dreary night in November, I beheld the accomplishment of my toils. For two years I had worked hard, for the sole purpose of infusing life into an inanimate body. Now it stood over me—a miserable monster whom I created. One hideous hand was stretched out to me, but I did not linger. I took quick refuge in the dreary night, trembling with fear.

Allow me to introduce myself. I am the renowned scientist, Dr. Victor Frankenstein. I abandoned my monster, only to later discover that my young brother William was murdered. Could this beast have murdered my dear William? I could not doubt it.

Prepare to hear my grisly tale of horror: **Frankenstein.**

Singer, Marilyn. *Josie to the Rescue.*

Illustrated by S. D. Schindler. Scholastic, 1999, 106pp. Upper Elementary & Up. Children's Books of the Year selection.

■ **HUMOR.** *Ethics; nature; pregnancy; rivalry; school.*

■ **RELATED BOOKS: Ramona** series and **Ellen Tibbets** series by Beverly Cleary; **Aldo** series (including **Aldo Applesauce** and **Much Ado About Aldo**) and **Lucas Cott** series (including **Class Clown; Teacher's Pet;** and **Class President**) by Johanna Hurwitz.

Note: The pregnancy of Josie's mother is discussed naturally, as is Josie's moral dilemma about honesty. Recommended as an enjoyable book for a beginning reader.

"Food is expensive."

That's what Josie heard Mom and Dad saying one day, when they thought she wasn't listening. Josie had the solution to that problem. Food was not expensive if you planted a garden.

That's what Josie would do. She would plant a garden for Mom and the new baby. Then Josie would be a thousand times more helpful than her younger, perfect sister, Mary Jane.

Of course, Josie didn't mean to plant vegetables in Mom's flower garden. Better "can" that idea!

OK, that idea didn't go over very well. What if Josie wrote to companies for free baby stuff? Of course, Josie didn't need 116 cases of diapers and neither did Josie's mom!

Lots of helpful ideas keep filling Josie's head. Ready or not, right or wrong, it's **Josie to the Rescue!**

Skurzynski, Gloria. *Spider's Voice.*

Atheneum Books for Young Readers, 1999, 200pp. Middle School & Up. YALSA Best Books for Young Adults; Children's Books of the Year selection.

■ **FOLKLORE AND ROMANCE.** *Disability (muteness); France; love; Middle Ages; sex and sexuality; sexual abuse.*

■ **RELATED BOOKS: Sirena** by Donna Napoli; **Othello** by Julius Lester; **Gawain and Lady Green** by Anne Eliot Crompton; **Joy in the Morning** by Betty Smith.

Note: The novel is based on the 12th-century love affair between the French lovers, Eloise and Abelard, which resulted in Abelard's eventual castration by Eloise's guardian. The book includes a Web site that posts the authentic love letters of this mythical couple. Recommended for mature romance lovers.

Throughout my life, I've usually gone unnoticed, like a spider on a wall. Like a spider, I have no voice. Thus, "Spider" became my name.

I may be mute, but I can see. I see my Master, Peter Abelard, and his lover, Eloise, meeting for another rendezvous. Like a spider, I would become enmeshed in the tragic web that linked Abelard and Eloise. One day the lovers would be discovered, and a tragic fate would await Abelard. I am powerless to stop his fate. I can only watch, like a spider.

How can I, a mute boy, untangle myself from this web of deceit? Somehow I must call up my strongest **Spider's Voice.**

Sleator, William. *Rewind.*

Dutton Children's Books, 1999, 120pp. Upper Elementary & Up. YASLA Quick Picks for Reluctant Young Adult Readers.

■ **SCIENCE FICTION.** *Adoption; bullies; death; pregnancy; time travel.*

■ **RELATED BOOKS: The Boxes; Singularity** and **Boltzmon!** by William Sleator; **The Dark Side of Nowhere** by Neil Shusterman.

Note: *The main character, Peter, makes three attempts to prevent the car accident that takes his life, only to discover that he must change his attitude and approach to change his fate. Highly recommended for reluctant readers who want a brief book with enough science fiction to keep them interested.*

I died today.

After the shriek of the tires and the sharp thud, I floated upward, following the white light. I even attended my funeral!

A voice said, *Peter, you're not permanently dead. You can go back to any moment you choose before death. You have 12 hours to choose the moment. Choose carefully. If you fail to fix your life, you will be permanently dead.*

It took me about 10 minutes to decide how I could prevent my death. "I'm ready," I said.

To which moment do you want to return?

"Two a.m., the night before I died."

So be it. Your attempt now begins.

Suddenly I was back inside my body. If I didn't act fast, I would die again—permanently. Now my life was beginning again, spinning on **Rewind.**

Smith, Betty. *Joy in the Morning.*

First published in 1963. HarperCollins Juvenile Books, 1976, 288pp. Middle School & Up.

■ **CLASSICS AND ROMANCE.** *Hobbies (writing); love; movies; pregnancy; sex and sexuality.*

■ **RELATED BOOKS: A Tree Grows in Brooklyn** by Betty Smith; **Daddy Long Legs** by Jean Webster; **Mrs. Mike** by Benedict Freedman and Nancy Freedman; **Rebecca** by Daphne du Maurier; **Jane Eyre** by Charlotte Bronte.

Note: *First published in 1963, this heartwarming romance occurs in 1927 and concerns a difficult first year of marriage between a 18-year-old girl from Brooklyn and a 20-something law student. The story ends on a happy but realistic note. Title is based on the Bible verse from Psalms: "Weeping may endure for a night/but joy cometh in the morning." Sexual situations are subtly mentioned. A must-read for romance lovers.*

"I don't feel married, Carl. I went into the town hall as Miss Annie McGairy and came out Mrs. Annie Brown. It was too quick."

"Listen, my child bride. We're married in the eyes of God, man, the nation, and the world."

"Honest?"

"I'll prove it." Carl put his arms around her.

"Not here, Carl."

"Why not? Pretend we're back in Brooklyn. Pretend we're not in this Midwestern college town. Pretend no one is watching." A group of college fraternity men stopped to watch the embrace. They loudly cheered as Annie blushed.

"OK, Annie. Now we're married in the eyes of the university too!"

"We sure are," Annie agreed. "OK, Carl, I'm ready. Let's begin our marriage and our new life."

Smith, Charles R., Jr. *Rimshots: Basketball Pixs, Rolls, and Rhythms.*

Dutton Children's Books, 1999, 32pp. For all libraries. ALA Children's Notable Book; Parents Choice Silver Award Winner; YASLA Quick Picks for Reluctant Young Adult Readers; Cooperative Children's Book Center Choice; Children's Books of the Year selection.

■ **SPORTS.** *Men's issues; sports (basketball).*

■ **RELATED BOOKS: Hoops** by Robert Burleigh (for younger readers); **Hoops** by Walter Dean Myers; **The Last Shot: City Streets, Basketball Dreams** by Darcy Frey; **The Moves Make the Man** by Bruce Brooks.

Note: *Poet-photographer Smith expresses his love for basketball by mixing poetry, memoir, short fiction, and photography. Sepia-toned pictures are purposely anonymous, giving the pages an artsy look. Recommended for all readers, especially reluctant readers who love sports.*

I REMEMBER
I REMEMBER this book: **Rimshots/Basketball Pix, Rolls, and Rhythms**
I REMEMBER pain, pleasure, poetry
    Cheering/jeering/crying
I REMEMBER snappy photo flashes
    Blurred/merged/cropped
I REMEMBER hectic basketball sounds
    Shuffling/scuffling/swishing

I REMEMBER this book: **Rimshots: Basketball Pix, Rolls, and Rhythms.**

Smith, Sally Bedell. *Diana in Search of Herself: Portrait of a Troubled Princess.*

Random, 1999, 368pp. High School & Up.

■ **BIOGRAPHY.** *Death; divorce; eating disorders (bulimia, anorexia); Great Britain; politics; single parents; stepparents; women's issues.*

■ **RELATED BOOKS: Diana: Her True Story in Her Own Words** by Andrew Morton; **The Real Diana** by Lady Colin Campbell; **Grace** by Robert Lacey.

Note: *Many readers can identify with Diana's insecurities due to divorce, eating disorders, and betrayal. Also recommended for biography readers and those who have suffered from eating disorders.*

Sometimes fairy tales have unhappy endings.

The Princess Di Story was a perfect example of a fractured fairy tale. After marrying Prince Charles in 1981, Princess Diana discovered her Prince Charming loved another woman. Feeling betrayed and abandoned, the Princess became self-destructive with suicide attempts and eating disorders. In 1997, Princess Di's story ended unhappily ever after when she was killed in a ghastly car accident during a high-speed chase.

That is the story that everyone knows. The real story is much more complex. Who was the real Diana? Was she victim or instigator? How much did she contribute to the marriage's failure? Was it true that she finally found happiness with Dodi Fayed?

Find out how the fairy tale began and ended. Read **Diana in Search of Herself.**

Spada, James. *Jackie: Her Life in Pictures.*

St. Martin's, 2000, 176pp. Middle School & Up.

■ **BIOGRAPHY.** *Death; politics; self-identity; women's issues; work.*

■ **RELATED BOOKS: Jack and Jackie** and **Jackie After Jack** by Christopher P. Anderson; **The John F. Kennedys: A Family Album** by Mark Shaw (photographer); **Jackie** by David Heyman; **Jackie O!** by Kitty Kelley.

> *Note:* More than 250 rare photographs are provided, with brief text that is free of gossip or innuendo. This is the perfect book for reluctant readers who need a biography.

What a great idea.

This biography tells the story of Jacqueline Bouvier Kennedy Onassis through photographs. After all, she is arguably the most photographed woman in the twentieth-century. (The only person who comes close is Princess Diana.)

So, here it is: Jackie as a beautiful baby, as a beautiful debutante, as a beautiful bride to John Kennedy, as a beautiful First Lady, as a beautiful widow (twice), and more.

Even the reclusive Jackie might have approved of this one: **Jackie: Her Life in Pictures.**

Spinelli, Jerry. *Knots in My Yo-Yo String: The Autobiography of a Kid.*

Alfred A. Knopf, 1998, 148pp. Upper Elementary & Up. VOYA Award; YALSA Best Books for Young Adults; Children's Books of the Year selection; National Council for Social Studies Notable Book.

■ **BIOGRAPHY.** *Hobbies (writing); school; sports (baseball).*

■ **RELATED BOOKS: Maniac Magee** and **Space Station Seventh Grade** by Jerry Spinelli; **But I'll Be Back Again** by Cynthia Rylant; **26 Fairmount Avenue** by Tomie DePaola.

 Note: The book's fast-paced, witty style makes this a great biography pick for reluctant readers as well as for aspiring writers.

I'm Jerry Spinelli, author of *Maniac Magee.*

Sometimes I can't believe I'm an author. I didn't read that much as a kid. Not books, anyway. Now, cereal boxes—that was another story. And comics. And the sports pages in the newspaper. Cereal boxes, comics, baseball stats—that was my reading.

I did write a poem. In the sixth grade our teacher assigned us a project: Make a scrapbook from Mexico. I wrote three stanzas about the beauty of Mexico, ending it with "Now, isn't that where you want to be?" My teacher told my mother that I didn't write the poem. She thought I had copied it from a book.

Hah! If my teacher only knew how few books I read, and never one with poetry! I'll tell you more in **Knots in My Yo-Yo String: The Autobiography of a Kid**.

Spires, Elizabeth. *The Mouse of Amherst.*

Pictures by Claire A. Nivola. Farrar, Straus, &Giroux, 99pp. Lower Elementary & Up. Children's Books of the Year selection; Publishers Weekly's Best Books.

■ **FANTASY.** *Animals (mouse); diaries; hobbies (writing).*

■ **RELATED BOOKS: Emily** by Michael Bedard, illustrated by Barbara Cooney; **Collected Poems of Emily Dickinson** by Emily Dickinson, edited by Mabel Loomis Todd and Thomas Wentworth Higginson; **Ben and Me** by Robert Lawson; **Beethoven and Me** by Barbara Nichol.

> *Note:* *Emily Dickinson was born in 1830 in Amherst, Massachusetts, and she lived with her parents all her life. As she aged, she became a recluse, publishing only a handful of her 1,789 poems. Four years after her death in 1886, Dickinson's poems were published, and became instant successes. This book, with its enchanting pen-and-ink drawings, imaginatively presents the poet's life. Recommended for all beginning readers and aspiring writers.*

Greetings. My name is Emmaline. I am a white mouse. I live in Emily Dickinson's bedroom, away from the kitchen and the cat.

It must have been fate that led me to this poet's room. Day and night, I watch her furiously write her poems, scribbling away, a blizzard of paper surrounding her. One day, in response to her poem, I write back a poem. She eagerly responds with another poem.

Since then, Emily Dickinson and I, **The Mouse of Amherst,** have become secret pen pals, sharing our mystical poetry.

Springer, Nancy (editor). *Prom Night.*

Daw Books, 1999, 309pp. High School & Up. YALSA Popular Paperbacks selection.

■ **SHORT STORIES.** *Love; magic; school; substance abuse; supernatural.*

■ **RELATED BOOKS:** (Romance) **Crush** and all other books by Ellen Conford; **The Unlikely Romance of Kate Bjorkman** by Louise Plummer; **Squash** by Joan Bauer. (Cutting-edge short story collections) **Black Cats and Broken Mirrors** edited by Martin H. Greenberg; **A Danger Magic** edited by Denise Little.

> *Note:* *Warn readers that book has little romance and instead offers fantasy, horror, and some science fiction. Most authors may be unknown, but the collection is varied and imaginative. Recommended for readers who like cutting-edge short stories.* ***Warning:*** *Profanity.*

Was your prom night the best night of your life or did you miss it? No matter. You are invited to 22 different and, well, strange proms in this collection of original stories.

In "Happily Ever After," a fairy godmother is prepared to transform some lucky girl into a prom princess—only this time, it's a "him"! In "Peggy Sue Got Slobbered," Peggy Sue's date acted like such a dog. In "Omar's One True Love," Omar's date for the prom was the most popular girl in school—who had been dead for two weeks!

That's just a taste of the weird and wonderful on that magical night, **Prom Night.**

Stevenson, James. *Mud Flat Spring.*

Greenwillow, 1999, 40pp. Lower Elementary & Up. Fifth book in **Mud Flat** *Series:* **Mud Flat Mystery; Mud Flat Olympics; Heat Wave at Mud Flat;** *and* **Mud Flat April Fool** *precedes.*

■ **FANTASY AND HUMOR.** *Animals; nature; seasons (spring).*

■ **RELATED BOOKS: Winnie the Pooh** series by A. A. Milne; **Petunia** series by Roger Duvonsin; **Henry and Mudge** series and **Poppleton** series by Cynthia Rylant; **Frog and Toad** series by Arthur Lobel; **Charlotte's Web** by E.B. White.

> *Note:* From Fergus the snail to Cheryl the earthworm, Lois the duck, Carol the skunk, and Serena the butterfly, Mud Flat's residents are graced with recognizably human personalities. Warm watercolor illustrations add to the humorous stories. Recommended for beginning readers who love animals.

"It's spring at Mud Flat!" rejoiced Burford.

"Ooh, I'm still tired," grumbled Morgan the bear. "It takes me a while to wake up after a long winter snoooooze."

A week later, the citizens of Mud Flat got a surprise. When they awoke, they discovered Mud Flat buried in snow!

"Uh-oh," groaned Morgan the bear. "Maybe I awoke for spring too soon. Back to the cave I go."

Not only was Morgan upset. Everyone in Mud Flat was sad that the ground was covered with snow.

"Now, Now," comforted Burford. "Remember when this snow melts, we'll have spring all over again. How lucky we are to have two springs in one year!"

He was right. **Mud Flat Spring** started all over again the next week.

Tan, Maureen. *AKA Jane.*

Warner Books, 1997, 326pp. First in a series; **Run Jane Run** *follows. High School & Up. YALSA Popular Paperbacks selection.*

■ **MYSTERIES/THRILLERS.** *Crime; death; Great Britain (Ireland); Ireland; love; revenge; sex and sexuality.*

■ **RELATED BOOKS: Run Jane Run** by Maureen Tan; **V. I. Warshawski** series by Sara Peretsky; **Elizabeth MacPherson** series by Sharyn McCrumb; **The Moon-Spinners** and **Nine Coaches Waiting** by Mary Stewart.

> *Note:* In this action-romance, Jane Nichols, a female James Bond, has a romance with Savannah's police chief. Meanwhile, she fearlessly tracks down an Irish terrorist who murdered her spy lover. Recommended for readers who like a strong heroine with a touch of romance. **Warning:** Profanity, but could be recommended to mature readers in middle school.

It was my fault that Brian died.

I died that day, too. I killed my spy name of Moura McCarthy. My next identity was as Molly Shanks. Meanwhile, I looked for Brian's killer, a red-haired Irish terrorist.

Seven years later, I discovered Brian's killer. Jim O'Neil was a respected businessman in Savannah, Georgia, but that didn't impress me. I knew he was a murderer.

In the meantime, I had become a best-selling mystery novelist under my real name, Jane Nichols. I moved to Savannah. My plans were simple. To rest. To write. And to kill.

Jim O'Neil will wish he never had the misfortune to meet

Moura, AKA Molly, **AKA Jane**!

Tashjian, Janet. *Tru Confessions.*

Holt, 1997, 128pp. Upper Elementary & Up. Children's Books of the Year selection.

■ **REALISTIC FICTION.** *Computers; diaries; disability (mental); family; show business.*

■ **RELATED BOOKS: Buddy Love, Now on Video** by Ilene Cooper; **Anastasia Krupnik** series by Lois Lowry.

> *Note:* Computer symbols and pages of lists will appeal to the computer literate. In addition, the main character, Trudy Walker, presents her brother's mental disability realistically.

101 Reasons (Not Dalmatians) Why I Am Keeping This Computer Diary:

1. So I can live up to my nickname: Tru. Trust me, it's hard to be Tru when it's so much fun daydreaming about starring in my own *Trudy Walker Show.*

2. So I can relive my torments again and again and still have a record on my hard drive.

3. So the entire world has a record of my secret desire: to be a documentary filmmaker who uncovers a new therapy for my twin brother Eddie to be un-handicapped. World, take note!

4. (Reasons 5-101 are still being compiled...)

That's enough for now. More details will follow in **Tru Confessions**.

Taylor, Theodore. *The Weirdo.*

Harcourt Brace, 1991, 289pp. Middle School & Up. Edgar Allan Poe Award; 1999 Battle of the Books.

■ **ADVENTURE.** *Animals (bears); crime; disability (burns); ecology; ethics; nature.*

■ **RELATED BOOKS: Wolf Stalker** by Gloria Skurzynski and Alane Ferguson; books by Will Hobbs: **Bearstone; Downriver; The Maze; Far North;** and **Ghost Canoe.**

> *Note:* In North Carolina's Great Dismal Swamp region, 17-year-old Chip Clewt (nicknamed "Weirdo") and Samantha (nicknamed "Sam") fight to save bears in the Potwen National Wildlife Refuge. Two alternating points of view tell the intricate plot. Issues such as ecology, prejudice against physical deformation, and family complexities also are explored. The author, who lived in Virginia and the North Carolina swamp area, incorporated his childhood experiences into the plot. The text includes maps. Recommended while studying ecological issues, and for adventure lovers.

"I know the way of the bears," said Chip Clewt. "I put myself into their skin when they are being hunted. I know that there are only about 250 bears left in the Swamp. I'm going to save them from the poachers."

Samantha shook her head in disbelief. "Chip, you could get hurt. There are hunters around here that might run you away at rifle point. My papa, for one. They think of bears as wild animals. If you get them mad, these guys could even kill you. Maybe that's what happened to your bear tracker friend, Telford."

Chip wasn't listening. "We can't convince the hunters. It's the Wildlife Service that needs convincing."

He's crazy, thought Samantha. Not only does he look strange with his half-burned face, but he's talking crazy as well. How can two teenagers save these bears from hunters? Hunting around here is like a religion. No wonder everyone around here calls him The Weirdo.

And yet...maybe **The Weirdo** makes sense.

Thomas, Rob. *Green Thumb.*

Simon & Schuster Books for Young Readers, 1999, 186pp. Upper Elementary & Up. Society of School Librarians International Honor Book; Children's Books of the Year selection.

- **ADVENTURE.** *Caribbean and Latin America (Brazil); science; ecology; bullies.*
- **RELATED BOOKS: Loch** and **Reef of Death** by Paul Zindel; **Z for Zachariah** by Robert C. O'Brien; **The Maze** by Will Hobb.

> *Note:* Thomas' underlying humor enhances this quick-paced adventure that is loaded with interesting scientific facts. Recommended particularly for the reluctant reader.

This letter changed my life:

Mr. Grady Jacobs,

Congratulations. You are invited to participate in a scientific project involving Super Trees. Super Trees are scientifically designed to replenish and regenerate the Amazon rain forest. Hope to see you in Brazil this summer for a life-altering experience.

Dr. Phillip Carter

Apparently, when I arrived in Brazil and met Dr. Carter, he was shocked to find out I'm only 13. He wasn't exactly happy with me, but what was he going to do? Send me back home through the Amazon jungle? Not likely.

Eventually I discovered that Dr. Carter was growing poisonous trees that could destroy the ecosystem. When I tried to stop this mad scientist, he went ballistic.

Now I'm running out of this jungle—running for my life. Grab a vine with me and hold on tight. It's going to be a wild ride—even if you do have a **Green Thumb**.

Ungerer, Tomi. *Tomi: A Childhood Under the Nazis.*

Roberts Rinehart, 1998, 224pp. Middle School & Up. ALA Notable Children's Book; Children's Books of the Year selection.

- **BIOGRAPHY.** *Europe (France, Alsace); Jews; racism; World War II.*
- **RELATED BOOKS: Anne Frank: Beyond the Diary, A Photographic Remembrance** by Rudd Van der Rol and Dian Vehoeven; **I Have Lived a Thousand Years** by Livia Bitton Jackson; **No Pretty Pictures: A Child of War** by Anita Lobel; **Eleanor's Story** by Eleanor Ramrath Garner.

> *Note:* Award-winning illustrator Ungerer presents both an oral and visual record of his childhood, with documents, 60 photos (40 in color), writing, and artwork of this time period. Of particular interest is the documentation of the Nazi propaganda machine, including French advertisements for the Nazi cause. This book is valuable as a primary source, autobiography, and photographic record of Alsace (at that time a part of France) during World War II.

I was eight when the Nazis marched into France. It was the 17th of June 1940.

Shortly after that unforgettable day, the doorbell rang. A German officer clicked his heels, raised his arm, and said, "Heil, Hitler." I had never heard that expression before, but, alas, I would hear it many times after that. He marveled at our beautiful chestnut trees, saying, "Are they not beautiful this time of year? One thing I promise you: The day will come when you will see a Jew hanging from every branch." Then he pulled out a piece of paper. "This is a wonderful recipe for carrot cake. You may keep it."

That's what I remembered about the Nazis. With one sentence they could rhapsodize about nature; the next sentence would talk about death to the Jews—and all said with a smile.

Varriale, Jim. *Take a Look Around: Photography Activities for Young People.*

Millbrook Press, 1999, 32pp. Upper Elementary & Up.

■ **NONFICTION.** *Hobbies (photography).*

■ **RELATED BOOKS: Click: Fun With Photography** by Susanna Price; **Cameras** by Chris Oxlade; **Camera Crafts** by Cyndi Finkle; **Click** by Gail Gibbons.

Note: This informative book includes the creative photography of young students at a Connecticut summer camp where the author taught photography. Accompanying each photo is a caption that points out its uniqueness and suggests an idea for a future project. The book includes a glossary and bibliography. Recommended by acclaimed photographer Richard Avelon, the book would be useful for photography buffs and art students, and those looking for an interesting hobby.

Without using words, good photographs can tell a story. In fact, the word "photography" is a Greek word that means "drawing in light."

You, too, can tell a story with photographs. Your photographs will show where you are right now—you don't have to go anywhere to produce a good photograph. First, you need to determine what interests you, what excites you. In other words, what do you see differently from others?

Then, grab your camera and **Take a Look Around**! Your world will never be the same again!

Velde, Vivian Vande. *Never Trust a Dead Man.*

Harcourt Brace, 1999, 192pp. Middle School & Up. YASLA Best Books for Young Adults; YASLA Quick Picks for Reluctant Readers; Children's Books of the Year selection.

■ **MYSTERIES/THRILLERS AND FANTASY.** *Crime; death; Middle Ages; rivalry; supernatural.*

■ **RELATED BOOKS: Ghost of a Hanged Man** and **Dragon's Bait** by Vivian Vande Velde; **The Cat Who Wished to Be a Man** and **Gypsy Rizka** by Lloyd Alexander; **To Visit the Queen** by Diane Duane.

Note: The tongue-in-cheek story contains supernatural elements of witches, spells of enchantment, and talking corpses. The creative plot was derived from Shakespeare's **Othello.** Selwyn and the corpse, Farold, become friends while on a journey to discover Farold's murderer. Farold's witty retorts and sarcastic replies add to the medieval whodunit. Recommended for mystery fans and readers who enjoy adventure stories with a humorous twist.

It's hard to have a decent conversation with a dead man. Much less a brought-to-life corpse that has transformed into a bat! Death certainly hadn't changed Farold. He still had that sassy mouth coming out of a bat's body. You try arguing with a bat!

Selwyn did try to talk to Farold, the corpse-that-is-now-a-bat. Selwyn needed to find out who murdered Farold because the village blamed him. Farold was no help. Farold claimed his back was turned while he was stabbed.

Who really killed the corpse-that-is-now-a-bat? Find out in **Never Trust a Dead Man**!

Velde, Vivian Vande. *There's a Dead Person Following My Sister Around.*

Harcourt Brace, 1999, 160pp. Upper Elementary & Up. Children's Books of the Year selection.

■ **MYSTERIES/THRILLERS.** *African Americans; Civil War; racism; runaways; supernatural.*

■ **RELATED BOOKS: The House of Dies Drear** and **The Mystery of Dies Drear** by Virginia Hamilton; **Barefoot: Escape on the Underground Railroad** by Pamela Duncan Edwards.

Note: *Velde does a commendable job of blending a ghost story into an American history lesson. The narrator, 12-year-old Ted, and his family live in a house in Rochester, New York, that was part of the Underground Railroad. He discovers his great-great-grandmother's diary in the attic. From the diary, Ted learns about Marella and her child, who were both runaway slaves. Recommended for mystery lovers and any reluctant reader.*

We have a ghost in our house.

It all started when my five-year-old sister mentioned her imaginary friend, Marella. Naturally, we didn't pay any attention. Then weird things started happening. A key to the attic kept moving, inside the attic a light bulb exploded, and behind me someone screamed. Scary, huh?

Listen to this. My older brother Zach, my cousin Jackie, and I were arguing over the TV programs, when suddenly I could see a person on the screen walking toward us.

"Zach, turn off the TV!" I shouted.

Jackie grabbed the remote control and turned off the power.

The screen stayed the same: black-and-white static with the ghost coming straight toward us.

Closer.

Closer.

Her face filled the screen.

Help! **There's a Dead Person Following My Sister Around!**

Voight, Cynthia. *Elske.*

*Atheneum, 1999, 256pp. Middle School & Up. YASLA Best Books for Young Adults. Last in **The Kingdom** series: **Jackaroo; On Fortune's Wheel;** and **The Wings of a Falcon** precede. Children's Books of the Year selection.*

■ **FANTASY.** *Class conflicts; Middle Ages; pregnancy; sexual abuse; women's issues.*

■ **RELATED BOOKS: The Kingdom** series by Cynthia Voight; **The Raging Quiet** and **Winter of Fire** by Sherryl Jordan; **The Midwife's Apprentice** by Karen Cushman.

Note: *This realistic fantasy is only linked loosely to the other books in the series and can be read alone. In the story, 12-year-old Elske has escaped her barbaric, Viking-styled homeland to become aide to the exiled queen. Due to its content of violence and abuse (including sexual), only mature readers should read this engrossing book.*

Elske was the chosen Death Maiden. When she reached puberty, she was to be a human sacrifice of the Volkarics. With her grandmother's help, she was able to escape her barbaric homeland.

She began her new life in Trastad as a handmaiden to Beriel, who was known as the Fiendy Princess and the "Queen that will be." Elske was the perfect servant to Beriel. Both were cleaver and independent and had no desire to marry. However, Beriel carried a secret known only to Elske: Beriel was "baby-swollen" with child.

Together, Elske and Beriel planned to hide the baby's birth. They also planned to assume Beriel's rightful place as Queen of the Kingdom.

Such an undertaking was unknown for females in the Middle Ages. That's just what they were counting on.

Follow the adventurous trail of two independent females, Beriel and her handmaiden, **Elske.**

Walker, Barbara G. *Feminist Fairy Tales.*

Illustrated by Laurie Harden. HarperCollins, 1996. 244pp. Middle School & Up.

■ **FOLKLORE, ROMANCE, AND SHORT STORIES.** *Africa; ethics; Ireland; love; magic; Middle Ages; Middle East; rites of passage; supernatural; women issues.*

■ **RELATED BOOKS: Restoring the Goddess; Women's Rituals;** and **Woman's Encyclopedia of Myths and Secrets** by Barbara G. Walker; **Women Who Run With the Wolves** by Clarissa Pinkola Estes.

> *Note:* Each retelling of the 28 fairy tales provides a brief explanation of the history and symbolism. Illustrations enhance the stories. Recommended for readers looking for strong, resourceful heroines. Also, good as a read-aloud and for Women's History Month.

Once upon a time Prince Puddocky went seeking the most beautiful girl to marry. If he saw a woman who did not meet his standards, he threw her into the river with the other ugly women. He finally found his dream girl, and they lived happily ever after.

Well, maybe the Princess found a happy ending, but what about all those other unfortunate women who failed the test? According to this old German fairy tale, female ugliness was a crime against the nation!

Maybe it is time to throw aside jealous stepmothers, helpless dames in distress, and superficial princes looking for beautiful mates. How about replacing these characters with feisty heroines like She-Wolf, Snow Night, and The Frog Princess? With **Feminist Fairy Tales**, we can still understand the symbols of classic fairy tales and receive a more positive message for today's women.

Now *there's* a happy ending!

Walton, Rick. *What to Do When a Bug Climbs in Your Mouth: And Other Poems to Drive You Buggy.*

Illustrated by Nancy Carlson. Lothrop Lee & Shepard, 1995, 30pp. Lower Elementary & Up.

■ **HUMOR AND POETRY.** *Animals (insects).*

■ **RELATED BOOKS: Animals, Animals** by Eric Carle; **Joyous Noise** by Paul Fleischman; **The Country Noisy Book** by Margaret Wise Brown.

> *Note:* These 20 brief poems teach respect of the animal kingdom, with bright cartoonist illustrations adding to the humor. Read "Billions of Bugs" aloud first. Recommended as a group read or a read-aloud.

Do Carpenter ants build houseflies? Do dragonflies breathe fire? If a firefly caught on fire, would a water bug put out the flame?

That all depends. It all depends if you know **What to Do When a Bug Climbs in Your Mouth.** These poems will drive you buggy!

Wells, H. G. *The War of the Worlds.* (Also known as *War of the Worlds.*)

First published in 1898. Mass Market Paperback, 1993, 204pp. Middle School & Up.

■ **CLASSICS AND SCIENCE FICTION.** *End-of-the-world; movies; science; war.*

■ **RELATED BOOKS: The Martian Chronicles** by Ray Bradbury; **The Moon Is a Harsh Mistress** by Robert Heinlein; **The Time Machine** by H. G. Wells; **The White Mountains** series by John Christopher.

> *Note:* *First published in 1898, this novel is first of the alien invasion stories. The plot is so ominous that when Orson Welles adapted it for radio broadcast on Halloween in 1938, many listeners believed Martians were attacking the Earth! Technology predicts tactical battlefield lasers, chemical weapons, armored mechanical fighting vehicles, interplanetary space flight, and computer controlled robots. Remember, this was written before automobiles, airplanes, and computers. A must-read for science fiction fans, as well as movie and adventure enthusiasts.*

"Read all about it! Spaceship from Mars!"

I quickly bought the newspaper and went to see the spaceship outside London. About 100 curious spectators were surrounding the spaceship.

Slowly, the big grayish bulk struggled to rise, standing on octopuslike tentacles. One of the tentacles pointed at the crowd. A flash of light with a surrounding greenish smoke gave an audible hiss: *sssss; sssss; sssss.* One by one, the people were turned into fire. Their charred bodies lay still and silent.

Now it was clear. Martians had invaded the Earth. How would we survive **The War of the Worlds**?

Wharton, Edith. *Ethan Frome.*

Buccaneer, 1998, 195pp. High School & Up.

■ **CLASSICS AND ROMANCE.** *Love; movies; rivalry; suicide.*

■ **RELATED BOOKS: Wuthering Heights** by Emily Bronte; **Jane Eyre** by Charlotte Bronte; **Rebecca** by Daphne du Maurier; **Anna Karenia** by Leo Tolstoy; **Madame Bovary** by Gustave Flaubert; **Romeo and Juliet** by William Shakespeare.

> *Note:* *First published in 1911, the novel vividly conveys the bleak, barren winter landscape of 19th-century New England. Ethan is tied to the demands of his farm and his tyrannical, sickly wife, Zeena; he passionately loves Zeena's young cousin, Mattie Silver, and these two star-crossed lovers are, of course, doomed. A must-read for all romance lovers.*

I'm Ethan Frome. I ain't never been called lucky. Since the trains quit stopping by Starkville, I found myself wantin' company during those cold winters. Sometimes I got so lonely that I wanted to join my family's tombstones. I thought marryin' Zeena would cure what wuz ailing me, but Zeena wuz as silent as Ma.

That all changed when Mattie came to take care of my wife. Mattie was a might purty gal with a love of life I never knowed before. When Zeena told Mattie to git out, I couldn't let my very last chance of happiness walk out, too.

That's when Mattie and me decided we would escape Starkville. Maybe the Lord and the neighbors wouldn't approve, but it's was our only way out.

Like I said before, nobody ever called me lucky. Nope, people just called me **Ethan Frome**.

White, Nancy. *Scholastic's The Magic School Bus Takes a Dive: A Book About Coral Reefs.*

Illustrated by Ted Enik. Scholastic, 1998, 32pp. Lower Elementary & Up.

■ **NONFICTION.** *Animals (marine); science.*

■ **RELATED BOOKS: Magic School Bus in a Pickle: Book About Microbes** by Nancy Krulik; **Magic School Bus Show and Tells: Book About Archaeology** by Jackie Posner; **Scholastic's Magic School Bus in the Arctic: Book About Heat** by Joanne Cole; **Magic School Bus Plays Ball: Book About Forces** by Joanna Cole.

 Note: *This series is an excellent and popular choice for students and teachers. Comic strip illustrations appeal to older reluctant readers as well. Both book and video formats are recommended.*

Ms. Frizzle wants our Science class to build a model of coral reek in a fish tank. Sound simple? With Ms. Frizzle as our teacher, nothing is simple and everything is fun. Especially when Ms Frizzle shows up wearing a diver's suit and pulls out a treasure map.

Is her treasure map real? There's only one way to find out. To the **Magic School Bus** we go!

Wilde, Oscar. *The Picture of Dorian Gray.*

First published in 1891. Tor Books, 1999, 256pp. High School & Up.

■ **CLASSICS AND HORROR.** *Aging; class conflict; crime; ethics; Great Britain; homosexuality; movies; substance abuse; secrets; supernatural.*

■ **RELATED BOOKS: Dr. Faustus** by Christopher Marlowe; **Faust, Part One** by Johann Wolfgang Goethe; **Interview With the Vampire** by Anne Rice and the rest of her series; **Canterville Ghost** by Oscar Wilde; **Wuthering Heights** by Emily Bronte.

 Note: *In this novel, the infamous author weaves morals, murder, and drugs into a spellbinding story, that reads much like a Greek tragedy. Wilde's jaunty wit provides many quotable lines about society and its conventional morals. Recommended for mature horror fans and readers looking for unconventional stories.*

A thing of beauty is a form of genius. With beauty, there is no need for explanation. Beauty cannot be questioned. It has Divine Rights.

Take The Picture of Dorian Gray. The portrait perfectly captured Dorian's finely curved lips, frank blue eyes, and golden hair. His youth's entire candor was there, as well as passionate purity.

However, Dorian was jealous of his portrait. Why should this inanimate painting stay beautiful while he ages? Why should this portrait mock him through the years? If only he could remain the same beautiful creature while his portrait ages!

Some wishes that come true can be the most horrifying. Read about **The Picture of Dorian Gray.**

Wilder, Laura Ingalls. *Little House Parties.*

Illustrated by Renee Graef. HarperCollins, 1999, 72pp. Lower Elementary & Up. Adaptation from **Little House** *series. This is the 14th book of the* **Little House Chapter Books** *series. Some preceding books are:* **Laura's Ma; Laura's Pa; Christmas Stories; Farmer Boy Days; Little House Friends; Animal Adventures; School Days;** *and* **Laura & Nellie.**

■ **HISTORICAL FICTION.** *Family; pioneer life.*

■ **RELATED BOOKS: Caddie Woodlawn** *by Carol Ryrie Brink;* **Dakota Dugout** *and* **Grasshopper Summer** *by Ann Turner;* **The Bread Sisters of Sinking Creek** *by Robin Moore;* **Trouble for Lucy** *by Carla Stevens; the original series by Laura Ingalls Wilder, including* **Little House in the Big Woods** *and* **Little House On the Prairie.**

> *Note:* *Another adaptation of Laura Ingalls Wilder's series, with seven self-contained stories. (Wilder's story was adapted in the 1970s as a TV series:* **Little House on the Prairie.***) Laura Ingalls Wilder was born in 1867 in a log cabin in the Big Woods of Wisconsin. She traveled with her family by covered wagon through Kansas, Minnesota, and the Dakota Territory. In 1930 she began to write about her pioneer girlhood, always encouraged by her daughter, Rose Wilder Lane. (Some believe Rose, a respected editor, actually rewrote scenes; she certainly was a strong contributor, as documented by John E. Miller in* **Becoming Laura Ingalls Wilder.***) This series is recommended for beginning readers as an introduction to Wilder's series.*

Laura wondered all week long what people meant when they talked about the upcoming "dime sociable." All she knew was that she had to pay a dime to go to a town party.

When she arrived, she saw her neighbors dressed up in their finest clothes sitting in nice chairs around the parlor. They didn't say a word until Reverend Brown entered, and when they talked, they talked about topics like the weather. Laura tried not to fidget, but she was so glad when she and Mary left early.

If this is a dime sociable, thought Laura, I wish I had kept my dime!

Would you like to join Laura and Mary at some fun **Little House Parties**?

Willis, Patricia. *Danger Along the Ohio.*

Clarion Books, 1997, 132pp. Upper Elementary & Up. Children's Books of the Year selection.

■ **HISTORICAL FICTION.** *Native Americans; pioneer life; racism; responsibility; survival; trust.*

■ **RELATED BOOKS: The Courage of Sarah Noble** *by Alice Dalgliesh;* **Caddie Woodlawn** *by Carol Brink;* **Rifles for Watie** *by Harold Keith;* **Out of the Storm** *by Patricia Willis.*

> *Note:* *In this rip-roaring adventure, a family endures two Indian attacks, rescues a Native American boy, and is taken prisoner by the Shawnee. History is interwoven into the plot, with respect for Native Americans. Issues of gun safety and bird extinction are also subtly addressed, and historical notes are included. Recommended for history buffs, adventure fans, and reluctant readers.*

"Why do Indians hate us?"

Amos thought for a moment before answering his seven-year-old brother and telling him what his father had told him. "Because they don't understand us owning the land. Indians use the land, but they don't own it. They're afraid if people like us keep coming, they'll be pushed out."

"Well, those savages better keep away from me!" declared his 12-year-old sister fiercely. "I'll use Papa's pistol if they get too close to me!"

Amos shuddered because he knew his sister was capable of shooting anything that disturbed her. As for himself, he was leery of guns since his accidental shooting of his best friend.

Soon Amos would face another terrifying fear. While traveling down the dangerous Ohio River, his family would be kidnapped by the Shawnee Indians!

Wilner-Pardo, Gina. *Jumping Into Nothing.*

Illustrated by Heidi Chang. Clarion, 1999, 64pp. Lower Elementary & Up. Children's Books of the Year selection.

■ **REALISTIC FICTION.** *Friendship; peer pressure; sports (diving).*

■ **RELATED BOOKS: Last One in Is a Rotten Egg!** by Leonard Wiseman; **Edward the Unready** series by Rosemary Wells.

> *Note:* *The author outlines simple solutions to fearful situations that are practical and encouraging. Add the humorous characters and dialogue, and the book is a satisfying read for all types of young readers.*

Do you know what's great about summer? All you have to worry about is the vending machine running out of grape soda.

Not always, though.

This summer Maggie and Jennifer dared me to jump off the high dive. I tried to, but I chickened out at the last minute. So I have a plan. If I do enough scary things, I might be able to tackle my biggest fear. Here's my list:

1. Do a math problem on the blackboard.
2. Sleep without my night-light.
3. Tell Matthew I think he's cute.
4. Eat some bugs.

Here goes! Wish me luck as I go **Jumping Into Nothing**!

Wilson, Diane Lee. *I Rode a Horse of Milk White Jade.*

HarperTrophy, 1999, 304pp. Middle School & Up. VOYA award; YALSA Best Books for Young Adults; YASLA Teens Top Ten Best Books; Children's Books of the Year selection.

■ **HISTORICAL FICTION.** *Animals (horses); Asia (Mongolia); China; disability (lameness); Middle Ages; women's issues.*

■ **RELATED BOOKS: Chinese Cinderella: The True Story of an Unwanted Daughter** by Adeline Yen Mah; **Bound Feet and Western Dress** by Pan-Meil Natasha Chang; **To Ride the God's Own Stallion** by Diane Lee Wilson.

> *Note:* *The main character, Oyuna, tells her granddaughter the story of her life in 14th-century Mongolia—a life filled with adventure. Full of period detail, with a glossary of Mongolian words, this novel is recommended for lovers of historical fantasy or horses.*

I always knew I belonged with horses.

Even when a black mare crushed my foot, I continued to love horses. Horses were not to blame for my bad luck. This bad luck hovered around me like a cat over a mouse hole, ready to pounce. I vowed if I ever had the chance, I would carry my bad luck far away from Mongolia.

My grandmother understood this. She claimed a horse crushed my foot to free me from the ground so I could ride its back, to travel with the wind, to another land.

One blindingly hot summer day, as usual, the horses alerted me to danger. I spotted Kublai Kahn's soldiers, hundreds of them. A solider tried to steal my horse of milk-white jade, but I undertook action. I cut off my long pigtail, hid my lameness, and enlisted in Khan's army—as a man!

I was bound for adventure, that summer day **I Rode a Horse of Milk White Jade.**

Wittlinger, Ellen. *Hard Love.*

Simon & Schuster for Young Readers, 1999, 224pp. High School & Up. Newbery Honor Book; Booklist Editor's Choice; Michael R. Printz Award for Excellence in Young Adult Fiction (Honor Book); Quick Picks for Reluctant Young Adult Readers; SLJ's Best Books; YALSA Best Books for Young Adults; Children's Books of the Year selection.

■ **REALISTIC FICTION.** *Divorce; homosexuality; love; self-identity; stepparents.*

■ **RELATED BOOKS: Whistle Me Home** by Barbara Wersba; **The Sun Also Rises** by Ernest Hemingway; the **Weetzie Bat** series by Francesca Lia Block.

> *Note:* *Wittlinger's award-winning book embraces the zine scene, self-published and self-designed underground magazines by young adults. The main character, John, tells of his star-crossed romance with a lesbian. The changing typeface and design gives the story a hip look, very much like a zine. **Warning:** Recommended for mature readers since the text includes profanity and sexual discussions.*

A stack of zines hit the floor. I glanced in that direction and then zeroed in. It's *her!*

I had been looking for Marisol since I read her zine, *Escape Velocity.* Now I have my own zine, *Bananafish,* and my own alias, "Giovanni." (No way was I going to put "John F. Garlardi Jr." It sounds like a dull stiff.)

In her zine, Marisol describes herself as a "Puerto Rican Cuban Yankee lesbian." As for me, I'm 16, straight, and totally uninterested in the opposite sex. Then I meet Marisol and fall like a ton of bricks.

What happens who two dysfunctionals meet? Sounds like **Hard Love.**

Wong, Janet S. *Behind the Wheel: Poems About Driving.*

Margaret K. McElderry Books/Simon & Schuster Children's, 1999, 44pp. Middle School & Up. YASLA Quick Picks for Reluctant Young Adult Readers.

■ **POETRY.** *Transportation (automobiles); responsibility.*

■ **RELATED BOOKS: Foreign Exchange: A Mystery in Poems** and **The Taking of Room 114: A Hostage Drama in Poems** by Mel Glenn; **A Lion's Hunger: Poems of First Love** by Ann Turner.

> *Note:* *Wong presents 36 poems in free verse, expressing her thoughts about the problems and joys of driving. Teachers could use these poems as examples for a writing exercise about driving. Recommended for purchase in all high school libraries.*

Everything you need to know
    You learn in kindergarten—
Not!
Instead
You learn
Everything you need to know
while driving.
Watch out for the other guy.
Keep your eye on your back.
Hey, you got my spot!
Everything you need to know
You learn **Behind the Wheel.**

Y

Yep, Laurence. *Dragonwings.*

Harper and Row, 1975, 248pp. Middle School & Up. Newbery Honor Book; ALA Notable Children's Book; Boston Globe/Horn Book Award; New York Times Outstanding Children's Books, SLJ's Best of the Best.

■ **HISTORICAL FICTION.** *Asian Americans (Chinese); immigrants; racism; transportation (airplanes); substance abuse (opium).*

■ **RELATED BOOKS: Dragon's Gate** by Laurence Yep; **The Year of the Impossible Goodbyes; Echoes of the White Giraffe; Gathering of Pearls,** all by Sook Nyul Choi; **The Joy Luck Club** by Amy Tan.

 Note: *Yep's young adult book is now a modern classic, which tells of a Chinese immigrant and his son, Moonshadow, building a flying machine. The story is set in early-20th-century San Francisco (including the earthquake). Recommended for any kind of multicultural project, (including ESL, or English as a Second Language classes), as a read-aloud, or for a group read.*

I was curious about the Land of the Golden Mountains because my father was there. I had not met my father because the White Demon didn't allow him to bring us from China.

My grandmother said my father was in a place called America that was far away from China. "It has mountains 3,000 miles wide and lets you scoop up gold lying on its surface," she said. "You have to work with those White Demons. Otherwise, you'll wind up poor."

My father is poor, but he sends me wonderful kites. I like to fly his kites because then I feel close to him. We both have the same dream: flying. We also are both curiously drawn to dragons. He once made me a majestic dragon kite.

Sometimes I fantasize that I can attach myself to my dragon kite and sail far away. These **Dragonwings** will take me to this America—if only to meet my father.

Yep, Laurence. *Ribbons.*

Putnam, 1996, 192pp. Upper Elementary & Up. National Council for Social Studies Notable Book.

■ **REALISTIC FICTION.** *Aging; Asian Americans; families; hobbies (ballet); rivalry; secrets; women's issues.*

■ **RELATED BOOKS: The Lost Garden; Dragon's Gate;** and **Dragonwings,** all by Laurence Yep; **Coming of the Bear** and **Ties That Bind, Ties That Break: A Novel** by Lensey Namioka; **Bound Feet and Western Dress** by Natasha Pan-Mei Chang; **Gathering of Pearls** by Sook Nyul Choi; **Ballet Shoes** by Noel Streatfield.

 Note: *The author intriguingly portrays sibling rivalry, sexism, and generational family tensions. The text includes historical notes about China's footbinding of young girls. Recommended for readers who enjoy realistic fiction and books about dancing.*

Dance is my life. I practice ballet every single day, no matter what. However, everything seems to work against my becoming Madame Oblamov's star pupil.

Yesterday my parents told me that I have to quit ballet lessons so they could afford my grandmother's ticket from China to America. Not only that, but I have to give up my room for her. Is life unfair, or what?

Put yourself in my place. (And I wish my Mom would do just that, for once.) If someone took away the very thing you love, how would you react? Will I ever again be able to put **Ribbons** on my ballet slippers?

Yolen, Jane. *Snow, Snow: Winter Poems for Children.*

Photographs by Jason Stemple. Boyd Mill Press, 1998, 32pp. Lower Elementary & Up.

■ **POETRY.** *Nature; seasons (winter); sports.*

■ **RELATED BOOKS: Owl Moon** by Jane Yolen; **Snowy Day: Stories and Poems** by Caroline Feller Bauer; **Snow** by Uri Shulevitz.

> *Note:* The book's dazzling photographs are by the author's son. Recommended as a read-aloud; choose "Snow on the Trees" and "Footprints" to read aloud first.

Do you like snow? Some people do. They enjoy its lacy feel, its shivery brightness, and its icy covering on the earth. Then there are others who might enjoy snow if it weren't so wet and cold.

Take a trip with me and enjoy the splendor of snow without even putting on your coat!

Zindel, Paul. *Rats.*

Hyperion Books for Children, 1999, 204pp. Middle School & Up. YASLA Top 10 Quick Picks for Young Adults; YASLA Quick Picks for Reluctant Young Adult Readers.

■ **HORROR.** *Animals (rats); death; ecology; end-of-the-world.*

■ **RELATED BOOKS: Loch and Reef of Death** by Paul Zindel; **The Rats of NIMH** by Robert C. O'Brien; **Redwall** series by Brian Jacques.

> *Note:* Zindel also wrote the young adult classic **The Pigman** in 1968. **Warning:** This novel about mutant rats changed by a buildup of Methane gas at a landfill may be shocking to some readers.

"What's that noise?" Michael asked.

His sister Sarah heard it too. It was like a buzz, coming from the asphalt-covered dump. *CHIRRR. CHIRRR.*

Before Sarah could answer, they saw their neighbor Mrs. Carson running out of the house carrying her son. "Help!" she called, hoarse and dazed.

Next door to the Carsons, young children were swimming in their pool. Suddenly, they began shrieking, "Rats! Rats in the pool!"

Something terrible was happening. Mutant savage rats had escaped from a dump in Staten Island and were on a rampage, killing all humans.

Who will rule, people or **Rats?**

Zmuda, Bob, with Matthew Scott Hansen. *Andy Kaufman Revealed! Best Friend Tells All.*

Little, Brown, and Co., 1999, 306pp. Middle School & Up.

■ **BIOGRAPHY.** *Movies; show business.*

■ **RELATED BOOKS: Lost in the Funhouse: The Life and Mind of Andy Kaufman** by Bill Zehme; **Taxi: The Official Fan's Guide** by Frank Lovece; **Saturday Night Live: The First 20 Years** by Michael Cader; **Backstage at Saturday Night Live** by Michael McKenzie.

 Note: The text includes an afterword by comedian and actor Jim Carrey. At times, Zmuda steals the spotlight away from his subject, Andy Kaufman, and self-promotes his contributions to Kaufman's comedy. However, this page-turning book is recommended for reluctant readers looking for a biography

"Ladies and gentlemen, applause for a new comic, Mr. Andy Kaufman."

Several times before, I had seen this shaggy-haired young foreigner begging the manager backstage for a chance to do stand-up comedy. I, along with the rest of the audience, sat back and waited for him to bomb.

At first, the guy was pathetic, doing lame impressions in a thick, unplaced accent, or "emetations," as he called them. After sorry imitations of Ed Sullivan and President Richard Nixon, this loser announced he was going to do "de Elbis Presley."

At that time, in 1973, Elvis was still alive and no one did impressions of Elvis. When Andy Kaufman combed his hair back and twitched his upper lip, the inhibited man disappeared, replaced by some sort of "Elvis life force." We all screamed with laughter when this Elvis persona said in a Southern fried voice, "Thank yeh verra much . . . you can just stare at me while ah catch mah breath."

I became an Andy Kaufman fan that night. I also became his conspirator. We cooked up some great gags, so real that people didn't know we were putting them on. Andy liked to pull people's chains, blending the line between life and art.

In fact, Andy was so effective at his craft that, when he died of cancer in 1984 at the age of 35, everyone thought it was a practical joke!

PART 5

Indexes

Author Index

Title Index

Reading Level Index

MIDDLE SCHOOL (GRADES 6-8)

HIGH SCHOOL (GRADE 9 TO ADULT)

Genre Index

HORROR

See also "Mysteries/Thrillers"

HUMOR

MYSTERIES/THRILLERS SEE ALSO HORROR

NONFICTION

POETRY

REALISTIC FICTION

ROMANCE

SCIENCE FICTION

SHORT STORIES

SPORTS

Subject Index

142   Keep Talking that Book! Booktalks to Promote Reading, Grades 2-12, Volume III